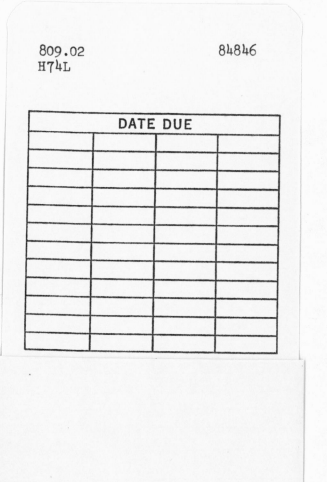

LITERARY PATRONAGE
IN THE
MIDDLE AGES

KARL JULIUS HOLZKNECHT

1966

OCTAGON BOOKS, INC.

New York

Originally published 1923 by The Collegiate Press

Reprinted 1966
by special arrangement with Eleanore B. Dreibelbies

OCTAGON BOOKS, INC.
175 FIFTH AVENUE
NEW YORK, N.Y. 10010

LIBRARY OF CONGRESS CATALOG CARD NUMBER: 66-28367

Printed in U.S.A. by
NOBLE OFFSET PRINTERS, INC.
NEW YORK 3, N. Y.

PREFACE

To treat literary patronage historically is, in large measure, to break virgin soil. Patronage as a custom is, of course, recognized, but no comprehensive or connected treatment of it has been undertaken and no investigation of its origin or early phases essayed. The present study was originally planned as such a comprehensive work, but the wealth of available material and the extensiveness of the field made it seem best to defer so large a task and to treat only the earlier and more neglected period at present. Beljame's admirable book, *Le Public et les Hommes de Lettres en Engleterre après de Dixhuitième Siècle,* breaks the ground very well for a most important era of patronage in England, while incidental treatments, such as that in Miss Phoebe Sheavyn's *Literary Profession in the Elizabethan Age,* or that in Wheatley's *Dedication of Books,* together with studies of individual authors or patrons, have sufficed for the Elizabethan period. But until now the Middle Ages have received little attention, though investigations concerning a few individual authors and nobles have yielded interesting results concerning the life of the time. Several years ago Professor R. K. Root promised an article on the subject in the *Publications of the Modern Language Association,* but other duties prevented the carrying out of his project. Professor Samuel Moore's Harvard dissertation (1911) was also originally planned as a study of the Middle Ages with especial reference to England, but he departed from his plan to examine certain Chaucerian problems only more or less connected with literary patronage. The work as a whole is still in manuscript, but all the material, somewhat enlarged, has been published in various journals, and references to it in these pages are made to the printed articles, which are readily accessible.

The present study attempts in its fashion to supply a connected account of this somewhat neglected phase of medieval literary life, and to look carefully in earlier ages for the origins of medieval patronage. As one may suppose, the ways in which a patron might be approached and the modes in which his favor might be extended were exhausted at a very early period, so that patronage of letters cannot be said to show much development or progress. In order to be significant as a study of the life and conditions of the early author, any treatment of this phase of the profession must rest on the painstaking collection and comparison of numberless instances, and it is hoped the ones here presented are sufficiently representative. Medieval patronage of letters, too, like other things medieval, was a custom undefined by the usual boundaries of country or tongue, and though English conditions are the first interest of this study, the close relation between England and the continent makes any strict distinction from the rest of Europe impracticable. Wherever it was possible, therefore, to draw illustrations from English life and conditions, I have done so, but whenever evidence was not readily to be had in England (or not so good as on the continent), I have felt free to substitute material outside of England.

As my work has proceeded I have, of course, incurred many obligations. To anyone who is acquainted with the members of the department of English at the University of Pennsylvania, my debt there will be obvious. To several I am more especially indebted. I wish to express my gratitude to Professor Felix E. Schelling, whose kindness, encouragement, and confidence in all things, has helped me in every way. In this particular work my greatest debt is to Professor C. G. Child, who sponsored it, and upon whose time and wide learning I have drawn extensively. To him, too, I am grateful for much encouragement and guidance, and that enthusiasm which he inspires in all his students. To Professor A. C. Baugh, likewise, I am under numerous obligations. He first introduced me to the methods of scholarship, and for his unwearied patience, searching criticism, and helpful suggestions, I am very thankful. To my fellow graduate students at Pennsylvania, also, I owe thanks for their interest and confidence. All the material for this study, I may add, was gathered during my tenure, in the years 1921-3, of the George Leib Harrison fellowship in English.

My debts elsewhere are various. To the authorities of the

Widener Library, I am grateful for access to much material at Harvard. Sir I. Gollancz, director of the Early English Text Society, kindly sent me Hoccleve's *Lady Money* roundels from the Ashburnham Hoccleve manuscript. To Miss Addie F. Rowe of Cambridge, Mass., I am indebted for various kindnesses. Finally, to name no more, to Miss Eleanore Butler of Philadelphia, I am especially grateful for the verification of material.

University of Louisville   K. J. H.

CONTENTS

LITERARY PATRONAGE IN THE MIDDLE AGES

INTRODUCTION

Patronage of letters, existing as a well-defined system, is not nationally restricted or dependent upon the spirit of any age but is the result rather of a few fairly obvious and universal social and economic conditions. Its most complete development is usually found within a highly aristocratic form of society, for obviously, inequalities of wealth and position only can bring about an exercise of individual largess or protection, and further, even in ancient times it is

> To growing wealth, the dedicator flies.

Literature in a wide sense had been pursued for ages before such a social condition was reached and before any individual ownership of literary property had become defined. There had been first of all a communal period of cooperative effort in which individual ownership gradually developed as the literary individual emerged from the throng. When literature came to be reckoned as a profession, however, it had to be adjusted to the existing economic system. In a homogeneous community, where power and wealth are widely or almost equally distributed, and where literary culture finally enforces recognition, means of rewarding genius come into use which are of a kind suitable to reach a large class of men. So among Semitic peoples from whom the oldest monuments remain and among whom individual authorship was unknown, literature was a growing thing, alive only so long as it grew. It was the product, not of individuals, but of schools of thought or of scribes of a particular temple, and it passed therefore with the thought which had produced it. Such production is purely communal, but parallel with group authorship there is the beginning of a more marked individual authorship, for books are also written at the order of kings and commanders, though with this qualification to be remembered, that literature is as yet a craft and not an art. Though there

I

may have been an art of well-rounded sentences and well-turned phrases in this old time, there is no reason to suppose that unusual literary skill at the service of an employer or lord was regarded as in any wise different from superior workmanship in bricklaying or carpentry.   Thus, in Chaldea the king kept in his household a scribe, with other duties beside literary ones, who wrote the record of his deeds and campaigns, but there is no trace of special compensation,[1] and obviously, where no favor is conferred, there is no patronage.   But this Chaldean practice is a great step in advance, for plainly, if art is to receive the real appreciation which leads to ducats in the purse or honors at court, it is to individuals that the poet must look—publics at best pay only in appreciation and are rarely remunerative.   It is only when the author perceives that his poetry is a ware which may possibly be sold, and decides, if he be commercially minded, to court an individual with it, that the real sense of literary property develops and patronage as a source of compensation comes into being.[2]

Turning to Biblical times, we may say that David's position in Saul's court was somewhat that of a patronized artist, and David himself and Solomon after him, to look no farther, were admirably equipped to patronize poetry and probably did.   In Egypt the change from communal to individual appreciation is most marked; until Rameses II and his son Menephthah literature was confined to the temples and was then removed to court and rewarded,[3] while in other lands the communal idea was never really displaced.   In ancient India[4] and Persia, literature and religion were

---

[1] Putnam, *Authors and their Public in Ancient Times,* (1894), 8.

[2] Speaking strictly, perhaps, it is only with the incoming of the publisher—'patron of literature' as Dr. Johnson called him—that property ideas develop; some one is needed to distribute and collect and assume the risk of investment of publication, but it may be recognized that in early times the patron assumed the function of publisher.

[3] Rawlinson, *History of Ancient Egypt,* (1882), II, 370-1.

[4] But the very literary priests of the Hindus were patronized by noble lords; the body of 'praises for gifts' or the Dànastutis of the *Rega Veda* are apparently panegyrics of the liberality of princes to the priestly singer. These poems are concerned chiefly with describing the gifts and their amount and praising the liberality of patrons, who are held up to the admiration and imitation of later generations. The poems are treated by Max Müller, *History of Ancient Sanskrit Literature* (1860), 493-4; and Macdonell, *History of Sanskrit Literature,* (1900), 127; and an interesting example is given by Frazer, *Literary History of India,* (1898), 26. It is likewise

closely connected; in Japan honor and prestige might be gained by an author, and in China there was state compensation for learning, economic necessity eventually forcing the poet into the meshes of the bureaucracy.[5]   Our own commercial age returns in a measure to the idea of communal approval and substitutes a royalty for what was earlier a gratuity.

Patronage, then, arises from this development of individual appreciation of art side by side with public appreciation of it, and is one of the early author's means of remuneration—alas, often the only one.   Hence, patronage, as we shall treat it, deals essentially with the economic phase of the literary profession.   In conditions of wide distribution of wealth and power, as in ancient Greece, genius is patronized by the public, and Pindar and Herodotus, decreed handsome gifts by the vote of the Athenian citizens, could be independent of individual benefactors, but with such conditions as prevailed under the early Ptolemies at Alexandria, under Augustus at Rome, and notably in Renaissance Italy, patrons of literature were a necessity—and it is only just to say that leaders of small wealthy cultured groups, willing to gratify their literary tastes by munificent payment for the luxury, have caused literary genius to flourish at least as well as in communities of less concentrated culture.

With even so brief a view of the conditions under which patronage may be said to have begun, it is easy to see that a superior-inferior relationship which was often not ideal might develop, and that a patron, as Dr. Johnson beheld him, could become "commonly a wretch who supports with insolence and is paid with flattery."[6]   But still on the other hand there was many a patron who lived his

age's ornament,
That with rich bounty and dear cherishment,
Supports the praise of noble poesie.

---

interesting to note that among the Hindus, as among the Teutons, poets, though of no special class, were looked upon as divinely created.   At the refined Gangetic courts minstrels and their poetry also held an honored place.

[6] Waley, *A Hundred and Seventy Chinese Poems*, (1918), 5.   The Chinese system of bureaucracy tended constantly to break up any literary coteries, and the Confucian idea insisted upon public service.

[6] *Dictionary*, s. v. *patron*.   Johnson's more famous definition belongs here also: "Is not a patron, my lord, one who looks with unconcern on a man struggling for

It is this fostering spirit, regardless of its motive, that is most frequently meant by that often loosely used word, *patronage.* For our purposes it denotes the employment of favor, protection, and influential support to advance the interests of art, limited generally to the habit of subsidizing authors, as is notable in 18th century England, and patronage almost always implies something of the relation of superior to inferior which existed between a wealthy and powerful Roman patron and his client. But this is only its material aspect. Patronage may omit the subsidy and may be simply an encouraging interest in letters extended by a person superior in wealth or position to an author, with or without donatives of money or honors. Hence, 'encourage by his patronage' need not always imply financial support and may be only the encouragement of a connoisseur's interest and approval. Where in the present investigation we find this to be the case, care will be taken to point out the fact. It is very questionable whether any man ever received social preferment, wealth, or position in the early time simply because he could write; he was probably merely hired as a craftsman when his services were wanted, as was Addison in Queen Anne's time. But there is no reason for supposing that his art might not recommend him, or even introduce him, to the attention of the great and so indirectly contribute to his wordly advancement, as in the case of Geoffrey Chaucer, if we allow patronage to him at all.

This brings up still another distinction which it is well to make at the outset, though more space will be devoted to it later, the distinction between patronage and those relationships just in the indeterminate zone between it and the more definitely commercial relationship of employer and employee, such as that of the court retainer mentioned above. In the Middle Ages we find *literati* at the courts of nobles serving as tutors, chaplains, clerks, secretaries, and what not, with duties which are often literary, but the relationship is essentially different from patronage. This was, however, one of the forms of medieval Maecenasship, as we shall see, for evidence shows that often a man was

---

life in the water, and when he has reached ground, encumbers him with help?" (Letter to . . . . the Earl of Chesterfield, Boswell's *Life,* Litchfield edn., I, 213.)

retained because he could write, and his other duties, in many cases very light ones, were secondary. We cannot call the relationship patronage, however, when the literary labors are secondary or unrecognized altogether. Further, there is nothing to prevent a literary man from being involved in affairs of state and having political backers or patrons; and in the case of a number of authors who presumably have both (the same man being perhaps both a literary and a political patron, as is possible notably in Chaucer's case), it is very difficult to determine where one left off and the other began, and such distinction is beset with dangers.[7] The problem is especially important and vexing in the Middle Ages when, as we shall see, patronage rarely took the form of the lavish support made famous by Maecenas.

It is the purpose of the present essay, therefore, after a glance at the early practice in classical times, to attempt to trace the development of the custom of patronizing arts and letters in the Middle Ages to the point where it becomes an institution, about 1500. While this study is to deal primarily with England and Western Europe, some attempt will be made to compare the patronage customs found there with those of other peoples. It will be necessary also to trace the gradual development of the literary patron as he emerges from the employer, from the nobleman who retained as a professional man a bard or minstrel at his court, to the man who favored a conscious literary artist largely on account of his art or learning. Finally, against such an introductory background, medieval patronage of letters in its general and special phases will be viewed more or less in detail.

[7] Moore, *M. L. N.,* XXVIII, 190, reviewing Hulbert's *Chaucer's Official Life,* first points out this distinction.

I

LITERARY PATRONAGE IN CLASSICAL TIMES

(a) *Greece*

Throughout the Greek and Roman world, the general opinion prevailed that wealth imposed the duty of fostering philanthropic and cultural enterprises. Hence, patronage was a natural thing, once individual authorship was recognized. After a bardic period as represented to us in the *Odyssey,* and indeed even through it, when the Greek bard, directly moved by the gods as was the bard of the Hindus and Teutons, sang in the halls of chieftains to the accompaniment of the lyre, it is safe to lay down as a rule that all Greek artists were professionals.[1] Professor Mahaffy (op. cit., 431ff.) summarizes the Greek attitude somewhat in the following way. Dilettantism and professional art were not fused into one another as in our own day but, be it said to their honor, the ancient Greeks were content to do their work for their own satisfaction and for the approval of their own generation, or for the chance of fame in future generations. In early times at least, nothing more tangible than fame came to them, but here it should be remembered that even the poorest citizen of Athens was in some sense an aristocrat with considerable leisure. The Seven Wise Men were nearly all poets as well as statesmen, and the turbulent Aristocrats could be both mercenaries and poets, like Archilochus and Alcaeus. Poetry in the early time was studied, not as an art, but as the only means of setting forth personal history, philosophy, and ethics. But leisure, instead of being spent in production, was spent in criticism, and the artist was not interfered with. So came about the conservatism, chastity, and reticence of the best of Greek art, for had there been any enticing rewards, its serenity would have been disturbed. The Greek artist was a tradesman, and a good one, who made

[1] Mahaffy, *Social Life in Greece from Homer to Menander,* (3rd edn., 1877), 431.

6

his work for an employer he was obliged to satisfy, but who when paid, admitted no further obligations of gratitude.

To be sure, art and literature were encouraged; the Greek tyrants, like their brothers in all ages, realized the need of making their position strong by a glorious court and a reign wherein culture developed. Thus Pisistratus at Athens encouraged architecture and poetry by restoring the Panathenic festival where the literary contests of the rhapsodists flourished,[2] and the drama made its appearance through the bringing of Thespis to Athens. His sons, Hippias and Hipparchus, ruled on the same principles as their father and surrounded themselves by many distinguished poets, as did the provincial tyrants, Polycrates of Samos, Hiero and Dionysius of Syracuse, Theron of Agrigentum, the Scopads of Thessaly, and the Macedonian monarchs. It is evident that there was no lack of patronage, but with Ibycus, Simonides, and Bacchylides, poets cease to be local poets, serving one state or deity, and offer their services to whoever seeks them. So likewise, for the first time, Simonides (early fifth century) introduced the practice of selling songs of praise for money, a practice which was apparently shocking to the Greek taste,[3] and at the same time poets became the friends and counsellors of princes. Petrarch did not occupy a more important place among the princes of medieval Italy than did Simonides in Greece,[4] and the last ten years of his life were spent at the 'home of geniuses,' the court of Hiero of Syracuse, a great patron of poets and philosophers, after he had enjoyed the favor, with Anacreon, of Hippias and Hipparchus at Athens. Similarly, Anacreon, living under the patronage of Polycrates, is said to have been paid the high honor of being sent for from Samos with a fifty-oared trireme when he accepted an invitation from Hipparchus to come to Athens. At this court of Polycrates also was the Rhegian poet, Ibycus, and a little later Dionysius entertained, though in a somewhat highhanded manner, the historian Philistus, the poet Philoxenus, and Plato, at his Syracusan court. Pindar, though

---

[2] Browne, *History of Classical Greek Literature,* (1857), 187.
[3] Plato, *Protagoras,* censures it as sophistic and illiberal.
[4] Symonds, *Studies of the Greek Poets,* 1st Series, (1877), 154.

a Theban, having felt enthusiasm for Athens in the Persian wars and expressed it in song, was by the vote of Athenian citizens made *proxenos* and given 10,000 drachmas, and it is said in addition that when the Thebans fined him for his implied reflections on them, Athens paid the fine.[5] Herodotus likewise was awarded ten talents on the motion of Anytus by the Athenian demos.[6] Though these are unusual cases, they show at least the fame and honor accorded the greater poets by the rulers of the great Greek cities. Both Pindar and Simonides carried on a trade in ode writing, for which they did not disdain to accept money,[7] Pindar writing for patrons after his own heart, among whom were the great merchant princes of Aegina.[8] It is not to be supposed, however, that they sang slavishly the praise of every bidder, and Pindar, at least, laments the necessity which drove him to do so outrageous a thing.[9] The drama seems to have been patronized and encouraged most. Prizes were offered by the state and contests encouraged, and the dramatists themselves were much in demand and held in high honor. Aeschylus visited Sicily on at least three occasions, once on invitation of Hiero, who was then founding the new town of Aetna, in honor of which event Aeschylus composed and exhibited the *Women of Aetna,* and again, a few years later, he gave a performance of the *Persae* at the request of the same prince. Euripides, shortly before his death, retired to the court of Macedon on the invitation of the king Archelaus for whom he wrote a tragedy. Finally, Plutarch, in the *Glory of the Athenians,* declares that the "Athenians spent more upon Bacchae, Oedipuses, and Antigones, and the woes of Medea and Electra, than in their wars against the barbarians and extending their Empire."[10]

It is matter of grave doubt, thinks Professor Mahaffy,[11] whether Greek art, flourishing as it did in tranquility under patronage in troublous times, could ever have attained all its greatness but

[5] Symonds, op. cit., 167.
[6] Murray, *Ancient Greek Literature,* (1908), 135.
[7] *Pythian Odes,* II.
[8] Murray, op. cit., 110.
[9] Proemium to the *Second Isthmian Ode.*
[10] *Plutarch's Miscellanies and Essays,* ed. Goodwin, V, 406.
[11] Op. cit., 440.

for the fostering and protection of the tyrants. Notable also is its backing both by individual and state, and, in fact, the direct successor of the tyrants as art patron was the Athenian demos, or perhaps more exactly, its leaders, Cimon, Pericles, and Lycurgus. At least it is certain that the work was not done to please private and peculiar taste or yet the taste of the particular coterie, but done for all—the fastidious, the vulgar, the learned or the ignorant.[12] In this, Greek Art, patronized as it was, differs essentially from art patronized in other ways, and this may explain perhaps why it is so broadly significant and eternal.

Nor did the old custom of individual patronage fail to persist in later times; rather it became much more substantial. Aristotle enjoyed the favor of several princes and was munificently assisted by Alexander to the amount of 800 talents toward defraying the expenses of his scientific investigations, and at one time the prince aided his researches in natural history by placing at his disposal a thousand men throughout Asia and Greece to collect and report details concerning the life and habits of fishes, birds, beasts, and insects. Similarly bounteous, the Ptolemies made Alexandria the great centre of Hellenistic literature and learning through their patronage. Such *literati* as Callimachus, Appolonius, Herondes, Theocritus, and Aratus were befriended by Philadelphus, the latter two having done literary work under the patronage of King Antigonus also. It was difficult for Greek authors to escape the magnetic influence of the great Academy and the powerful and munificent Philadelphus, for

> The best pay-master for a free-born man
> Is Ptolemy.[13]

But even into such a Paradise the serpent of indifference and disregard had already entered, and the poet was not always well-

---

[12] Ibid., 440.
[13] Theocritus, *Idylls*, xiv., (tr. Hallard). The passage goes on:
> And what besides is he?
> A kindly man, a friend of art and song,
> A lover, and the pink of courtesy;
> A man that knows his friend, his enemy
> Still better, giving largess unto many,
> Nor aught denies, that may beseem a king,
> To him that craves a boon.

treated. Theocritus, after having visited several courts, writes his plea:

Who will to-day be a friend to the singer that hymns his praises?
I know not; for men no longer desire as aforetime
Glory for noble deeds; but money is monarch and master. . . .
'Homer's enough for us all, and who would list to another?'
'Best of the bards is he that takes no part of my substance.'[14]

Alas, no longer did men wish for their praises to be sung by their poets, and no longer did they remember that those who have gone before would be completely forgotten had their deeds not been sung, for

Only the Muses grant unto mortals a guerdon of glory.

, Thus patronage in Greece is unique in its development. Arts, which were professional, were fostered by the patronage of the tyrants until public taste and sentiment was strong enough under the proper leaders to become a kind of demos-patron in the Golden Age, but there is a return to the system of individual patronage, with all its possible vicissitudes, in later times.

(b) *Rome*

Poverty has ever been the stepmother of learning, and it was advantageous to the poet that in ancient times at Rome princely generosity was especially expected, though on the whole early patronage of letters at Rome seems to have been a very unsubstantial affair. During the early Republic the patricians had extended their patronage to a favored few among writers. Literature had hardly come into its own until the interval between the first and second Punic wars, when the Romans first had leisure to contemplate the marvellous results of Greek culture. Then a gradual emancipation of the poet took place; his worth was discovered, and he at the same time became aware of his own value. Thus, when Scipio Africanus drew about him a circle of aristocratic liberals whose chief interest was Greek poetry and philosophy, and patronized Ennius, just as his son afterward did Terence, the relationship was honorable and not at all bind-

---

[14] Ibid., xvi.

ing. It was a fostering friendship purely, thoroughly consistent with the author's self-respect, and the poet neither sought nor attained wealth from this intimacy. Such also was the relationship which was maintained by Lucullus, who extended his patronage to all the arts and to scholarship. So, under conditions the poets or men of learning remained independent, and when they found no patron or could not support themselves by their own means, as Catullus and Lucretius did, until the time of Valerius Cato, at least, they maintained themselves by teaching and playwriting.

But in the troublous times of the late Republic it is to be doubted if such a system was fully efficient in producing literature. At any rate it was far from profitable; the matter-of-fact Roman could hardly be expected to spend much labor in a profession of small return, and, with the growth of the client system under the empire, poets no longer remained independent, but became members of a clientele. Instead of being satisfied with the joys of labor, many now expected to receive splendid presents from the emperor and other wealthy men, and also a certain profit from their works.[15] There was a time when it seemed possible that patronage would make literature remunerative. In the age of Augustus, as in the time of the Ptolemies in Alexandria and, in modern times, in the age of Louis XIV in France and our own Tudor age in England, poets wrote to please individual patrons. Patrons of arts have for the most part been men of high tastes, who demand a high degree of finish; hence, courtly ages of private patronage produce works of highest craftsmanship and have given the world much of its finest literature. The advantages of patronage are immense, but it is indispensible that the patron himself be great. In this respect the age of Augustus was ideal. A book-trade had grown up, but to make a living on book-sales without a private income was a sad business; the author needed a patron.

Most prominent stands Maecenas, whose name has become

---

[15] These statements refer to professional literary men only; the fact that men in all generations have done work or written simply to satisfy themselves is not to be overlooked.

synonymous in all ages for the great patron of letters. In Augustus' time other forces were making themselves felt besides political ones, and one of these was the literature of a class of men to whom letters was a profession and not a relaxation, and who now appear as a force in Rome. Augustus saw the immense advantage of enlisting these men on his side to become an instrument in his policy; he could pass laws and inflict punishments, but he could not reach the hearts of his people unless he found persuasive voices to preach for him and his reforms. And here about him was assembling a band of highly cultured, but threadbare poets. Maecenas, his friend, was well-fitted by his amiable address to be the attractive centre of such a circle. By the exercise of a patronage at once liberal and thoroughly consistent with the self-respect of its recipients, in time he gathered together with a very discriminating taste[16] a literary coterie of the rarest quality. He was thronged with parasites—musicians, buffoons, and *mimi* with Bathyllus at their head, but poets, such as Horace, Virgil, Varius, and Valgius, were also his companions and intimates. Other men did likewise. Messalla had a similar following, among whom were numbered the poet Tibullus[17] and the younger poets of the period; and similar groups were headed by Agrippa and by Pollio, who first encouraged public and private recitation of literary creations, and, indeed, by Augustus himself,[18] who thoroughly understood how to make poetry subservient to his aims by frank recognition and excellent judgment. Virgil, through the liberality of Augustus, lived in opulence, and Horace was happy in his Sabine farm, the gift of Maecenas.[19]

[16] Nine months elapsed between the introduction of Horace to Maecenas by Virgil and Varius, and his final enrollment of the poet in his circle, showing that he was not hasty in awarding patronage. The difficulty which Propertius encountered in gaining a footing shows that talent itself was not sufficient recommendation to his regard.

[17] Tibullus, however, with his private income, was probably above patronage.

[18] The eclogues of Calpurnius are an excellent example of the violent praise offered the later Caesars by needy poets.

[19] Horace, however, seems to have held aloof from the Emperor, and we hear of Augustus complaining: "Why is it that you avoid addressing me of all men in your poems? Is it that you are afraid posterity will think the worse of you for having been a friend of mine?" (Suetonius, *Horatii Poetae Vita*.) In *Epist*, II, 1, he declines to write the epic of Augustus' achievements.

It is pleasing to observe the entire absence of ill feeling in these great circles and the ideal manner in which poets and great men met on terms of equal companionship.[20] Servile compliment and eternal obligation were definitely not expected of the patronized as only too frequently in later periods; patronage and its acceptance were voluntary and honorable.[21] But there are always some vulgar pushing people. A delightful tale is told of Augustus and a Greek who would not allow him to go out of his palace without offering him a poem. The act was repeated again and again, until the emperor himself rapidly wrote an epigram and gave it to the Greek as he passed. The poet went into ecstacies on reading it, applauding by voice and visage; and approaching the royal litter, he put his hand into his purse and drew out several denarii which he offered saying, "Here is a little something for you, my lord, if I had more I should give you more." How could one be stone-hearted against such audacious impudence? Augustus turned to his dispenser and the poor Greek was happier by 10,000 sesterces.[22] Likewise, Horace gives us a picture of how importunate some folk are when he mentions the troublesome acquaintance, probably Propertius, who besought him for an introduction to Maecenas.[23] But the poet was not the only beneficiary by this ideal relation; he returned with interest the favors bestowed upon him, for honor and fame in the present, and immortality in the future, have always been confidently promised by even the meanest scribbler of verse in return for a livelihood. This patronage by Augustus and his friends did really in the end amount to a great deal. It produced Virgil and Horace, notably, and made the reign of Augustus a golden literary age, but such select cultivation per-

---

[20] Horace's ninth satire of the first book is a panegyric of the principles upon which Maecenas conducted his patronage.

[21] When Maecenas became impatient and reminded him of his obligations, Horace gently asserted himself. "I would not exchange my independence and quiet for all the riches of Arabia." (*Epist.* I, 7.) Further, not one word of commendation is there in Horace of Maecenas the poet (and a bad one) by whom it would, no doubt, have been gratefully received.

[22] Macrobius, *Saturnalia*, II, iv.

[23] *Satires*, I, 9. Of course, he finally got into the circle and addressed several grateful poems to the great patron. (II, i; III, ix.)

haps reacted unfavorably on thought and imagination. At any rate, this nursery developed a cultured literature, different from the current popular trend, but artificially delicate as is seen by its almost immediate collapse at Augustus' death.

There are certain features common to these Augustans, however, which indicate a need of patronage, and which differentiate them from the writers of the late Republic. The latter were mostly men of eminence, while the Augustans were mostly Italians and provincials, of humble origin even, and of peaceful quiet natures devoid of ambition and wishing only to be left alone to their art.[24] Such spirits would not have risen to eminence in the fierce contests of the Republic, and in most cases they do not appear to have had the opportunity of finding out whether apart from patronage they could actually have made their livings by their poems. The remarkable development of their genius is perhaps a definite indication of how much literature had suffered from unsettled times, justifying to a certain extent at least, the standing apology of later times:

Let there be many a Maecenas, many a Maro will not fail, and even your fields will give you a Virgil.[25]

At the death of Augustus the Golden Age soon passed away. Though under an imperial master literary expression could not be so free as in the days of the Republic, the amount of the restraint depended upon the Emperor, and from Augustus to Hadrian the ruling princes were nearly all poetical amateurs, who, aside from the celebration of their fame, felt it incumbent upon them to show a practical interest in poetry. Besides, patronage had become a fashion which fitted well into the client system. Though the good old custom of rewarding poets fell into disuse,[26] there is no reason to believe that there were not many

[24] Virgil prays he may live without glory among the woodlands and streams he loves (*Georgics*, II, 486), and Tibullus (I, i.) and Propertius (I, vi, 29) assert in strong terms their incapacity for active careers, praying for nothing more than enjoyment of love and song.

[25] Martial, VIII, lvi; and in I, cvii, he pleads for leisure. Juvenal, resting his hopes on Caesar, has a similar complaint. (*Satire* vii.)

[26] The younger Pliny, writing to Cornelius Priscus of Martial's death, laments that the old practice of heaping pecuniary rewards on poets for their verses has grown out of fashion, though he himself had kept it up and felt it his duty to pay Martial's

and generous patrons among the emperors and nobles. Martial had many liberal protectors,[27] and there is reason to believe that poets forced themselves upon the later emperors by flattery,[28] and exploited on a large scale their liberality, while the emperors, with the best of intentions, could satisfy but a small part of the entreaties addressed to them.[29] In the later Empire, when the relation of poet and patron was not distinguishable from that of client and patron, not only did the noble appreciation of poetic genius in high circles disappear,[30] owing to the decay of cultured as well as popular taste, but under Domitian at least, distinguished men had to guard against arousing suspicion by too lavish a generosity and too numerous a clientele. Under such conditions, of course, a political backer is worth more than a poet. Hence, Juvenal's complaint that poverty and want were avoidable, is not correct, for though poets probably enjoyed on the whole as much

travelling expenses home in return for a very flattering poem. His attitude is very interesting: "Do you not think that the poet who wrote in such terms to me deserved some friendly bounty *then,* and that he merits my sorrow *now?* For he gave me the most he could, and it was want of power only, if his present was not more valuable. But to say truth, what higher can be conferred on man than fame, and applause, and immortality? And though it should be granted, that his poems will not be immortal, still, no doubt, he composed them upon the contrary supposition." (*Letters,* III, 21, ed. Melmouth.) Martial himself complains of the outrageous habit his friends were falling into of decreasing their gifts or of giving them to mistresses instead. (VIII, lxxi; IX, lxxxviii; X, xxix and lvii; XI, cv.)

[27] Each Caesar. he tells us with pride, bestowed rewards upon him and gave him the privileges of a father of three sons, (III, xcv; ix, xcvii; and II, xcii) and he begs for more. (IV, xxvii.) He tells Priscus Terentius that what Maecenas was to Flaccus and Varius and Maro, he is to Martial. "You create my genius, you create whatever power I seem to show; you give me the free man's right of idleness." (XII, iv.) The difficulty in Martial's case is to distinguish his friends and his political patrons from his literary ones.

[28] The method is seen in Martial. "A certain individual, Faustinus, whom I praised in my book, pretends he owes me nothing. He has cheated me." (V, xxxvi.)

[29] That they did not allow such pleas to go unrewarded is evident. Tiberius handsomely rewarded the knight Gaius Laberius for an elegy on the death of Germanicus; Claudius must have been liberal since poets lament his death, which they would probably not have done if he had not been; and an epigram of a Greek poet living in Rome reads: "Had not the emperor Nero given me some ready money, it would have gone ill with me, O Muses, daughters of Zeus." Vespasian gave Saleius Bassus 500,000 sesterces, and the Greek poet Oppian is said to have received a piece of gold from Marcus Aurelius for every line of his poems he read in his presence. (Friedländer, *Roman Life and Manners under the Early Empire,* III, 54.)

[30] The increasing divergence from popular taste due to Augustan patronage meant practically that when the appreciation of the cultured was gone, all appreciation was gone, and a popular poet now would necessarily have been a bad one.

favor as they deserved or formerly had,[31] they were too many in number, and too entirely dependent on favor and generosity. They were perhaps themselves largely to blame, though they lacked a confident feeling of their own worth. And so, at Rome, when the hopes of patronage were finally abandoned, the profession of poetry seems for a time to have been practically given up.[32] When we read of the authors of this period we are inevitably reminded of the literary man of 18th century, afflicted by

Age, envy, want, the patron, and the jail,

and of Dr. Johnson waiting for hours in Chesterfield's office and returning home to write as scathing a satire as ever Martial or Juvenal wrote. In the flattering addresses of Roman poets, we are likewise reminded of the flattering dedications of later times, so liberally or illiberally paid for. In fact, the entire system of Roman patronage represents a development, if we may call it so, which affords an interesting parallel to the development of medieval and modern patronage in general, and in particular to conditions in England. Early Roman patronage bears in some respects the same marks of instability, indefiniteness, and unsubstantiality that characterized medieval patronage; it is sporadic, unorganized, and individual. The Augustan age compares favorably with the Elizabethan and Tudor ages in England or that of Louis XIV in France, where the custom has become an institution, already struggling to meet the demands made upon it; and finally, Roman patronage of the later Empire finds its parallel in 18th century England, where it definitely can no longer bear up under its duties and collapses for the same reasons that Roman patronage collapsed.

(c) *The Literary Man in the Dark Ages*

With the decay of power in Rome, as has been indicated, came a decay of taste, and with the entrance of Christianity, pagan

[31] It seems a great pity that because of the age and environment, poets like Martial should make their muse shamelessly mercenary and prostitute great genius to the poor business of court poet.

[32] Men still wrote, however, to fill in leisure hours and to amuse themselves or their friends.

literature and all things corrupt were suppressed, and study of what was good of the ancients discouraged. Thus art, literature, and hence thought, decayed, and what little learning there was was entrusted to the monks and other ecclesiastics. What literary men there were were clerics, and their subjects are either religious or at least tinged with theology and religious ideas. But even in the fifth century many of the Christians themselves felt the lure of pagan perfection. For many of the early Fathers the classics were beautiful horrors possessed of the double potency of attraction and repulsion; we see Jerome fearfully shrinking from his love of Cicero, and Augustine from Virgil. In Italy with the disappearance of paganism, the devout horror of profane literature gradually died down, though not until culture and much that is worthwhile were almost past rebuilding. In the East, likewise, literature remained to a certain extent, and with it also a semblance of patronage of letters. We find dedications, panegyrics and encomiums of nobles, addresses to emperors, and flattery galore,[33] and between 886 and 963 Constantinople was ruled by the so-called 'literary emperors' during whose reigns literature became the fashion of the court.[34] But the idea of patronage is one which does not decay or die, and just as soon as a leader rose who was strong enough to enforce peace and had time to look about him for means of making his court glorious, literature and learning again came into their own. Thus, Charlemagne, with an interest which was rare among Frankish kings, loved learning though he could not read, and spared no pains to revive what was fast passing away. He drew Alcuin to his court from Northumbria, and Paul the Deacon and Peter of Pisa from Italy, where learning, if inert, was not dead. These men, it is true, were valued by their patron chiefly as teachers of grammar and because they were men of learning, and not because they could write. Perhaps, too, Charlemagne felt his dignity as Roman emperor. At any rate, nothing perhaps is more touching than to see this rough old warrior, now that he had brought about peace, endeavoring to encourage learning in others by his gener-

[33] Krumbacher, *Geschichte by Byzantinischen Litteratur*, passim.
[34] Putnam, *Authors and their Public in Ancient Times*, 286.

osity, and attempting to acquire it himself, recognizing that a
reputation for liberality and the reward of renown amply com-
pensated all conveniences.[35]

In England in the next generation there was an equally famous
figure in Alfred the Great. Like Charlemagne he encouraged
the fine arts and learning, and like Charles the moment he had
the power and leisure he set to work to gather together "those
who might assist his righteous intention and aid him to wisdom."
These helpers were all Mercians. Werforth became Bishop of
Worcester and translated from Latin the *Dialogues* of Pope
Gregory at the king's command; Plegmund, "one indued with wisdom," became archbishop of Canterbury, and Athelstan and Wer-
wulf both were the king's chaplains.[36] To these four were
afterwards added several foreignors. From Gaul he summoned
Grimbald, "an excellent singer,....very learned,....and adorned
with every good quality." From the continent too, he summoned
John the Old Saxon, "a man of very cunning mind, and very
learned in all the rules of the art of letters." Finally, Asser was
summoned from Wales. All these learned men were held in
high honor by the king, who richly rewarded them. Grimbald and
John were given rich abbacies, and Asser, who speaks of his
own fortunes more in detail, shows Alfred to have been very
liberal. On his first visit Asser received the monasteries of Con-
gresbury and Banwell, a "pall of silk most precious," and as
much incense as could be borne by a strong man, with the promise
of greater gifts. Later he received the whole see of Exeter in
addition to countless daily gifts of all manner of earthly goods.[37]
Further, Johannes Scotus is said to have been allured from the
court of Charles the Bald by the munificence of the English
king.[38] Hence, as a result of Alfred's revival of learning Eng-

---

[35] Eginhard, *Charles the Great,* Section 21. He also collected, wrote out, and committed to memory the rude old songs of the exploits and wars of kings of old, and
began a grammar of the speech of his country. (Ibid., Section 29.)

[36] Asser, *Life of King Alfred,* ed. Jane, (1908), 57.

[37] Ibid., 59-64.

[38] William of Malmesbury, *Chronicle of the Kings of England,* (Bohn Lib.), 119.
Besides scholars, Alfred also patronized other artists, and architects were especially
dear to him. To his artificers he devoted a large portion of his income. (Asser,
op. cit., 83.)

land for many years had an educated governing class, lay as well
as clergy, and one may judge of his efforts from the fact that
they were still bearing fruit in Dunstan's time, fully three generations later.

A similar patron of learning is to be found on the continent in
the tenth century. Like Charlemagne and Alfred, Otto the
Great not only built up his empire, but found time to encourage
art, owing, no doubt, to his ties in Italy and the East.[39] Learned
men and artists were summoned from beyond the Alps and from
Constantinople, and their number and influence were increased
when Otto's son married a Greek princess, who reflected in her
German home the learning and splendor of the Byzantine court.
Notable among those encouraged by Otto was the nun Hroswitha,
who besides writing plays wrote a panegyric on Otto's family,
which we find her presenting to him.[40]

Thus it is seen that the tradition persisted, but of more interest
to us than these few remnants of the old time, are instances of
encouragement offered by men to a very corrupt form of ancient
entertainer, the mime, who has come down even into modern
times. This notorious Roman and Greek entertainer, though
beset on all sides by the hostile forces of the church, yet managed,
by his clever policy of being all things to all men, to keep himself
safe and well-cared for. He had been much honored in Rome
in the last days and continued to be so at Constantinople where
he commanded every luxury.[41] Then when the theatres were all
closed he chose to wander out in the world, and make the best
of it. He was still in vogue, however, if no longer in the theatres,
then at banquets and public merrymakings or even in the streets
—wherever he could collect a remnant of his old audiences.[42]

[39] Like Charles, Otto was himself a man of little culture, but he had a taste for
literature, and through his means there came about a revival of Latin letters to which
the first beginnings of German literature were united. In this he was aided by his
youngest brother Bruno, Arch-chancellor and Arch-chaplain of the Empire and Archbishop of Cologne.

[40] A wood-cut, by Dürer, 1501, representing Hroswitha, attended by the abbess of
Gandersheim, presenting her poem to Otto I, is reproduced in Kemp-Welch, *Of Six
Medieval Women.*

[41] Reich, *Der Mimus,* 755 and passim.

[42] Chambers, *Medieval Stage,* I, 24.

Attila the Hun in 448 entertained the imperial ambassadors at a banquet where they were first moved to martial ardour and to tears by the recital of ancient deeds of prowess, and then stirred to laughter by the antics of a buffoon;[43] Sidonius tells how *mimici sales* found a place in the festivities of Theodoric, King of the Visigoths in Gaul, 462-66,[44] and in 507 Clovis the Frank sent to Theodoric for a *citharoedus* trained in the music of the south.[45] At the hands of Charlemagne the mime won at least some recognition, for the emperor personally took a distinct interest in minstrel performances, and the later jongleurs looked upon Charles as the great patron of their order who had given them all the fair land of Provence in fee.[46] But more often, instead of being fostered, the mime had to contend for denarii with low sorts of persons such as jugglers and rope dancers and beast tamers, and he had to learn anything that might amuse. Essentially, the mime was just as he had always been—a buffoon, a jester, and ever an obscene person. Now he travelled in small groups, making for himself a welcome at castle or tavern or wherever he found it profitable to be, and so became absorbed into that amiable body of nomad entertainers upon whom the Middle Ages depended largely for entertainment. The features of the minstrels of medieval Europe are essentially those of the Roman mime. One parent of the medieval jongleur, however, was much more respectable than the other, for, like other factors in medieval society, in the minstrel as well were merged Latin and Teutonic elements; he inherits the traditions of both the *mimus* and the Teutonic *scop*.

[43] Priscus, *Hist. Goth.* (ed. Bonn), 205, cited by Chambers, op. cit., 34-5.
[44] Chambers, op. cit., I, 35.
[45] Cassiodorus, *Variae*, II, 40-41, cited by Chambers, op. cit., I, 35.
[46] Philippe Mouskes, *de Poetis Provincialibus*, quoted by Du Cange, s. v. *leccator* and cited by Chambers, op. cit., I, 37.

II

THE SCOP, THE SCALD, THE BARD, AND THE MINSTREL

In the society of the Teutons, gathered about its chieftains, room was found for one honored as the maker of song and of praises of the king, which he chanted to the accompaniment of the harp. He was not a soldier, perhaps, but he was a thane, and he was rich in dignities and rewards and essentially different from the scurrilous *scenicis infamis* of Rome. Just when he came·into being is not known; by the fifth century he was thoroughly established, though he doubtless existed in the fourth and, we hear of him, not from Latin sources, but from those early English poems, which in origin at least, date before the time the Teuton changed his dwelling place. Because the English remained until a comparatively late date remote from Roman influence, it is in these poems that both the original development of the Germanic *scop* and his later contamination by the *mimus* are to be traced.

Our old Teutonic ancestors seem to have been a singing people, for in all accounts of them we hear of their singers and poets, who were held in very high respect and esteem. This fact had its origin perhaps, in an intense and universal veneration for literature, for poetry was looked upon as a gift from the gods. When we consider what the scop or bard meant in the old time, we must admit that his range of activity was large and that he was worthy of all the respect that came to him. He was the court singer, with all that the term means—'maker' and composer—both extemporal and traditional; he was the teacher and critic of his time; the conserver of knowledge; the historian and genealogist; the journalist; and often the traveller and bearer of news. In war he went into battle, sometimes as a warrior, but more often as the inspirer by his noble songs to deeds of valor. Like the

bard of classical times, the Anglo-Saxon scop also was looked
upon as divinely inspired for the purpose of setting forth the
noble deeds of his hearers, and of raising their thoughts to higher
things.[1]   He held a high place in the court[2] as a thane and a
member of the king's household, and his dignity and worth stand
out in marked contrast to the disrepute of his successors in later
times.   The mere fact that he was the preserver of tradition with
something of the priestly about him,[3] was sufficient, perhaps, to
account for part of his high esteem, but one of the main reasons
was the influence exerted upon public opinion.   It is almost safe
to say that glory among men and the possibility of immortality
in the future—in short that "world's mighty Monarch, Good
Opinion" to whom Marston unceremoniously and directly made
his dedication—is behind much of literary patronage.   So it was
among the Anglo-Saxons, and though as a general rule the poet
was retained at the court of his lord, wandering about has its obvious advantages when glory is to be peddled; hence the scop
yielded to the wanderlust with royal consent and travelled, there
apparently being no distinction between the scop as retainer and
as wanderer.   Testifying to his importance in Anglo-Saxon life,
three of the old poems, the *Beowulf, Widsith,* and *Deor's Lament,* give us a very full account of the scop and his means of sub-
sistence.   As has been said, he was a man of repute who adopted
poetry as a profession,[4] and from the *Widsith* notably we know
he held lands, even the lands of his fathers.[5]   Widsith's position
toward his king, too, is that of an advisor.[6]

> ¹Þonne þy læs þe him con leoþa worn
> Oþþe mid hondum con hearpan grētan,
> hafaþ him his glīwes giefe, þe him god sealde.
>   —*Gnomic Verses* (Exeter), 170-72.
>
> Compare *Elene,* 1247-52.

² In *Beowulf* the scop is named after the king (210 ff.), and while a self-respecting
Roman citizen, treading the boards or performing publicly, was immediately stamped
with *infamia,* Hrothgar's thanes and Hrothgar himself take their turns in telling a
wondrous tale.

³ The Anglo-Saxons in writing of Biblical patriarchs, prophets, etc., represented
these as singers. (*Elene,* 337, 561-2; Anderson, *Anglo-Saxon Scop,* 35.)

⁴ Deor and Hrothgar's scop are spoken of as professionals.

⁵ Land grants would serve to attach a singer permanently to his lord.   Widsith
received grants of land not only from his king, but from his queen also, (1. 971),
and the land of Deor seems to have been attached to the office of scop, passing into
the hands of the more successful Heorrend. (*Deor's Lament,* 1. 39.)

⁶ *Widsith,* ll. 11-13.

The scop was wholly dependent upon gifts for his sustenance, and we find numerous mentions of presents for songs, usually gold rings.[7] In return for a living he celebrated heroic deeds in song,[8] for renown as a leader was the greatest thing in life to the old Teutons. The ideal chieftain, moreover, was he who availed himself of the opportunity the scop's art gave for glory, and recognized the poet's power of increasing the chief's prestige in the eyes of his subjects.[9] Hence, it is natural that there are many references to the king as the giver: *brytta, beaga brytta, sincesbrytta, goldes brytta, goldwine gumena, gold-gifa, sinc-gifa, beaggifa, hringa Þengel.* A throne is a *gif setl* or a *gifstol,* and even the hall where the scop sang is called the *beah-sele* or the *goldsele.*[10]

---

[7] Cynewulf states he received presents of gold (*Elene,* 1258-9) and of Widsith we hear much as to his rewards:

> oft he (on) flette geþah
> mynelicne maþþum.   (ll. 3-4.)

Again:

> Forþan ic mæg singan on secgan spell,
> mænan fore mengo in meoduhealle,
> hū mē cynegōde cystum dohten.   (ll. 55-7.)

or:

> þær ic bēag geþāh;
> mē þær Gūðhere forgeaf glædlīcne māþþum
> songes to lēane.   (ll. 65-7.)

That this riches was, like booty taken in war, to be brought to the scop's original lord is seen in this passage:

> sē mē bēag forgeaf, burgwarena fruma,
> on þām siexhund wæs smætes goldes
> gescyred sceatta scillingrīme;
> þone ic Eadgilse on æht sealde,
> minum hlēodryhtne, þā ic tō hām becwōm,
> lēofum to leane, þæs þe hē mē lond forgeaf,
> mīnes fæder eþel, frēa Myringa.   (ll. 90ff.)

Compare *Widsith,* 74 and 97, *Wanderer,* 33 ff. The *Fates of Men,* (Exeter Book), ll. 80 ff., also refers to reward. *Riddle* 95, if one accepts the solution 'wandering singer,' contains a reference to largess. On the "Autobiographical Element in the Cynewulfian Rune Passages," see C. F. Brown, *Englische Studien,* XXXVIII, (1907), 196 ff.

[8] *Beowulf,* ll. 872 ff.

[9] Widsith states of the queen Ealhild, who was gracious to him, that:

> Hyre lof lengde geond londa fela,
> þonne ic be songe secgan sceolde
> hwær ic under swegl(e) sēlast wisse
> goldhrodene cwēn giefe bryttian.   (ll. 99 ff.)

[10] *Beowulf,* 11, 35, 168, 352, 607, 1012, 1170, 1171, 1177, 1342, 1476, 1507, 1602, 1922, 2071, 2311, 2327, 2329, 2419, 2587, 2652; *Wanderer,* 22, 25, 35, 44; *Elene,* 100, 1199; *Genesis,* 1997; *Andreas,* 1657; *Guthlac,* 1326.

Such phrases commendatory of princely generosity as

næs þæt sæne cyning[11]

give us an insight into the relation of poet and patron, for in such
connection phrases are not to be taken merely as bits of praise,
but also as reminders of duty. Presents were not always of great
value, perhaps, and by no means certain, and some means of in-
citing bounty—delicate, of course—had to be devised. Few noble
qualities are so frequently referred to as generosity; all true
heroes possess it, and acts of munificence are the ones most dwelt
upon.[12] Perhaps the best summary of the scop's patronage and
his activity are the closing lines of the *Widsith:*

> Thus wandering, they who shape the songs for men
> Pass over many lands, and tell their need,
> And speak their thanks and ever south or north,
> Meet some one skilled in songs and free in gifts,
> Who would be raised among his friends to fame
> And do brave deeds till light and life are gone;
> He who has thus wrought himself praise shall have
> A settled glory underneath the stars.

Likewise, poetic skill seems to have been a national trait among
the Scandinavians. Though kings and warriors frequently break
into spontaneous verse,[13] poetic talent was confined to a stated
profession, that of the *scald,* or 'verse smith,' who had much in
common with the scop and the southern troubadour, and who
was equally honored and rewarded. Literary talent was not a
matter merely of amusement; it was a means to favor in the
courts, and naturally the scald was more especially caressed by
those princes who were distinguished warriors. Hence, the scald
is often more the historian of his patron than the poet, having
recourse to poetry only to immortalize his king. Scaldic activity
in the early time seems to have centered around the court of

---

[11] *Widsith,* 67, etc.

[12] Widsith abounds in references to particular acts (ll. 65-7, 70-4, 89-92, etc.), and
Hrothgar possesses this virtue (*Beowulf,* 80). The hint is broader yet in *Beowulf,*
18-25. Cf. also, *Beowulf,* 71 ff., 1020 ff., 1050 ff., 1089 ff., 1193 ff., 1866 ff., 2018 ff.,
2190 ff., 2633 ff., 2865 ff., 2994 ff.

[13] Volume II of the *Corpus Poeticum Boreale* contains numerous examples; Warton,
History of English Poetry, ed. Hazlitt, (1871), I, 117 gives a few.

Harold of the Fair Hair, a most liberal prince, who gave the highest patronage.[14] People whose object was glory could not fail to show great respect for those who published it abroad and made them immortal.[15] Hence, the prince often exposed his life recklessly only to be praised by his scald whom he brought into the field of action.[16] And it is interesting to note, in view of what has been seen of ancient times and of the Anglo-Saxons, that apparently no scald ever went without being recompensed with glittering armor, rich apparel, and rings and armlets.[17] Largess, of course, brought forth expressions of gratitude and praise in the sagas, all of which added to a prince's reputation abroad.[18]

[14] Poets are listed according to their patrons in the *Skalda-Tal, Corpus Poeticum Boreale*, II, 442. A description of Harold's court scalds with their gold rings, red cloaks, shields, swords, gilt belts, chased helmets and armlets is found in Thorbjöron's Hornklofi) *Fagrskinna*, quoted by Metcalfe, *The Englishman and the Scandinavian*, 385.

[15] A good example is found in the epilogue to *Atli-mal in Granlenzko, Corpus Poeticum Boreale*, I, 346.

[16] Thus Olaf of Norway placed three around him in battle and exclaimed: "You shall not only record in your verses what you have heard, but what you have seen." (Warton, op. cit., I, 127.)

[17] Respect often extended so far as to remit punishment of crime on condition that the scald sued for his pardon in verse. (Mallet, *Northern Antiquities*, 235. An example is given by Warton, op. cit., I, 127-8.) That the scald was honored very highly is shown in that he even married kings' daughters. (*Landnama*, V, ch. 1.)

[18] These references are usually at the beginning as prologue: "Hearken, O Raven-kettle, to my praise of the brightly painted Shield and of the king *that gave it me*: so that the son of Sigrod may learn the song I have made in return for the ring-naved buckler." (*Bragi's Shield Lay, Corpus Poeticum Boreale*, II, 6.) Again at the end of the same song as Epilogue: "I got gold at the king's hands in return for my song. He (*the king*) was the worst friend to gold and the best to me." (Ibid., I, 9.) Again, "How can . . . . my mouth render thanks to Thorleif for the bright-ringing shield!" (Prologue to Thiodwolf's *Haust-Song*, Ibid., I, 14), and as a refrain in the same song are introduced such lines: "Lo, this is painted on my shield. I received the colored buckler from Thorleif's hands," (Ibid., I, 16), or, "Clearly I see all these adventures on the shield. I received the colored buckler at Thorleif's hands." (Ibid., I, 17.) So also in a song of Olaf Tryggrason's (995-1000) we find the mention: "I know that the wide-ruling king gave the poet a naked sword for a certain thing [for his song?]. I have a precious jewel now. The hilts of the king's gift are costly mounted. A fine sword I have; I got a brand from the king." (Ibid., I, 96.) Again, when Thorarin the Flatterer made the encomiastic *Stretch-Song* on Cnut, well might he record in his Epilogue: "I have gotten fifty marks of the king as a fee, which he gave me for my song that I delivered on him. I made the Stretch-Song on the Gold-giver," for the piece sounds it. Also in the *Laxdala Saga* we hear: "Ulf Uggoson was of the bidden guests, and he had made a poem on Olaf Huskoldson and of the legends that were painted round the halls, and he gave it forth at the feast. This poem is called the 'House Song' and is well made. Olaf rewarded him well for the poem. Olaf gave

The process of obtaining this patronage, happily, is described to us in one of the sagas. Gunnlaug of the Snake's Tongue went to Ireland, and after having greeted the king well and worthily, announced that he had made a song on him and desired silence. And strangely enough, this king of the land of bards answered: "No men have ever before now come forward with songs for me and surely will I hearken to thine," whereupon Gunnlaug sang a stanza dealing entirely with rings and rewards and kingly generosity. The king was pleased and thanked him, and calling his treasurer to him, asked:

"How shall the song be rewarded?"
"What hast thou to give lord?" says he.
"How will it be rewarded if I give him two ships for it?" said the king. Then said the treasurer, "This is too much, lord; other kings give in reward of songs good keepsakes, fair swords, or golden rings."[19]

So the king gave him his own raiment of new scarlet, a gold embroidered kirtle and a cloak lined with choice furs and a gold ring which weighed a mark.[20] Gunnlaug then moved to Orkney and received for lay reward a broad-axe all inlaid with silver, and was asked to abide there.

That the scalds were entertained at English courts seems undoubted. In the same *Gunnlaug Saga* we hear of the hero at the court of King Ethelred, son of Edgar,[21] on whom he makes a song and who gave him a scarlet cloak lined with the costliest furs and gold embroidered down to the hem. The Danish king Canute was also their patron.[22]

---

great gifts to all the chief men who came. Olaf was considered to have gained renown by this feast." (tr. Muriel A. C. Press, 90.)

[19] It is interesting to note this early example of the avariciousness of treasurers, and to recall how badly Spenser fared at the hand of Elizabeth's, who grumbled, "So much for a song!" (Manningham's *Diary*, May 4, 1602, and Fuller's *Worthies*, II.)

[20] *Gunnlaug Saga, Three Northern Love Stories and other Tales*, tr. Magnusson and Morris, 32 ff.

[21] *Op., cit.,* 28. The fact is carefully explained so: "But in those days was the same tongue in England as in Norway and Denmark; but the tongues changed when William the Bastard won England, for thenceforward French went current there, for he was of French kin." (Ibid., 27.)

[22] Numerous scalds made songs on Canute. Their names are listed by Du Chaillu, *Viking Age*, 390. Further, we are told that Thorarin the Flatterer made the good king angry by writing too concise a poem upon him. Cnut bade him make a full

Among the Irish and Welsh, to the bard in addition to the various functions of the scop and the scald, was added something of the magician, law-giver, judge, counsellor, priest, or favorite of the gods. So learning shared honors with royalty. The laws of Howel the Good of Wales,[23] though given c. 940 indicate something of the privileges of the bard among Celtic peoples in early times. He is a domestic officer and has a horse from the king and garments from the king and queen; if a booty is taken and he is present, he receives a choice bullock. The gifts to the king are to be given literally for a song, and he is a land holder by the grace of his office, that he may live in independence and ease. We hear among other things that "a natural genius who shall achieve nothing less than an exploit in respect to art, for the benefit of a community" is one of the three accidental objects of free support.[24] Three persons are not to engage in war: a bard, an artist, or a scholar and a judge, for neither one or the other of the three can be dispensed with.[25] Furthermore, rewards for bardic songs were established by law. Finally, even if he were a murderer a minstrel could not be put to death.[26]

The profession was hereditary, but when the bard died, his estate devolved, not to his oldest son, but to that member of his family most talented for poetry and music. Thus poetry and its professors were an appanage to the feudal lord of every small domain, and every castle was its seat. In Wales the bards had fixed places of abode, but in addition they made a tour of the the country once in three years. In Ireland, though generally attached to a patron, the poet at certain intervals with a retinue of twenty-four of his disciples, was entitled to go on visitation. The kings and chiefs visited were expected to lodge and entertain him lavishly, and on his departure to give him a valuable present

---

encomium by the next day's dinner or his head would be the penalty. Thorarin was equal to the occasion and received fifty marks of silver in fee, whereupon he wrote the *Stretch-Song* on Cnut in commemoration. (*Corpus Poeticum Boreale*, II, 158-9.)

[23] *Ancient Laws and Institutes of Wales*, tr. and ed. A. Owen, 2 vols, (1841).
[24] Ibid., II, 548-9 and 524-5.
[25] Ibid., II, 556-7.
[26] Ibid., II, 626-7.

for his poetry, in particular for the eulogy of his host presented by the poet on his arrival.[27]

Perhaps one reason at least for the high esteem of the bard was his influence on public opinion. Oisin, at once a hero and a bard, felt equally the dignity and importance of his talents which had the power to confer the immortality of fame, that, as a hero, he ardently desired, and he recurs, with pleased, yet melancholy retrospection, to the happy days when he encouraged the art of which he was a master.[28] There are those who would make the panegyric of noble deeds the earliest form of poem, and likewise find in it the origin of the epic; whatever the case may be, it is true that the old poetry is full of panegyric. If a Louis XIV gratified himself by eulogies written to order by Molière, it is not inconceivable that the early chieftains in the days before Christianity had reached England liked them too and were willing to pay for them, since the military chief was the sole patron by whom the author might live. But with such easily abused privileges obviously the bard was at no time an unmixed blessing. He was unproductive economically, and as early as the seventh century, in Ireland at least, he was looked upon as constituting an intolerable drain on the nation's resources.[29] His silver pot 'of avarice' into which the unfortunate victim was expected to throw his largess of gold while the bard chanted a poem in his laudation,[30] was not to be evaded.[31] Woe indeed for him who refused, for a scathing satire was at once forthcoming. Under no circumstances is a lampoon agreeable, but a bardic satire was indeed venomous, for current belief held that it had the power of inflicting actual physical or mental mischief, and that the poet's *aer* could blight crops, dry up milch-cows, raise ulcerous blisters,

---

[27] Instances are given by Joyce, *Social History of Ancient Ireland*, I, 449. The last visitation was made in 1808 by the bard O'Kelley, who made a circuit of Connaught, extorting subscriptions, and writing on his return some verses mostly in praise of those who gave him money or in scurrilous abuse of those who had the spirit to refuse.

[28] 'The Chase: A Poem,' Brooke, *Reliques of Irish Poetry*, (1789), 81 and note.

[29] Hyde, *Literary History of Ireland*, 488.

[30] Examples of these panegyrics and their insinuating references to the lord's generosity are to be found in Wilkins, *History of Literature in Wales*, passim.

[31] Hyde, op. cit., 489.

or bring ruin or disgrace.[32] This terrific weapon was often wielded with curious and elaborate ceremonies which served to make it still more deadly, and though several attempts were made to suppress the bards, their power was so great that they were only checked,[33] their number was limited, and the amount of the reward which they were allowed to receive for their poems legally settled.[34] So with his system of enforced patronage, one might say, the family bard, originally a retainer, remained from the 13th to the close of the 16th century the most important literary man in Ireland.[35] In Wales, where the bard's reputation was perhaps not so high as in Ireland, he appears to have lived with his patrons, and, as usual when literature depends upon the uncertainty of the patron's caprice, begged and lived by his praises, just or unjust.[36]

Such then was the patronage accorded to the more respectable ancestors of the medieval minstrel or jongleur. So long as the scald and the scop[37] remained in their own territories or wandered about under the patronage of their lords, they united in themselves the various functions described. When, after the

[32] In the 'Reign of Bres,' in Lady Gregory's *Gods and Fighting Men*, we hear of such a curse. "And from that day there was no good luck with Bres, but it is going down he was forever after. And that was the first satire ever made in Ireland."

[33] Keating, *History of Ireland*, 371-2, quotes from poems in praise of Connor and Maolchabha, Kings of Ulster, who protected the bards from banishment.

[34] Hyde, op. cit., 489-90.

[35] Even so late as Spenser's time we hear of these abuses and the outrageous greed and unscrupulousness of the bards. "There is amongst the Irish a certayne kind of people called Bards, which are to them insteede of poetts, whose profession is to sett foorth the prayses and disprayses of men in theyr poems and rimes; the which are had in soe high request and estimation amongst them, that none dare to displease them for feare of running into reproche through theyr offence, and to be made infamous in the mouthes of all men. For theyr verses are taken up with a generall applause, and usually songe at all feasts and meetinges, by certayne other persons, whose proper function that is, which also receave for the same greate rewardes and reputation besides." (*View of the Present State of Ireland, Works,* ed. Trent, 790.)

[36] Notable and interesting examples of this relationship are the explicit poems of Taleisin, written to Urien. "May I never smile if I praise not Urien" is the refrain of many of his pieces. (*Book of Taleisin,* xxxi-vi and xxxix, in Skene, *Four Ancient Books of Wales,* I, 344 ff.) Poseidanus relates an amusing story of Luern, king of the Arvernians, which shows us generosity aroused by panegyric. Versions of the story are reported by Warton, op. cit., I, 135 n. and Van Laun, *History of French Literature,* (1876), I, 39.

[37] The same is not true in all ways of the bard, though he was not uninfluenced, for on the whole he remained isolated from the effects of the fall of Rome.

fall of Rome, tribal institutions and classical traditions were brought into contact and ancient culture had begun to be assimilated by the invaders, the simple character of the old poets expanded. In the early times there was no distinction between *scop* and *gleoman;* Widsith is at once resident singer and wanderer.[38] Later in the glosses *joculator, mimus, iocista, scurra, pantomimus* all equal *gligmon,* while *scop* is reserved for the dignified *vates* or *poeta.* The inevitable had happened. The wandering gleeman, while still singing the ancient tribal lays, had taken another stock in trade, the tricks which had diverted the rich and corrupt Roman, and had become a mime. Minstrelsy too took on in course of time other instruments besides the harp, and the scop of the court became the king's minstrel whose business it was to amuse his highness: in fact he was a kind of slightly dignified court fool. Hence, with the characteristic differences between the Teutonic and Roman entertainer in mind, it might be assumed that there were two types of minstrel in the Middle Ages: (1) the amiable wandering entertainer of the folk, or modified Roman mime, and (2) the professional retained minstrel or more direct descendant of the old scop or bard. But no such clearly drawn distinction can be traced. The minstrel was all things to all men; he was retainer or wanderer as it was advantageous to him, and the two types blend hopelessly into one another.

The minstrel in his itinerant capacity is the less important in a study of patronage. No student of the medieval entertainer will ever believe that showmanship began with Barnum. By the thirteenth century minstrelsy had grown definitely into a profession for all sorts and conditions of men who wished to live by their wits, and it knew no national bounds. Its means of support was patronage of the unsure, capricious kind, and its methods of arousing generosity were various. The minstrel's main business, of course, was to tell stories and amuse, but as in earlier times he often clothed in verse the deeds that fell under his eye and lauded the conduct of the patron who had been kind to him.

---

[38] Widsith calls himself *gleoman,* and the etymology of the two words suggests no vital difference.

Generally, too, he felt the spirit's call to lampoon him who had been niggardly. Minstrels speak of themselves as going from castle to castle depending on the liberality of the lord and his guests, and from the romance of *Richard Coeur de Lion* we hear something of the method of procedure of these wanderers:

> Whenne þey hadde drunken wel afyn,
> A mynstralle con þer in
> And saide: "Goode men wyttyrly,
> Wol ȝe have ony mynstralsy?"

The company is not so disposed or very hospitable, and:

> The minstralle took in mynde,
> And sayde: "ȝe are men vnkynd,
> And ȝiff j may, ye schall forþynk
> ȝe gaff me neyþer mete ne drynk!
> Ffor gentyl men sholde bede
> To mynstrall þat abouten ȝede
> Off here mete, wyn, and ale!
> Ffor los ryses off mynstrale."[39]

The last sentence of the minstrel's pronouncement, of course, is the one great cause of his profession—fame. John of Salisbury in the reign of Henry I writes approvingly to a friend because "he had not, like the triflers of the age, lavished his wealth on minstrels and mimes and suchlike monsters, in order to purchase fame and the propagation of renown."[40] William de Longchamp, the much-hated Bishop of Ely and Chancellor of Richard I, enticed singers from France by his presents to have them sing his praises in the streets.[41] Going about as they did in public places these disinterested peddlers of glory for those who would pay largely undoubtedly exercised their influence on ideas

---

[39] Ed. Karl Brunner, *Wiener Beiträge*, XLII, (1913), ll. 663 ff. and ll. 669 ff.

[40] Courthope, *History of English Poetry*, I, 433, quoting from Du Cange, s. v. *Ministelli*. A similar passage is found in Chaucer. "Soothly what thyng that he yeveth for veyne glorie, as to mynstrals and to folk, for to beren his renoun in the world, he hath synne ther-of and noon alemesse." (*Parson's Tale*, 814.) Glory is also alluded to in the *Brut* of Layaman, ed. Madden, ll. 18853 and 23033 ff. The instances might be multiplied indefinitely. Compare Hamlet's remarks on the wandering players, II, ii, 549 ff.

[41] Roger de Hovedon, *Chronicon*, (R. S.) III, 143. William doubtless needed it. The effect of such glorification is likewise seen further in the same passage, for we hear: "but lately it was everywhere said that there was not such a person in all the world."

and manners of their time, and they had a facile avidity of comprehension. Nothing could be easier than to introduce all sorts of panegyrics into a *chanson de geste,* and these rogues set up a trade in it, the price depending on the development of the eulogy.[42]

The gifts bestowed on them were of course spontaneous and usually clothing, arms, horses, and the like, often the very robes their hearers wore,[43] and the minstrel sometimes named his own reward.[44]   In fact, so much was expended that we are asked to believe the public treasuries were drained,[45] and Matilda, queen of Henry I, lavished so much on them that she had to oppress her tenants to procure more revenues.[46]   The garments and rewards they did not fail to carry with them to other courts to excite to similar liberality, but the chief method of doing so was to make the heroes of their pieces exceedingly bountiful to minstrels,[47] such descriptions being generally near the end of the

---

[42] Gautier, *Les Épopées Françaises,* II, 119, gives an example. *La Chanson d'Antioche* and *La Conquête de Jerusalem,* both by Le Pelerin Richard, are probably illustrations in point.

[43] Examples of reward in kind are too numerous to mention. Many are to be found in Grossman, *Frühmittelenglishe Zeugnisse über Minstels,* passim; and Gautier, *Les Épopées Françaises,* II, 132.   Others are *Piers Plowman,* ed. Skeat, C passus xvi, ll. 202 ff.; *Richard Coeur de Lion,* ed. Brunner, ll. 3775; *William of Palerne,* ed. Skeat, E. E. T. S., ll. 5070 ff., and 5354 ff.; *Sir Ysumbras,* ed. Zupitza and Schleich, *Palaestra,* XV, ll. 19 ff., and *Sir Orfeo,* ed. Ritson, *Ancient English Metrical Romances,* II, ll. 467 ff.

[44] *Sir Orfeo,* ll. 411 ff.

[45] Strutt, *Sports and Pastimes,* 275.

[46] William of Malmesbury, *Chronicle of the Kings of England,* ed. Giles, (Bohn Lib.), 453-4.

[47] *Lyfe of Ipomedon,* ll. 2269 ff., ed. Kölbing:

> Ipomedon gaff in þat stound
> To mynstrellis V C pound,
> And othyr yiftes of grete nobley
> He yaff to other men þat day.

Romance of Sir Eglamour of Artois, ed. Halliwell, *Thornton Romances,* Camden Society, ll. 1327 ff.:

> The mynstrels that were of ferre londe
> That had mony robys, y undurstonde,
>   And mony a ryche gyfte.

or: (ll. 1336 ff.)

> Mynstrels that were in that stounde
> Ther gyftys were worthe iij. c. pounde
> The bettur myght they speede.

end of the poem. Naturally the minstrel had an intense horror for small coins, and if what he thought proper was not forthcoming he reminded his audience of it.[48]

Such extensive privileges as the minstrel enjoyed were, of course, open to abuse. Public favor inflated his pride and made him insolent, and we find him demanding a reward and setting its amount according as he valued his abilities and the affluence of the nobleman into whose castle he had intruded. In case of refusal he wielded a terrific weapon—satire, which took away a man's reputation in a breath, not only close at home, but wherever the minstrel travelled as well.[49] Because of the prosperity of the profession many unattached peoples[50] everywhere pursued the

---

Romance of Sir Degrevant, ed. Halliwell, op. cit., ll. 86 ff.:

> And mensteralus her in halle,
> He yaff hem robes off palle,
> Off gold and off ffee.

and: (ll. 1861 ff.)

> Mynstrallus hade in halle
> Grete gyftys withalle,
> Ryche robus of palle,
> With garnementus hale.

[48] Such references are very amusing. In the *Gui de Bourgogne,* ll. 4136 ff., we hear:

> Qui or voldra chançon oïr et escouter,
> Si voist isnelement sa boursse desfermer,
> Qui'il est hui mès bien tans qu'il me doie doner.

and in the *Huon de Bordeaux* (ll. 5482 ff.) the minstrel after reciting slightly over five thousand lines, dismisses his audience till another day, recommending that next time they bring their purses with them. In an Anglo-Norman version of the *Old Testament* (MS. Egerton, 2710, f. 11.) quoted in the *Bulletin de la S. A. T. F.,* XV, 76) there are these lines:

> Brefment l'ai dit par tut sanz mentir,
> Del son me done qui mès voldrat oïr.

[49] The Sarum statutes of 1319 lay especial stress upon the flattery and evil speaking with which minstrels rewarded their entertainers. Sometimes they overreached themselves, for Henry I put out the eyes of a Norman jongleur, Lucas de Barre, who made songs against him. (Ordericus Vitalis, *Historiae Ecclesiasticae,* XII, ed. Augustus le Provost, (1852), IV, 459-60.)

[50] The Goliardi are an excellent example of wanderers turning minstrel to get what they wanted. Begging students were common in the Middle Ages, and helping them was a deed of merit. (*Piers Plowman,* C passus x, 35. Cf. Chaucer, *Prologue;* 301-2.) A scholar, wishing patronage, turned minstrel to get it and begged realistically and poetically as Erasmus and the Humanists later begged, not for himself, but for learning. Examples of the begging poems are numbers XCI and CXCIV of the *Carmina Burana,* (ed. Litt. Vereins in Stuttgart, 1847.) Others are given by Grimm, *Kleinere Schriften,* III, 1 ff.; Spiegel, *Die Vaganten und ihr 'Orden,'* (1892); and

vagabond life, and so mischievous did this become that in 1315 Edward II passed an order of restraint. No minstrel was to be retained unless he came on invitation or belonged to a lord, and he was to be satisfied with the reward given him.[51]

When all is said, there was no place in the social status of the Middle Ages for men of intellect and genius who were not in the church, and such persons were compelled to depend on the patronage of courts. Nor did the nobility depend merely on the stray visits of wanderers for entertainment, but in keeping with their idea to live extravagantly and to support a large household, they domesticated some—*ministri* in the true sense of the word—in their households.[52] The duty of this hall minstrel was to amuse the prince and the court and to compose or recite songs and poems that would please them. In short, he was patronized for his art of entertainment, and because he could make compositions in which the glory of the house would live. To us he is interesting, for from him, a patronized artist, may have developed the man of letters of later days, his race culminating in "le grand jongleur du Moyen Âge"—Chaucer.

Of course, the retained minstrel was not required to remain always at court; he wandered about too, for vagabond life in

---

Wright, *Anecdota Literaria*, 39. A delightful translation of *Carmina* XCI is to be found in Symonds, *Wine, Women, and Song*, 59. These poems will be more fully discussed in the general treatment of begging poems.

[51] *Calendar of Patent Rolls, Edward II, A. D. 1313-18*, 306. (IX Edward II, 1315, August 6.) Edward IV likewise found it necessary to forbid his minstrels to be too presumptuous or familiar in asking rewards, supporting his ordinance by quoting a similar prohibition made by the emperor Henry II. (*Black Book of Edward IV, Household Ordinances*, 48, quoted by Chambers, *Medieval Stage*, I, 52.)

[52] From the various account books and Issue Rolls we hear of minstrels in the employ of the king and his barons and duchesses, even of clothes and other things given to the king's minstrels. (Grossman, op. cit., passim.) King's minstrels are mention in some of the early poems. We hear of Bishop Grosseteste's love of minstrelsy and of his harper's room next his, (Robert Mannyng, *Handlyng Synne*, 209 ff.); Chaucer, (*Squire's* Tale, 78), pictures Cambuscan holding a feast with minstrels; they are mentioned in *Piers Plowman*, (C viii, 97 ff.) and the *Romance of the Rose*, (B. 2035) and Lydgate, (*Troy Book*, ed. Bergen, E. E. T. S., 393) speaks of Agamemnon's minstrels. Mention is made of the "eorlus owne mynstralle" in the *Romance of Sir Degrevant*, ll. 1566, ed. Halliwell, *Thornton Romances*, Camden Society. Furthermore, the minstrel guild at Beverly in Yorkshire would take in no minstrel "except he be brother to some man of honour or worship or waite of some town," etc. Mention is likewise made of the "minstrels of the Duke [Humphrey] of Gloucester," (Vickers, *Humphrey of Gloucester*, (1907), 416.) The privy purse expenses of Henry VII also mention retained minstrels. (Bentley, *Excerpta Historica*, passim.)

the Middle Ages was not so disreputable as it later became.[53] But with the breakdown of the feudal system, the minstrel, like other retainers could feel independent and dispose of his art wherever he could get the best price, and the same held true of the lord; he could reward him for a piece of work without any obligation to do so the next time. So, the medieval man of letters later wrote his work for a particular patron and satisfied his needs, and the relationship ended as abruptly as it began. The more dignified entertainer, not always, but whenever possible, remained attached, if only loosely, to the lord, and gradually became the more dignified man of letters. When he was retained, his art was the chief cause of his retention, though his duties often involved other things;[54] and though sometimes he was a learned man, his learning he bore with a difference, for his duty was to amuse. Alongside of him in the Middle Ages was the purely learned man, invariably an ecclesiastic, who practiced the literature of fact rather than that of power; generally he had to do his work for the love of it or from another incentive than patronage, for entertainment being chiefly in demand, patronage of him was often neglected.

[53] Perhaps the livery of his lord gained him entrance into the courts of other nobles. There is a medieval Latin story of how a minstrel sought his supper at a castle. Asked what lord he served he replied "God" and was refused entrance by the porter unless he served some other lord. But minstrels were always men of quick wits, so this one announced thereupon that he was the devil's own servant and was received joyfully "quia bonus socius erat." (Wright, *History of English Culture*, (1874), 198.)

[54] Often, as he was generally learned, he was chaplain, secretary, tutor, or scribe, or, as in the case of the man mentioned in the *Paston Letters*, only a 'man,' kept because he could play *Saint George* and *Robin Hood* characters. (ed. Gairdner, V, 185.)

III

TROUBADOURS, TROUVÈRES, AND MINNESINGERS

An interesting phase of this process of adaptation is represented by the troubadour, the trouvère and the minnesinger, types of singer more dignified by far than the common jongleur, but still not yet stationary enough to be called patronized artists in the real sense. As the troubadour represents not only a large class in the Middle Ages, but, when his singing was a profession, one whose sole remuneration was the largess of the great, it is necessary here to treat evidences of a system of troubadour patronage apart from other medieval patronage systems. The distinction between the troubadour proper and his northern French counterpart, the trouvère, and his German counterpart, the minnesinger, is largely nominal; in all cases their function and their treatment was the same.

The question of date and period alone need for a moment trouble us. The Provence and southern France were already in possession of a well-developed lyric poetry when north of the Loire the first trouvère began to sing; the German minnesinger is likewise of late date. In short, the poetry of the trouvère and minnesinger may be looked upon as a direct borrowing or imitation originally of the Provençal troubadour, and what changes came about were due to differences in civilization and environment. How troubadour poetry spread northward is not to be determined; perhaps the medieval journalist, the jongleur, or the crusade of 1147 had something to do with it, and perhaps patronage itself aided its spread. Eleanor of Acquitaine, the granddaughter of the earliest known troubadour, was, as is well known, a most munificent patroness of troubadours, and was for a time queen of France; her daughters, Marie and Aelis, married Henry I of Champaigne and Thibaut of Blois respectively, and inspired a love of court poetry in the north as well as protected poets at their courts. Further than this the subject need not interest us.

Moreover, our isolation of the troubadour literature is not an unjustifiable distinction. Whatever may have been the origins of this exotic type, it was definitely fostered by feudal society, and at the beginning of the 12th century it appears as a poetry essentially aristocratic, intended for nobles and courts, with only a rare appeal to the middle classes or peasants at all. Kings, princes, and other nobles, pursued the art or became the patrons of those troubadours who had risen from the lower classes.[1] Though this is true, for our purposes there were two great classes of troubadours, trouvères, and minnesingers; those who sang by inclination and those who sang by profession. Among the troubadours by inclination are to be included the great barons of Poitou, Provence, and Toulouse, Richard I of England, Alfonso El Sabio of Arragon, and an infinite number of small yet powerful chatelains, such as Bertrand de Born or Savari de Mauleon, or such men as the Monk of Montaudon, whom love and pleasure at length induced to leave their old way of life to wander from court to castle making songs. To this class also belong most of the early minnesingers. Differing from their southern brothers slightly, they seem to have been more largely knights and nobles, and hence not until the time of Walther von der Vogelweide is there evidence of patronage of them. Occasionally there also existed troubadours with sufficient resources to be independent and above the need of seeking patronage, such as Folquet de Marseilles, who seems to have been a merchant of wealth; and obviously ladies who professed the art did so from love of it and from inspiration of feeling. But the troubadour by inclination, if he were powerful and wealthy enough, was admirably fitted to become the patron of his less fortunate brother in Apollo, the professional singer. Thus Raimbaut d'Aurenga, besides being a troubadour, patronized poets, as is shown by allusions in Guiraut

---

[1] This point of appeal was the subject of some discussion among the troubadours themselves, as shown by the *tenso* between Guiraut de Bornelh and Linhaure. Chaytor, *The Troubadours,* (Cambridge Manuals of Science and Literature), (1912), 39.

de Bornelh's poems.[2] So also Cercamon fostered Marcabrun,[3] and Peire d'Auvergne and Peirol lived with the Dauphin d'Auvergne.[4] Alfonso of Arragon, Richard of England, and Duke Raymond of Toulouse sheltered numerous poets. The list might be multiplied indefinitely, as instances both in the *Lives* and in the poems show these relations, but it is interesting only to note that no jealousy existed between the troubadour prince and his less fortunate vassal; a kind of literary democracy existed, and in the overlord there was always sympathy, often of a substantial kind, for other troubadours.

Beside these wealthy singers are to be placed such men as Bernart de Ventadorn, Marcabrun, Peire d'Auvergne, Guiraut de Bornelh, or Walther von der Vogelweide, of whom some were noble though poor—so poor that they had to make of their art a profession of which patronage was the sole means of remuneration. Some of the most celebrated of the poets were of lowly origin.[5] More of them were of the nobility, but in most cases, they were not of the highest nobility, and in several instances poverty is distinctly mentioned as the reason they adopted the profession and sought their sustenance in song.[6] There was scarcely a noble family in southern France without one member at least in this singing profession.

Vagabond life was by no means disreputable in the Middle Ages, and roving was the prime characteristic of all these poets,[7] but the famous troubadour, trouvère or minnesinger rarely recited

[2] Smith, *Troubadour Poets,* 125.
[3] Farnell, *Lives of the Troubadours translated from the Medieval Provençal,* (1896), 22.
[4] Ibid., 39 and 151.
[5] Bernart de Ventadorn was said to have been a stoker; Perdigon, the son of a fisherman; Marcabrun, a foundling; Guiraudon the Red, the son of a poor knight, as were Raimbaut de Vaquieras and Sordello. Others were of similar birth.
[6] Thus Gaucelm Faidit became a jongleur because at dice he had lost all he had (Farnell, op. cit., 169); Arnaut de Mareuil, because he could not earn his bread by letters, took to wandering through the world and well knew how to sing and rhyme (Ibid., 67); and Peirol, having lost favor with the Dauphin d'Auvergne, and finding himself unable to maintain himself as a knight, became a jongleur and "passed from court to court, receiving of the barons raiment and money and horses." (Ibid., 151.)
[7] Thus Guiraut de Bornelh, 'Master of Troubadours,' spent his winters in school and his summers in journeying from court to court with two singers who sang his songs. His case is typical. (Farnell, op. cit., 78.)

or sang his own pieces. Instead, he circulated his poems by the mouth of a jongleur or meistersinger, who was often sent long distances by his master. The troubadour confined himself to the dignity of composition, becoming jongleur only by necessity; and when he travelled he was accompanied by a jongleur or a troop of jongleurs whose part it was to turn their master's songs into profit.[8] The jongleur is no other than our old friend the minstrel who has ceased to be an attached servant. Jongleurs were received by the courts on terms of equality with their more exclusive brethren, the troubadours. The same gifts were meted out to them; as a whole they did not themselves compose, but took the compositions of others, often begging a troubadour acquaintance for a song.[9] The two professions, however, were frequently united in the same person,[10] at least they merged to

[8] The distinction, a recognized one, is clearly made in the answer of the king of Castile to a complaint of Guiraut Riquier. The king finds three classes of entertainers: (1) The first and lowest are those who hang about the village green, (2) then the reciters of stories who contribute to the amusement of nobles by their act. These alone should claim the title of *joglar* and ought to be received at court and liberally remunerated according to their merit. (3) Finally there are those who have the gift of inventing verses and melodies, who are called *troubadours*. (translated by Hueffer, *Troubadours*, (1878), 74.)

[9] Thus Raimon de Miraval addressed the jongleur Bayonna: "I know it is for a sirventes you have come among us. And counting this there will be three, for two I have made already by which you have gained much gold and silver, Bayonna, and many a warm coat and other clothes good and bad." (quoted by Hueffer, op. cit., 64.) He goes on further to enumerate the various princes at whose court it will be advisable for Bayonna to stop, describing fully what he may expect of each. (Rutherford, *Troubadours*, 208-9.) Petrarch likewise complains of those "persons of no great ability, but of retentive memories; of great industry too, but of greater audacity. They haunt the antechambers of kings and potentates naked if it were not for the poetic vesture they have filched from others. Any especially good bit which this one or that has turned off, they seize upon, more particularly if it be in the mother tongue, and recite it with huge gusto. In this way they strive to gain the favor of the nobility, and procure money, clothes, and other gifts." These he goes on to say, pester writers of renown for songs. "Some of those I had been induced to assist, and who had left me with their wish fulfilled, but otherwise poor and ill clad, returned shortly after arrayed in silks, with well-filled bellies and purses, to thank me for the assistance which had enabled them to cast off the burden of poverty." (Robinson and Rolfe, *Petrarch*, 198.)

[10] Both Rutebeuf and Colin Muset, considered from a social point of view, seem to have been both trouvère and jongleur. Rutebeuf in his works describes how he and his companions journeyed from castle to castle begging to be allowed to recite their poetry, yet he writes poems and complains of niggardliness. ("C'est' de la Povretei Rutebeuf," *Works*, ed. Jubinal, I, 1.) Colin Muset likewise is a true trouvère, for he wrote and composed, yet we find him attached and complaining to his baron of his want of liberality to him. (Tarbé, *Chansoniers de Champagne aux*

such an extent that strict differentiation is almost impossible. A jongleur of originality might become a troubadour, and a troubadour fallen on evil days might sink to the profession of jongleur. The troubadours did not write narrative poems; their field was the lyric, and when business required it, the jongleur came forward with a *chanson de geste*. Later he degraded his profession by introducing mimic tricks.[11] The same distinction on the whole held between the minnesinger and the meistersinger,[12] and in the north the same result came about: like the jongleurs, the meistersingers organized and became minstrels.

As our discussion has indicated, the profession of troubadour, even though dependent upon the fickle generosity of princes, was probably one of the best remunerated of the age. In general, the rewards, as in the case of minstrels, were spontaneous and only infrequently in money. Under the influence of a song the noble recklessly doffed his goodly apparel and other gear, including jewelry, or forgot how valuable or how dear to his heart his charger was; perhaps he even tossed the poet his entire purse.[13] Exceptional merit, or more correctly, perhaps, exceptional appreciation by the lord, brought higher reward. Aubert de Pucibat,[14] Perdigon,[15] and Raimbaut de Vaqueiras won knighthood;[16] Sordello was given a good castle and a noble wife;[17] Elias and Oliver

XIIe et XIIIe Siècles: Colin Muset, 78.) Peire Rogier and Elias of Barjol also combined the two professions, (Farnell, op. cit., 52 and 247) and probably Raimbaut de Vaqueiras. (Ibid., 141.) Hugh de St. Cyre was likewise first a jongleur. (Ibid., 208.)

[11] In fact Giraud Clanson advises such a repertory in a poem quoted by Rutherford, op. cit., 211.

[12] The former did not reach beyond the courts and castles of princes while the latter reached the middle and lower classes.

[13] Often the troubadour demanded his own reward. Of the Monk of Montaudon, the *Life* says: "and whatsoever it pleased him to ask of them, that gave they." (Farnell, op. cit., 159.) It seems hardly necessary to remember that even down to the 17th century to accept gifts of clothing from a superior was not degrading, but honorable. The Monk of Montaudon, however, rails at a brother poet for accepting *manh vielh vestimen*, though his scoffing perhaps is at the fact that the garment was previously worn to rags by the economical patron. (Hueffer, op. cit., 59.) In the travelling accounts of Bishop Wolfger of Passau there is this entry: "Walthero cantori de Vogelweide pro pellico V solidos longos." (*Ency. Britt.* s. v. *Walther von der Vogelweide*.)

[14] Rutherford, *Troubadours*, 197.

[15] Farnell, op. cit., 250.

[16] Letter to Marquis de Montferrat, Farnell, op cit., 39.

[17] Farnell, op. cit., 228.

of Barjol were given wives and land;[18] Walther von der Vogelweide got a fief; and Guilhelm Baye, Arnaud de Cotignac, and
Gaucelm de Mastiere were made influential rulers.[19] Raymond
de Miravel was lord of the house of Count Raymond of Toulouse, of King Peter of Arragon, of the Viscount of Beziers,
of Lord Bertran of Saissac, and of all the great lords round
about.[20] Some gained comfortable priories, and there is record
of a large estate changing hands literally for a song.[21] On the
whole, however, the most frequent form of patronage was retention at court, for the discoverer of genius was sure to take
credit to himself for it.[22] The promising young aspirant or his
more seasoned brother of the road was often taken into the service of a powerful lord, and indeed might find it temporarily advantageous to tarry while his favor lasted. If three or four
neighboring lords vied with each other in liberality, he might
attach himself to the highest bidder, or continue a career of
caprice and uncertainty until he had gathered a competence.[23]
As a rule, however, the troubadour ever felt the wanderlust, and
cases of more or less permanent establishment under a patron are
few. Sometimes even, personal attachment to a patron and

[18] Ibid., 247.
[19] Rutherford, op. cit., 197.
[20] Farnell, op. cit., 179.
[21] Tarandet de Flassons purchased an estate from Folquet de Ponteves for a piece
entitled "Lous Ensegnamens per se garder contra las Traysons d'Amor," concerning
which the Monk of the Golden Isle remarks that its instructions must have been of
little value since both men were alike deceived by their mistresses.
[22] Sometimes a pleased patron recommended the poet to other barons. Thus, Sir
Guilhem de Berguedan after having advanced Aimeric de Peguillon and given him
his palfrey and raiment, made him known to King Alfonso of Castile, which way
greater honor lay. (Farnell, op. cit., 214.) So also, Colin Muset, in recommending
himself to the lord of Waignonmt, says that through him his verses had reached the
good count of Widemont. (Tarbé, *Chansonniers de Champagne aux XIIe et XIIIe
Siècles,* 78.)
[23] It is not to be supposed that all these singers met with unlimited favor—far
from it. To cite only a few examples of failure to win patronage, the *Life* tells us
that though Guiraut de Caleneo was a "right learned man" and "subtle in the making
of poetry," his canzones, though made with great cunning, were ill liked in Provence
and "small fame had he." (Farnell, op. cit., 236.) So likewise Gaucelm Faidit,
before his fortune was made by the Marquis de Montferrat, though he "sang worse
than any man in the world, yet made many a good melody and many a good canzone,"
for twenty years and upward received small favor of any. (Ibid., 169.) Elias Cairol,
though also of great learning and subtlety in making poetry, because of his scorn
of the barons, was not favored as his work merited. (Ibid., 256.)

roaming abroad might be combined as when the troubadour followed his patron on expeditions or on the crusades.[24] Rewards won by the power of song cannot be passed without a mention of the romancing of Nostradamus on Pietro di Castelnouvo. Reporting "vn' authore degno de fide," he tells how the poet fell among thieves, who stripped him of all he had and were about to finish their work and leave him for dead for some good Samaritan. Unfortunately, after the manner of thieves, they yielded to his entreaties to be allowed to sing one of his songs before he died. Pietro, clad only by the sombre woods, be it remembered, extemporized so sweetly upon the merits of thieves and thieving in general and upon his thieves in particular, that their hearts within them were moved, and they returned his horse, his clothes, his money and all they had taken from him.[25]

Under certain conditions, however, the troubadour's position was far from one of dignity, for when the generosity he thought his talents deserved was not forthcoming, he was not ashamed to stoop to threats or adulation to stimulate tardy liberality; in fact, largess thus won had a special name, *messio*.[26] But of such complaints and their effects, more later. On the whole there was a definite opportunity for the musical vagabond. If he possessed any real talent he could be certain of its being at last recognized and rewarded and his fortune made secure, not to speak of having his fame trumpeted abroad by the proud patron.

It seems safe to say that to patronize these singers of love was a fashion, and at the courts of princes and nobles the troubadour was eagerly welcomed. When he chose to stay at a castle, his

[24] Examples are numerous. The story of Richard and Blondel is well known, and other references both in the *Lives* and elsewhere make it clear that Richard had many poets in his service in the Holy Land, and Louis VII of France took some in his retinue when he embarked. In a letter to his lord of Montferrat, Raimbaut of Vaqueiras speaks of having ridden through all Greece and having endured the dangers of war with him. (Quoted by Farnell, op. cit., 139.) So also Adam de la Halle became companion and secretary to Robert Count of Flanders on his diverse voyages to the Holy Land. (Dinaux, *Trouvères, Jongleurs, et Ménèstrals* . . . (1837-63) I, 48.) Among the minnesingers both Friedrich von Hausen and Albrecht von Johannsdorf followed Barbarossa on the Crusade of 1189, though, being nobles, most probably not as patronized poets. (Robertson, *History of German Literature,* 117-8.)

[25] Jean de Nostradamus, *Le Vita della Piv. celebri et antichi primi poeti Provenzali* . . . (1575), 145.

[26] Chaytor, op. cit., 12.

relation to the lord of it was that of an equal; the relationship
was practically that of guest and host, and of the same order as
that which Horace and Virgil enjoyed with Maecenas. The poet
had no distinct charge or office, no irksome duties to perform and
was free to come and go as his wayward mood directed him. A
position such as that of the laureate of a later period, bound
for certain emoluments to grind out a certain amount of verse,
would have been quite unsuitable to the disposition of the medieval wanderer. Bertran de Born addresses the sons of Henry II
by familiar nicknames,[27] Raimon de Miraval did the same with
Raimon VI of Toulouse, and, in general, the ease of intercourse
between the singer of the lowest rank and the mightiest prince is
as amusing as that between king and jester.

Then, too, thoroughly in keeping with this kind of poetry and
appropriately enough too, since they benefited most by it, women
came forward as patronesses of the *gai saber*. The *Life* tells us
that Bernart de Ventadorn, out of favor with his prince,

"got him to the Duchess of Normandy, who was young and of great
worth, and who loved virtue, and honour, and the singing of her praise.
And the vers and canzones of Sir Bernart did greatly please her, and she
received him at her court and gave him hearty welcome. Long did he
dwell there singing many a good song of her."[28]

This lady with the admirable qualifications was none other than
Eleanor of Acquitaine, the most famous of the patronesses of the
troubadours. Both by tradition and temperament the grand-
daughter of the first known troubadour, Guillaume IX of Poitiers, was fit subject for the poems of praise which many poets
offer her. Her career was varied and her moving about from
place to place may have had much to do with the spread of the
gay science into foreign parts, for troubadours like Bernart and
Bertran de Born went with her, and her court thus became the
centre of Provençal influence in northern France. She was queen
of France and then in 1152 was divorced by Louis VII and married to Henry, Duke of Normandy, who became King of England
in the same year. It is through her, if through anyone, that
troubadour poetry penetrated England, but of this more later.

[27] "Rassa," "Yea and Nay," and "Sailor." (Farnell, op. cit., 92.)
[28] Farnell, op. cit., 28.

Important in literary history, too, are the two daughters of Eleanor, Marie and Aelis, the former married to Henry I of Champagne and generally known as the famous Marie de Champagne, whose court was a kind of experiment station of Provençal ideals, and the latter to Thibaut de Blois. At both of these courts troubadours were constantly present. The later husband of Marie, the illustrious Baudouin IX, Duke of Flanders and Hainault,[29] also composed in the language of Provence, an unusual thing for a man of the North, but his wife far outshone him in her patronage. Chréstien de Troyes is her most famous protégé, in whose works the theory of courtly love finds expression. He began at her bidding the romance of *Lancelot de la Charette*, which was finished by Godefrey de Lignal, and dedicated to Marie.[30] Jeanne, the daughter of Marie and Baudouin, likewise encouraged trouvères.[31] And there were more. Ermengarde, viscountess of Narbonne, was "in those days much honored and prized of men" welcoming among others, Peire Rogier;[32] Adelaide, daughter of Raymond V of Toulouse, and countess of Beziers, patronized Arnaut de Mareuil, furnishing him with "goodly apparel and other gear, and greatly honored and pleased him."[33] Later in the North, Marie de Brabant, at one time wife of Philip le Hardi of France, was famous[34] as was the Duchess Bonne de Luxembourg,[35] and if we are to believe an old poem on Louise de la Tour, we have in Canaples in the 13th century

---

[29] He was the sixth duke of Hainault of that name.

[30] Dinaux, op. cit., 88, 65.

[31] To her is dedicated the *Romance of Percival*, commenced by Chréstien and finished by the trouvere Manessier:

> Si com *Manessiers* le témoigne
> Qui a fin traist ceste besoigne,
> El non *Jehane*, la contesse,
> Qui est de Flandres dame et maistresse,
> Et par ce que tout ie apris
> Des ses bones mours à dèlivre,
> Ai en son nom finé mon livre. (quoted by Dinaux, op. cit., II, 66.)

[32] Farnell, op. cit., 52.

[33] Ibid., 67.

[34] Li Rois Adenez dedicated to her *Les Enfances d'Ogier le Danois*, (Dinaux, op. cit., IV, 132.)

[35] The trouvère Adam Raymont dedicated to her *L'Arbre d'Amor et de ses Fruits bons et mauvais*. (Dinaux, op. cit., II, 69.)

a beautiful woman, who appreciated verse, inspired it, received
it, and maybe recompensed it.[36] Take it all in all, the list of
ladies who acted as patronesses is quite impressive.

The chief seat of troubadour patronage, of course, was its
cradle, Provence. Each little court seems to have bade the troubadour welcome, and, possibly because the feudalism of Languedoc was more democratic than that of the north, poetry flourished. In spite of his poverty the Dauphin Robert I of Auvergne
made himself famous for generosity,

"and by his bountiful gifts he lost the half and more of his country, but
by his prudence and thrift he knew thereafter to win unto himself all
that he had lost, yea, and eke much more."[37]

Among the lesser barons who were munificent were Blacatz and
Savaric of Mauleon.[38] Of Blacatz the *Life* says:

"Never was there a man who loved better to take than he to give, ...
and the more he grew in years the more he grew in bounty."[39]

but by far the most famous and able as patrons were the counts
Raimond Berenger II, Alphonse II, and Raimond Berenger IV.

Second in importance are the counts of Toulouse, of whom
the most prominent were the three Raimons—Raimon IV of St.
Gilles, who took the cross in 1096; his grandson, Raimon V, who
befriended Peire Rogier, Bernart de Ventadorn, and Peire Raimon; and Raimon VII who also loved poets, among them Raimon
de Miravel. In southern France also, the courts of Richard
Coeur de Lion, William VIII of Montpelier, Barral, Viscount of
Marseilles, and the princes of Orange, William IV of Baux and
Raimbaut, were famous. In Spain we have several famous
patrons, as well as poets. In the later days Spain became a
refuge for those driven from southern France by the Albigeois
Crusade, and their treatment was always royal.[40] In Arragon

[36] The poem, B. N. MS. 7613 f. 147, is quoted and thus speculated upon by
Dinaux, op. cit., III, 63.

[37] Farnell, op. cit., 61.

[38] He is called the "most bountiful of the bountiful." (Farnell, op. cit., 199.)

[39] Farnell, op. cit., 197. Sordello on the death of Blacatz invites to the funeral
feast the Roman Emperor Frederick II, the kings of France, England, and Arragon
and the counts of Champagne, Toulouse, and Provence, urging them to eat the heart
of the dead man that they might gain some of his courage and nobility. The poem
is quoted in extract by Farnell, 228 ff.

[40] Guiraut Riquier's description of Catalonia is interesting. "I must needs enter
upon the road of true love and I can learn it well enough in gay Catalonia among

the most important protectors were Alphonso II, Pedro II, Jaime I, ("Conquistador") and Pedro III, at whose courts many gay singers found consolation for the arduous labor of loving. At Castile and Leon are found Alphonso VIII, IX, and X, the last of these, "El Sabio," being especially praised for his enlightened interest in matters intellectual. Among others Sancho I of Portugal is said to have had French jongleurs in his pay in the 12th century and Diego Lopez de Haro of Vajcaya is praised by several troubadours.

Also, when poetry was crushed out in Languedoc, the states of northern Italy which had ever been most hospitable to troubadours, now gave them a last refuge. The family of Este is spoken of as munificent, especially Azzo, as are the Marquises of Montferrat, Bonificius, and William IV, as well as the counts of Verona, Savoy, and Malaspina. But most especially to be noted in Italy as a patron is Frederick II in Sicily. Besides being a poet and a man of unusual culture and keen interest in things literary, he perhaps favored the troubadous because of their animosity to the papacy, aroused by the Albigeois trouble. Blasting sirventes, such as Guillem Figuerra and others could pour forth, were probably useful to him in his business of outwitting the pope.

In the North love fared just as well. Baudouin IX of Flanders[41] has already been mentioned in connection with his wife. In Flanders, also, was Philippe d' Alsace, who patronized Chréstien de Troyes and Gautier d'Épinal. The courts of the dukes of Brabant were renowned from very early times for their encouragement of literature, and it is natural that under brilliant and generous Maecenases, themselves agreeable poets, that the new poetry from the south should flourish also. At the court of Luxembourg trouvères were fostered, the most notable patron being Wencelas, best known as the early friend of Froissart. Further, the nephews of the Jeanne, daughter of Marie de Cham-

---

the Catalonians, men of worth, joy, gratitude, gallantry, sense, knowledge, honor, fair speech, fair company, liberality and love, learning and grace find maintainance and support in Catalonia entirely." (quoted by Chaytor, op. cit., 119-20.)

[41] Baudouin also gathered certain compositions—*Histoires de Boudowin*—which unfortunately have not been preserved. (Dinaux, op. cit., IV, 69.)

pagne, spoken of above—Gui and Guillaume de Dampierre—carried out well the ideals of their aunt and protected jongleurs and trouvères, who returned thanks in well-sounding eulogies. Finally, one must not forget Philip Augustus, who, though a patron of poetry, would rather give his old clothes to the poor.[42]

Germany was not far behind her sister country in generosity when patronage was necessary, but as a rule the minnesinger was above the need of it. The best and most gifted of the later *spielleute,* however, and the later minnesingers and meistersingers, were dependent upon generosity. The case of Walther von der Vogelweide is notable. Tired of wandering and poor, but influential, he begged poetically for a home, and Frederick, recognizing his merits, gave him a property and a title, for which Walther was duly and poetically thankful. As a rule, however, the court of the Hohenstaufens of the house of Suabia encouraged poetry with the highest favors, if not actually with money. But with the accession of the house of Hapsburg an era of decline set in; the German nobility ceased to be interested in minnesong, and the meistersingers took up the neglected *geige.* The case is one which is admirably adapted to the drawing of a moral on patronage. German vernacular literature was rich in promise, but its early beauty gave way to artificiality. All troubadour poetry was frankly aristocratic, the product of the caprice of aristocracy and an excited feeling of society, but in Provence inspiration had not been denied to men outside of the nobility, and princes awarded favor on the democratic principle of merit with no regard for rank. In the North, far otherwise. Could it be that when the protecting hand was removed a force which had pushed appreciation and respect for art beyond its natural level was removed too?

With regard to the meistersingers an essential feature is to be noted, the singing contest. The oldest literary example is the description of such a contest in the *Wartburgkrieg,*[43] dating c. 1300 or earlier. The chief minnesingers, Wolfram von Eschenbach, Walther von der Vogelweide, and others are represented

---

[42] Dulaure, *Histoire Civile, Physique, et Morale de Paris,* II, 447 and 448 n.
[43] Ed. Simrock, Stuttgart, 1858.

as assembled at the court of the Landgraf Hermann of Thuringia. A certain Heinrich von Ofterdingen, probably a fictitious character, challenges all comers to a contest of praise of great lords, and eulogy is heaped by the basketful. About all one can draw from such a work, besides seeing in it a custom, is that the Landgraf Hermann of Thuringia was a patron of literature, who had as guests at the Wartburg at one time Wolfram von Eschenbach and Walther von der Vogelweide.

But what about the troubadors in England? Little is to be said. Of Eleanor of Acquitaine something has already been noted, though there is no evidence save a most probable possibility that she invited trouvères and troubadours to her court.[44] Her son Richard was more French than English, and besides being a troubadour himself is known to have been a munificent patron of troubadours as were his brothers Henry and Geoffrey,[45] but Richard spent less than six months of his reign on English soil, and we do not know if he was followed to England by any of his protégés.[46] Further, Alix de Brabant became the wife of Henry I of England in 1122, and, as she had leaned to poetry in her father's court where she protected trouvères, probably invited them to England. It is impossible that England should not have known the troubadour influence. Of opportunity for it to come to England there was no lack, for during the period of general stimulus to lyric poetry throughout western Europe, Norman French was the literary language of England and there was free intercourse between the two countries. England could not fail

---

[44] Bernart de Ventadorn may have crossed the channel. In one poem he says: "The *vers* has been composed fully so that not a word is wanting, beyond the Norman land and the deep wild sea; and though I am far from my lady, she attracts me like a magnet, the fair one whom may God protect. If the English king and the Norman duke will, I shall see her before the winter surprise us." (Chaytor, op. cit., 47-8.)

[45] Notable among Geoffrey's protégés is the trouvere Gace Brulé who addresses some of his chansons to the "comte Geoffroi." (Chanson xxx, 1, 57 and xxxv, 1, 36 are examples, Huet, *Chansons de Gace Brulé*, S. A. T. F., 74, and 86.) The "contesse de Brie" at whose command Chanson xxxix was written, may be Marie de Champagne, uterine sister of Geoffrey. Guiraut de Clanson and Bertran de Born were perhaps in personal relationship with the same Geoffrey de Bretagne.

[46] The *Life* of Arnaut Daniel tells an amusing story of Arnaut's thievery of a song from another jongleur at Richard's court, but the incident is only possible in England. "Now it chanced upon a time, that he was in the court of King Richard of England." (Farnell, op. cit., 165.)

to feel the influence. There are several political poems written against John and Henry III which may fairly be called *sirventes*, but not until the 13th century does English lyric poetry appear, and in this French influence is apparent.

It is never to be supposed in any system of patronage that the poet is the sole beneficiary; it certainly was not the case with the troubadours and their French and German brothers. Praise was the coin in which they paid, with the assurance expressed or implied, that the patron's fame would spread. The relation of patron and poet was one of give and take,[47] and largess was definitely expected.[48] At bottom in all this lordly poetry there is but one lordly virtue—*milte, donar, dos,* and one lordly vice—*karcheit avareza escarsedatz; larcx* is a favorite term of eulogy and is the term of which Alexander in the early time stands the type. It is ever praised, while *escas,* represented by Darius, of the poem of censure, is ever blamed.[49] The prince must busy himself getting *milte;* honor is his already in the praise of the poet, if he will but avail himself of it.[50] The excessive praise of

[47] So Raumsland says: "Ich wil den hêrren singen unde sagen unde lachen, daz sie gedenken mîner kunst, ich denke ir milte." (Nickel, *Sirventes und Spruchdichtung, Palaestra,* LXIII, 82.)

[48] Guillem Magret closes a canzone of praise to the King of Arragon with these humble words:

> Reys Aragones,
> Legatz de romanha,
> E ducx e marques,
> E coms de Serdanha,
> Gent avetz esclarzit l'escuelh
> E del fromen triat lo juelh,
> Qu'el luec de San Peir'etz pauzatz
> E drechuriers reys coronatz;
> E, pus dieus vos a mes lay sus,
> Membre us de nos que em sa jus.   (Mahn, *Werke der*

Troubadours, III, 244.) Boniface Calvo in the middle of the 13th century systematized the art of giving for the King of Castile thus: the giver must think who he himself is, who the receiver is, and what the gift is. (Nickel, op. cit., 91.)

[49] Nickel, op. cit., 81. The eulogy of Aimeric de Peguillon on Frederick II is illustrative. (Bartsch, *Chrestomathie Provençale,* 162; Farnell, op. cit., 212.) Characteristic of this attitude also is the tenzone in which Guiraut Riquier takes part as to whether valor or generosity are best. Needless to say the claims of generosity are sustained. See further Miss M. P. Whitney's, "Queen of Medieval Virtues: Largesse," *Vassar Medieval Studies,* (1923), 181 ff.

[50] So Peire Vidal: "And he will have great honor if he has me as his servant, for I can make his praise known to the entire world, and increase his fame more than

many of these old poems is not to be put aside as inconsequential. Its recurrence probably had the purpose of inculcating generosity toward the reciter much as in the poetry of the scop, but the troubadour had a more powerful means of making his patron bow to his wishes. The wandering poet was the journalist of the Middle Ages; where we now have a leading article, in the old time there was the jongleur's song, and just as songs of praise spread from court to court and even in the streets, so spite at the niggardliness of the great might pass, and reputations might be made or marred in a song. The rich Zorgi warns those who would guard against 'mesprendre' to give to their jongleurs,[51] and certainly many high lords profited by the eulogy of minstrels. But there were equally many who fared badly. The old poetry is full of vituperation, and demands and appeals are numerous.[52] Such a system went well unless the stingy patron happened to be a poet himself and then the troubadour got at least as good as he gave.[53] We know from a poem of Cadenet's

---

anyone in the world." (Nickel, op. cit., 82.) So also Walther von der Vogelweide:

"Die nôt bedenkent, milter künec, daz iuwer nôt zergê."

(Ibid., 82.) Lady Audast says to Gaucelm Faidet: "Right worshipful am I of honor, and for love of one that may win me praise and renown. I wot you are he of whom I may have all this, and I am she that can well reward all. I would have you then for lover, and do make you gift of myself and of my love." (Farnell, op. cit., 171.)

[51] Nickel, op. cit., 84.

[52] Bertrand de Born to the great shame of Alphonso says: "Of Alphonso have the jongleurs told me that they would have praised him much, but he never gave them clothes or money," and we hear that Frederick was generous before he was rich, but now those who come from him say that he holds his havings close together. Other interesting examples are given by Nickel, op. cit., 83-5.

[53] So it happened once to Hugh de St. Cyrc. Coming to the count of Rodez, he experienced a less warm and liberal reception than he had formerly had and composed a delectable lay and got back an equally forceful one:

> Don't be afraid my mettlesome blade
> Nor raise your eyebrows or straighten your leg—
> I assure you I have not come to beg.
> Of this world's goods I have all I need—
> As for yourself—if you're short of pelf—
>   For so it may be
> That times have changed with you as with me—
>   I do not object my pockets to rifle
>   In order to hand your countship a trifle:
> I verily think it would be a good deed!

To this the count replied:

> You wretched scamp! you inveterate tramp!
> Do you indeed forget, or no

also that the Count of Burlatz drove off all the troubadours from his court because he was satirized by one of them.[54]   Then when flattery, begging, and finally the *sirvente* had failed, the poet indulges in self-pity over his fruitless unrewarded service.[55]

But it must not be supposed that real feeling did not exist between the poet and his lord. The elegies or *planhs* upon the deaths of famous patrons are sufficient proof often of a high and noble attachment.[56] Finally, it must be noted that the poet served his lord very often in a quite material way by taking his side in a private or political struggle, turning journalist with his poetry. He might even be a means of preaching crusades. The most notable example of a poet taking a patron's part in return for munificence is that of Walther von der Vogelweide, who though not the first to draw political events into poetry, was the first to write political verse. At the death of Kaiser Henry VI

> Entering my castle some years ago
> Naked without and empty within—
> A very scare-crow ragged and thin?
> To fatten you up and set you to rights
> Cost me more than the board of a couple of knights,
> Including their tail of archers and squires—
> And now—by the soul of all my sires!—
>   Those who hear you I know will believe—
> You inveterate screw! you worse than a Jew!
> If I were to offer a palfrey or two,
> By jingo, you're just the sneak to receive!

(Rutherford, op. cit., 199.)

[54] Nickel, op. cit., 91.

[55] Thus, Raumsland sighs: "In dienet maniger hande man, der nie ze lône heil gewan" and Frauenlob likewise: "swer boesen hêrren dienen muoz, des heil sich überbüeget," or Heinrich von Mügeln: "wer bôsen hêrren dienen wil, der hât den lôn wol halp von him verloren." These and other complaints are given by Nickel, op. cit., 83-4.

[56] The attachment of Bertran de Born for the young prince Henry, son of Henry II of England is most touching. The *Life* tells us how Bertran, warring against Henry is taken, treated ill by the king, and taunted: "Full well I ween your wits are now to seek." "My lord," answered Sir Bertran, "you speak true." "And wherefore?" quoth the King. "My lord," answered Sir Bertran, "on that same day that the most excellent young king, your son, died, I lost all sense and wisdom and understanding." (Farnell, op. cit., 100-1.) Bertran also wrote a dirge in which he expresses his grief at the death of Henry. A translation is found in Farnell, op. cit., 110 ff. Sordello's *planh* on Blacatz has already been mentioned; Folquet de Marseilles wrote on the death of Barral of Marseilles (Ibid., 129 ff.) and of the highest order is the lament of Gaucelm Faidit on the death of Richard Coeur de Lion. (Ibid., 174 ff.). Hartmann von Aue's elegy on his liege lord is one of the most sincere expressions in early minnesong. (*Minnesang's Frühling*, ed. Vogt, (1920), 240 ff.)

in the north two rivals arose, Philip of Suabia and Graf Otto of Poitou, while in the south Innocent showed himself capable, to put it mildly, of a wider political activity than Italy afforded him. Walther employed his art in the interest of the Duke of Suabia. The cause was won, and Walther ceased to write. When the emperor again changed, and Otto IV was under ban of the pope, he became his advocate though he received small thanks for his pains. When under Frederick II the Empire again reverted to the Staufens, he had a more generous patron, and when in 1227 the inevitable rupture between Emperor and Papacy came, Walther once more wielded his pen and urged Frederick to undertake the crusade the pope had forbidden.

But the close of the 12th century saw the passing of the golden age of troubadour poetry. Complaints of lack of refinement and avariciousness of patrons are commonplaces. A commercial class was rising, and the Albigeois Crusade was stamping out all desire for court poetry, while the patrons struggled for existence. The troubadour's occupation was gone.

It is interesting, in passing, to note the prevalence of a custom of patronage in the Orient, closely similar to that of the troubadours. Poetry in the East seems to have been in the air much as it was in Provence in the time of the troubadours, and both king and subject practiced it. As in ancient Rome, so in the great Mohammedan cities, public recitation was the means of making one's talents known. The mosques were customarily used for this purpose, but better accommodation was provided by the courts of generous princes. About the Caliphs were hosts of minstrels and bards whose well-timed, tactful panegyrics were liberally rewarded. During the Ghaznawí period, literary men were highly esteemed and each independent ruler strove to emulate his rivals and peers in the brilliancy of his court. But the palaces alone were not responsible for this abundance of minstrels, for they were received at the houses of average citizens, merchants, and even the poor. Most of the literary men wandered from court to court, dedicating a poem wherever profit was like to come of it.[57] Similar conditions brought similar results,

---

[57] Thus Abú Mansúr ath-Tha 'alibi of Nishápúr dedicated to several. A list is given in Browne, *Literary History of Persia*, II, 101. A similar list of patrons and poems

and panegyrics, gentle hints, and begging poems are numerous,[58] and rewards likewise were for the most part spontaneous and ever generous.[59] For the usual favors the poet promised the usual things.[60] Lastly is to be noted the *qasída,* or "purpose

---

is given for Dhahiru'd-Din Faryábi. (Ibid., II, 414.) Ibn al-Khayyât travelled about and made eulogies on his hosts. (Huart, *History of Arabian Literature,* 109.) The historian Elmacian assures us that Hároun al-Raschíd never undertook a journey without carrying with him at least a hundred men of science. (Sismondi *Literature of the South of Europe,* I, 51.) Hafiz of Shiraz (14th century) was invited to visit India by two kings, one of whom sent him money for his journey. This Hafiz spent and gave away and then abandoned the trip. (Browne, *History of Persian Literature under Tartar Dominion,* 285.)

[58] Thus Farrukhi of Sístán wrote a *qasída* in the branding ground of Amir Abu 'l-Mudhaffar of Chagháneỹan in which he says:

> But, though on one side he brandeth, gives he also rich rewards,
> Leads his poets with a bridle, binds his guests as though with cords."

(Browne, *Literary History of Persia,* II, 127.)

[59] Thus Zobeir Ibn Dahman received 20,000 dirhems from Hároun al-Raschíd for a single composition on a favorite slave. (Rowbotham, *Troubadours,* 14.) On another occasion the same poet received 50,000 dirhems for a song, and on being told to demand whatever further he wished, asked for a country house and was given two villages. (Ibid., 14.) Hafiz, mentioned above, was not wholly indifferent to royal favors as the following extract shows:

> The king of Hurmúz did not see me, yet showed me a hundred favors
>   without a word (of praise on my part);
> The king of Yazd saw me, and I praised him, but he gave me nothing.
> Such is the conduct of Kings: be not thou vexed, O Hafiz:
> May God, the Giver of daily bread, vouchsafe them His Grace and Aid!

(Browne, *History of Persian Literature under Tarter Dominion,* 290.)
A delightful story is told of the old time which well illustrates the spontaneity and amount of these gifts. On one occasion a poet came to Mahdí, heir apparent, (8th century) recited a panegyric in his honor, and was given 20,000 dirhems for his pains. Mansúr, the Caliph, was informed, and he wrote to his son, reproaching his extravagance. "What you should have done," he said, "was to let him wait a year at your door, and after that time bestow on him 4,000 dirhems." Then he arrested the poet and the following conversation is reported:
"You went to a heedless youth and cajoled him?"
"Yes, God save the Commander of the Faithful, I went to a heedless generous youth and cajoled him, and he suffered himself to be cajoled."
"Recite your eulogy to him."
The poet obeyed, not forgetting to conclude his verses with a compliment to Mansúr, who cried, "Bravo! but they are not worth 20,000 dirhems. Where is the money?" It was produced, he made the poet a gift of 4,000 dirhems and confiscated the remainder. (Nicholson, *Literary History of the Arabs,* 258-9.) The shameless treatment of Firdawsí in the writing of the *Sháhnama* is well known. (Warner, *The Sháhnama of Firdawsí,* I, Intro.) Cf. Gosse, *Firdawsí in Exile,* (1886.)

[60] "It is by words of the poet that monarchs are saved from oblivion," (Gibb, *History of Ottoman Poetry,* V, 81.) So also the lines from one of Rúdagí's poems:

> "Surely are renown and praise a lasting gain,
> Even though the royal coffers loss sustain."   (Browne, *Literary*

poem"—the *sirvente,* in a manner, of the East. Usually it was a panegyric, and included as an essential part of the poem, generally at its conclusion, a petition for the patron's favor or generosity and a prayer for his long life. Every good *qasída* contained such a passage,[61] and the hint for reward, when neatly introduced, was called *husn-i-talab*—"beauty of demand."[62]

Even from this brief outline it can be seen that in the East there existed a form of patronage essentially similar to that of the troubadour and dating in its beginning much earlier. Whether or no the Crusades with the imitation of Mohammedan and Oriental customs they occasioned had anything to do with the system of patronage developed in France, we leave as an open question. It is interesting at least to note so striking a similarity.

History of Persia, II, 16.) The worth of poetry is attested by such a passage:
"Your gifts have vanished, but his poems live on. They are robes of honor which Time cannot decay." (Huart, op. cit., 16.)

[61] Gibb, op. cit., III, 151, n. 2. Compare Ibn Qutayba's account of the contents and divisions of a *qasída:* "And when, after representing all the discomfort and danger of the journey, he knew that he had fully justified his hope and expectation of receiving his due meed from the person to whom the poem was addressed, he entered upon the panegyric (*madíh*), and incited his generosity by exalting him above his peers and pronouncing the greatest dignity in comparison with his to be little." (Quoted by Nicholson, *Literary History of the Arabs,* 77-8.)

[62] Browne, *Literary History of Persia,* II, 33.

IV

GENERAL AND SPECIAL PHASES OF PATRONAGE IN THE MIDDLE AGES

Having treated at some length the scop and the troubadour and their brothers and, in general, phases of medieval patronage which are best spoken of apart from the general manner of literary patronage in the Middle Ages, it is our purpose now to deal more generally with evidences of patronage of literary men as they manifested themselves in the old time. We have passed over rapidly the decline of Roman letters and the almost complete absence of learning in the Dark Ages, due not altogether to the invasion of the barbarian, but likewise to decay within. A complete mouldering away, however, was postponed perhaps by the artificial health given by the patronage, such as it was, of the Roman emperors, who looked upon a fostering of art as part of their duty as emperor. In the darkest time, as we have seen, the lamp of learning was tended by such great figures as Charlemagne, Otto, and the English Alfred. Finally, viewing more especially the literature of entertainment, we have noted the court retainer, the bard, and the scop, as he developed into the conscious literary artist, while his less reputable brother became a wandering minstrel. It is our purpose now to discuss patronage as it affected this higher type in the Middle Ages.

At the beginning of our study it was noticed that patronage arose with the development of individual appreciation of letters, side by side with the more impersonal public appreciation, and that hence patronage flourished best in a highly aristocratic form of society. In these respects medieval society was ideal. What had been a communal culture now centered quite naturally about certain courts, but rarely if ever was medieval patronage of letters a lavish system after the style made famous by Maecenas.

55

Rather it was sporadic and uncertain, seldom general or indiscriminately given, but almost always individual, and the Renaissance ideal of patronage was as far removed from the early method as was the Maecenasship of the Augustans from the early Roman practice. Were materials available and were this the place to do it, it is probable that a gradual growth of patronage could be noted among the Romans, beginning, say, with Ennius and culminating in Horace and Virgil. But even if there were princes in the early Middle Ages who preserved learning in troublous times, Europe so lapsed from high civilization to a semi-barbarous state with consequent decline of intellectual power, that the high individualism of Empire slipped back into an almost communal condition. Hence, when we deal with the literary man we must recognize a gradual awakening or emergence from this medieval Teutonic communalism, parallel in a way to what must have been the circumstances under which the individual artist emerged from the primitive throng. Further, a gradual regrowth of the conditions of classical times slowly came about. Early medieval patronage of letters was largely patronage of the scop, but with the decay of the early feudal system came inevitably a decrease in the importance of the retainers. Now retainers were no longer vassals, but hired servants, bound not by oath of fealty, but by the receipt of wages or at least the hope of reward; hence only rich men could afford to have dependents of this kind. It is only when the individual artist freed himself from the shackles of communalism that there was possible those distinctly modern ideas of fame, of glory, of individual achievement, literary property, and individual worth which characterize the Renaissance.

But it must not be supposed that it was necessary to reach this ideal state for literary talent to be recognized by those who were in the position to become patrons. Medieval emperors, because they were Roman emperors, perhaps, lent an encouraging hand as did other kings and princes, though as a whole it was individual fondness for literature and not tradition that prompted Maecenasship. With such royal encouragement, patronage of arts became a fashion. Other wealthy nobles satisfied their own literary tastes by contracting with a poet for a work or two, and churchmen—

cardinals, archbishops, bishops, and abbots—likewise recognized
the value of patronizing letters, though when they did so individually, it was a temporal princes that they patronized, and not as
ecclesiastics. Finally, with the rise of the middle class, in addition to these patrons there were also a few bourgeois like Nicholas
Rolin, chancellor of Philippe le Bon, and Jacques Coeur, finance
minister of Charles VII in France, who were in a position to help
the struggling author through having acquired wealth by mercan-
tile or financial transaction, and accordingly vied with the nobility
in their luxury and patronage of the arts. Hence, in a popular
poet such as Lydgate, Monk of Bury St. Edmunds, we find the
list of patrons often an imposing one, reaching from the unknown
"worthy citeseyn of London" who wished *Bycorne and Chichevache* for his 'parlor' walls, to none less than the Victor of
Agincourt himself, for whom, while still Prince of Wales, the
Troy Book was written, and it includes the Earls of Warwick and
Salisbury, the great Duke Humphrey of Gloucester, and the
Countess of Suffolk.

Italy in the time of the Renaissance may be cited as a significant
example of conditions which were suitable for the development
of a grand system of patronage, and hence for the birthplace of
the Renaissance. Geographically its situation was perfect, but
there were more potent reasons within. Just at the time of the
Renaissance, Italy was broken into many little principalities.
Venice, Florence, Milan, Rome, and Ferrara were all distinct
centres, at the head of which was a prince, struggling for a firm
foothold. Much like the tyrants of classical times, many of these
men arose from the lower strata of society and had to establish
themselves by brute force; many had risen to power through commercial activity, and all were wealthy. Hence, such men as the
Medici, once fairly well established, looked about for a way of
tightening their hold, and by means of their wealth to use their
authority to please the people and to cover their tyranny by the
lustre of institutions of national glory. Thus, individual talent
was stimulated, and even if freedom was on the decline, what had
originally individual glory as an end now became the incentive to
civic glory. Though Florence was nominally a republic, Cosimo

de' Medici had one object steadily in view, that of increasing the growth of the Medici power on the foundation of popular favor. That the flowering of the Renaissance under such princes as the Medici, the Sforza, the Visconti, and others was due to the aristocratic organization of their governments, is clearly seen by a comparison with the Italian republics. In them nothing akin to the glory of the aristocratic centres is to be found. Sienna and Pisa produced great artists, for ornamental arts were encouraged by governments of every form, but literature found neither a cradle nor an asylum. Literary talent was left to its own resources, while in aristocratic communities, it was gathered about the courts and fostered. Hence, when it seemed that Alfonso of Arragon would become master of Italy, Aeneas Sylvius, writing to Marino Socino, a citizen of Sienna, states his preference clearly: "I had rather that Italy attained peace under his rule than under that of the free cities, for kingly generosity rewards excellence of every kind.[1]

Such are in brief the political and social conditions under which patronage in the Middle Ages flourished, but there were in addition some important economic aspects. Aside from uncertain and capricious patronage, nothing material could come to the author from his writings, and his very public oftentimes depended upon his patron. Hence, to practice literature as a profession was a highly impractical undertaking unless the author had some other means of support. The more practical made literature an avocation rather than a vocation. The great figures among medieval poets such as Chaucer, Gower, Hoccleve, and Lydgate, all had commercial or other responsible positions, and only a few poets in the Middle Ages lived by their pens. In the early time such writers as Sanson de Nantueil, Benoit de Sainte Maure, Marie de France, and others seem to have had no other duties, though so little is known of them outside their own works that any assertions concerning them are unsafe. Giraldus Cambrensis definitely had other duties, and Wace, Geoffrey of Monmouth, and William of Malmesbury were churchmen. In later times

[1] Epistle 39, quoted by Burckhardt, *Civilization of the Period of the Renaissance in Italy*, tr. Middlemore, I, 311.

Trevisa was a chaplain, and Capgrave, Burgh, Metham, and Bokenham were members of religious orders which obviously imposed obligations. These duties often meant very little actual time spent in their performance, and such men as Froissart in reality became men of letters purely, while Christine de Pisan, through the products of her pen which she presented to the nobility, was able to make her living by literature. Men of letters generally are an impractical lot, and many in the Middle Ages, with the impulse to write upon them, gave themselves up to it without much thought of conditions. Hence, we hear complaint after complaint, and find much shameless importunity and open begging on the part of the writer. The frequency of such appeals testifies to the large number of writers who depended upon letters for support, and it is indeed pitiful when we remember that the plaints come from men practicing a profession which was unrecognized.

The invention of printing, of course, made a difference, for it gave the author such a public as his patron could not supply, and made possible remuneration from book sales. Hence, the Elizabethan Age, to digress for a moment, differs greatly from the preceding centuries. As a result of various causes the Elizabethan poet could find that being a poet was the real function of his life, and that the support of the natural man was a necessary evil to be contended with. To be sure, such men as Wyatt, Surrey, Greville, Sidney, and the gentlemen authors of the period, were dilettanti in the very best sense of the term. They practiced literature during ample moments of leisure for the love of it, and because it was a polite gentlemanly accomplishment, and a man like Sidney, by no means wealthy himself, patronized needy talent from a devout sense of duty. Sincere and serious they certainly were, but not unnaturally so, and their works were not intended for publication. But the case is different with other authors of the period. Though a great deal of medieval literature was by no means uninspired, the Renaissance spirit made the Elizabethan surer of his art. Spenser's real occupation was that of writing the *Faerie Queene,* and to him his state positions were merely a means of supplementing the earnings of his pen, if indeed there were earnings. Bacon's real life work was the composition of his *Instauratio Magna*, though incidently he had to be a lawyer and a statesman. Ben Jonson, the recipient of a comparatively munificent patronage, was definitely a literary man. So likewise was Daniel. Nashe, Dekker, Greene, Lodge, Breton—in fact all the prose writers and dramatists—were very definitely professionals, negotiating with a bookseller or a theatrical manager for a living.

But while the advantages of printing were beginning to give the Elizabethan writer a wide reading public and hence a great patron, he attempted to become a professional writer under the old conditions, and wished to live by patronage which was fitted only to the medieval system. As Miss Phoebe Sheavyn has shown,[2] professional writers increased out of proportion to the class among whom patrons were to be found, and quite naturally, there were changed relations between patron and protégé. Instead of quietly creating a literary work for his patron's circle of friends, the Elizabethan writer became now merely one of a crowd of unattached suitors, striving to snatch for himself a share of the bounty which not all could possibly obtain. He lived in perpetual rivalry and availed himself of extravagant eulogy and flattery (means not always necessary before) to bring about artificially what had once been a natural relationship. And with so many persons to be cared for, quite naturally patronage was incapable of bearing up, and we hear complaint after complaint.

But non-professionalism, as Professor Moore points out,[3] is not the most important economic fact in literary circles of the Middle Ages. He stresses rather the fact that the medieval writer addressed his work, not to the world in general, but to a very definite and restricted circle, a circumstance explainable by the fact that there was no book-buying public. Libraries were small and the demand for books small also, that in general they were written only to order. In the main the statement holds true for both the early and the later Middle Ages, but in spite of these conditions, the medieval author was not without his desire for

[2] *The Literary Profession in the Elizabethan Age*, 19 ff.
[3] "General Aspects of Literary Patronage in the Middle Ages," *The Library*, 3rd Series, IV, 369 ff.

fame through his writings, and he expected to be read more widely than in an immediate circle of understanding readers. The books of chronicles, of religious commentary, and of encyclopedic learning, were intended to have universal significance, and the address to "al who hit read or heren it red" appended to many a manuscript begging that the faults be excused and the author held blameless, indicate a wider audience than that of immediate acquaintance. At least the author hoped that his work would be copied, and it can be shown that he definitely expected his patron to act somewhat in the capacity of publisher. In later times the press and the booktrade assured an author of a hearing abroad, and he was not dependent upon the patron for the currency of his work, but the medieval man of letters sought a patron, if not in hope of gain, at least in the hope of winning a public, and hence some remuneration.

But this could never be more than a hope, and the author found his compensation generally in satisfaction; never would it have occurred to anyone in the Middle Ages to choose literature as a lucrative profession. That the author did expect some return from the work of his pen will be evident as we proceed, but he looked to a patron and not to the public. It is something of a universal condition that Giraldus Cambrensis describes when he concedes the statement of his friend Walter Mapes, that while Mapes talked in the vulgar tongue, he reached many people and had some advantage from his sermons, but Gerald, writing in Latin, reached few, and addressing himself to princes, was not able to secure any sort of reward for works which merited it." "It is true indeed," sighs Gerald,

"that my best years, and the prime of my life have been spent without any remuneration or advancement arising out of my literary labours, and I am growing old, and standing, as it were, on the threshold of death; but I neither ask, nor expect, worldly recompense from anyone. My only desire is, and it is all I ought to desire, that, first, and above all, I may partake of the divine mercy vouchsafed to me by Him who giveth all things freely, through good works; his grace co-operating, nay, being the sole efficient cause; and next, that through my poor literary works I may obtain favor with the world, if ever the pursuits of learning should again be held in esteem, and recover their former eminence; although my reward may be deferred till further times, when posterity is sure to award honour to every man according to his just deserts."[4]

It is too sweeping a generalization, however, to assume that no medieval author ever found himself without a patron. Though the gain or fame arising from writing books in the Middle Ages never amounted to very much without the patron, it is to be remembered that books are produced also for self-satisfaction, or because of the call of duty. By far the largest body of literature in the Middle Ages is of a religious character, and excluding such works as may have been used as homilies or dissertations from the pulpit, there is much more that has no such connection. Many of the poems on religious subjects have addresses which indicate that the author used his talent for the good of his parishioners,[5] and the "Munk of sallay" who wrote the *Myrour of Lewed Men*, translated it,

"out of a frenche romance that sir*e* Robert; Bisshop*e* of lycolñ, made; and eked mekel therto, as him thoght spedeful to edificacion and swettenes of deuocio*n*, and lering of lewed men."[6]

Further, the author of *St. Bernard's Lamentation on Christ's Passion*, looks about and sees that:

> Lewed me*n* be not lered in lore,
> As Clerkes ben in holi writ;

and he reflects:

> 3if Crist haue send mon wit at wille,
> Craft of Clergye, for to preche,
> Alle hise hestes scholde we fulfille
> As ferforþ as we mihten areche. . . .
> Þerfore ichaue on Englisch wrou3t,
> Saint Ber*n*ard witnesseþ in Latyn.[7]

Further, the author of the *Spore of Loue*, "þat profitable is to

---

[4] Preface to the third edition of the *History* addressed to John, *Historical Works of Giraldus Cambrensis*, ed. Wright, 177.

[5] "Mirror of the Periods of Man's Iife," ll. 649 ff., in *Hymns to the Virgin and Christ*, ed. Furnivall, E. E. T. S.; "Prouerbes of diuerce profetes and of poetes and of oþur seyntes," *Minor Poems of the Vernon MS.*, II, 522; (E. E. T. S.) Many other examples could be cited.

[6] *Minor Poems of the Vernon MS.*, I, 40. The poem itself is from MS. Egerton, 927.

[7] Ibid., I, 298.

soule behoue," after invoking a blessing on those who hear him, adds:

> ffor, lewed and lered, more and lesse,
> How wol ow teche holynesse;
> To loue God wiþ fyn chere
> How wol ou teche, my leoue and dere.
> ffor mony a tyme ȝe cone me preye
> Þer-of a lesson ow to seye;
> ȝoure dulnesse sumwhat to scharpe
> ȝe han me preyed for to carpe. . . .
> Þerfore þis bok to ow I make
> ȝoure discumfort for to slake
> Þat is cald "þe spore of loue,"
> Þat stureþ or loue to god aboue.[8]

Finally, to cite no more evidence, the author of the *Myroure of Owre Ladye* begs the prayers of his readers,

"that lyke as trew charyte to your soulles helth, & comfort, forsothe hathe styred me to thys laboure, and none other erthly thynge."[9]

Therefore, it seems that Barbour in his prologue to his legend of *Mary of Egypt* has stated the general principle which moved many a medieval author to write:

> It ware spedfule, quha-sa cuthe,
> To put in wryt ore tel be movthe
> It þat mycht mene gere lef syne
> & wiþ god sa sauchtnyne wyne.[10]

while the author of *How to Hear Mass,* sets the matter of remuneration at rest:

> Of my trauayle is me nouȝt;
> Wolde ȝe þenke it in ȝor þouȝt.[11]

Nor were religious works the only ones produced without patrons. While one would like to think that the authors of the ambitious medieval encyclopedic works had some remuneration other than inward satisfaction, we have no evidence, and because men are the creatures they are, it seems not unlikely that much

---

[8] Ibid., I, 268-9.
[9] Ed. Blunt, E. E. T. S., 7.
[10] ll. 1 ff. *Barbour's . . . Legendensammlung . . .* ed. Horstmann, (1881), I, 143.
[11] ll. 655 ff. *Minor Poems of the Vernon MS.*, II, 510. Another important illustration in point is the prologue to the *Ormulum*, ed. White (1852).

work was done purely for the love of it, and for the consciousness of good done to posterity.   But we have other evidence besides conjecture.   Nennius, in the preface to the *History of the
Britons* says that his work is compiled from a wish to benefit his
inferiors, and he hopes

"that the prayers of my betters will be offered up for me in recompense
of my labour."[12]

Layamon likewise bids "alcne æþele mon þet þeos boc rede &
leornia þeos runan," that he pray for the author and his parents.[13]
But often the writer is more specific.   Robert of Brunne repeats
a common formula when he tells us definitely that his *Chronicle*
was translated "not for the lerid bot for þe lewed" who cannot
understand strange English:

> I made it not forto be praysed,
> bot at þe lewed men were aysed. . . .
> ffor þis makyng I will no mede
> bot gude prayere when ȝe it rede;
> Þerfore [alle] ȝe lordes lewed
> ffor wham I haf þis Inglis schewed,
> Prayes to God he gyf me grace,—
> I trauayled for ȝour solace.

At the end of his preface he carefully reminds us again that he

> did it wryte for felawes sake,
> whan þai wild solace make.[14]

Likewise the author of the *Eulogium (Historiarum sive Temporis)* (14th century) carefully informs us that the higher in-
ducements to historical research are ineffective in his case; he
speaks of how history and writers kept memory from oblivion,
and adds that the tedium of monastic life and the request of his
prior that he do something in "modo chronico" led him to undertake his work.[15]   In this case, obviously, the work is due to the

---

[12] *Six Old English Chronicles,* tr. Giles, (Bohn Lib.), 384. Bede, who availed
himself of another kind of patronage, makes a similar wish in his *Ecclesiastical
History.* (tr. Giles, Bohn Lib., 4.)

[13] *Brut,* ed. Madden, I, 3.

[14] *Story of England by Robert Manning of Brunne,* ed. Furnivall, (R. S.), ll.
83, 128, and 143 ff.; I, 3 ff.

[15] Ed. Haydon, (R. S.), (1858), I, 1 ff.

encouragement of the prior, and the evident sincerity of Robert of Brunne's work leads us to believe him implicitly.

But be that as it may, it is interesting to note that one class of work at least, histories, lost their reputation for veracity in later times if they were too obviously conferring immortality on a patron. There are, of course, many historical works which are known to have been patronized, and which will be treated as our study advances. Ethelweard's *Chronicle* is addressed to Matilda, daughter of Otto the Great,[16] and its object is definitely to point out the glorious lineage of that princess. Giraldus Cambrensis affirms his object of making the glory of his princes live. William of Malmesbury avows a similar purpose, assuring his dedicatee that in his work he may contemplate himself as in a glass.[17] Other historians, Geoffrey of Monmouth, Henry of Huntingdon, William of Newbury, Rigord, Jehan de Waurin, Thomas of Walsingham, and Capgrave, were all patronized writers. The life and opinions of Froissart, as they are reflected in his *Chronicle* even, were determined by the favor of his patrons as we shall see, and it is no surprise to find authors stating that their histories had no patron, as a recommendation of truthfulness. At the end of the *Schir William Wallace*, Henry the Minstrel states the case quite clearly:

> All worthi men at redys this rurall dyt,
> Blaym nocht the buk, set I be wnperfyt.
> I suld hawe thank, sen I nocht trawaill spard
> For my laubour no man hecht me reward;
> Na charge I had off king nor othir lord;
> Gret harm I thocht his guid suld be smord.
> I haif said her ner as the processe gais;
> And fenȝeid nocht for frendschip nor for fais.
> Cóstis herfor was no man bond to me;
> In this sentence I had na will to be,
> Bot in als mekill as I rahersit nocht
> Sa worthely as nobill Wallace wrocht.[18]

In regard to inaccuracies, "two knychtis," he says, "suld blaymyt be for this"—his authorities—who "gert me mak [wrang] rec-

---

[16] *Six Old English Chronicles*, tr. Giles, (Bohn Lib.), 1.
[17] Tr. Giles, (Bohn Lib.), 478.
[18] Bk. XI, ll. 1431 ff., ed. Moir, S. T. S., 376-7.

ord." Recognizing the bad light of patronized histories, John Major, dedicating his *History of Greater Britain* to James V, is most apologetic, and from him we learn the popular attitude:

"for my justification in the eyes of those who pretend that it is not fitting to dedicate a historical work to any person, seeing that he who seeks for a patron must put on a mask of a flatterer rather than that of a historian, whose first law it is to write the truth; all that these objectors urge in support of their contention is this: that neither Sallust, nor Livy, nor any of the ancients made dedication of his works."

This Major concedes, but suggests that the dedications may have been lost, or, he reflects—Sallust had no occasion to dedicate since in his time there were no kings, while Livy probably thought it was more glorious to accomplish his work for the gods and for posterity than for any mortal man. But the poets, he adds, all dedicated, and Valerius Maximus in his *History* was not silent concerning his dedicatee; neither was Augustine, Bede, or almost all of the ecclesiastical historians.

"For which reason, seeing that to your Highness and to your ancestors we owe all that we have, I think it right and proper to dedicate this work now undertaken to the same. Yet lest my work should contain any suspicion of flattery, I have left untouched, to be dealt with by other hands, matters of most recent date."[19]

Though Major's apology might be most necessary in the later Middle Ages, that the fact was recognized earlier is to be seen by the attitude of William of Malmesbury, who though a most fulsome dedicator himself, objected to panegyric in others. In Book V of his *Chronicle of the Kings of England* he speaks disparagingly of one David, Bishop of Bangor, a Scot, who wrote a history of Emperor Henry V's expedition against the pope, which has been lost. This, William says, was written "far more partially to the king than becomes an historian," and truly if one may judge from the samples William gives of it, his judgment was probably sound when he determined "to make allowances for him, since he has not written a history, but a panegyric."[20]

It is clear then that not all works in the Middle Ages were

[19] *A History of Greater Britain* . . . tr. Constable, Publications of the Scottish History Society, (1892), X, cxxxiii ff.
[20] Tr. Giles, (Bohn Lib.), 458.

patronized. Much of the religious literature was written solely for the purpose of instructing men or at the call of duty, while secular works were sometimes written to benefit those who were ignorant, or for the possibility of fame in future ages. Sometimes, too, the author was careful to deny a patron, and histories, as noted above, that were known to have been patronized, were in ill-repute as to truthfulness, a fact arising perhaps from a servile relationship which the author felt toward his patron.

Too much stress has been laid upon the unworthiness of the relationship between many patrons and their protégés, who had no duties save just to live at court, and write if they chose, and though such conditions led to mercenary flattery, the principle was at basis only too ideal. Professor Emerton[21] has pointed out this ideality in the case of the Humanists, showing that the poet need not feel humbled by this relation, for the very essence of such patronage was the reflection that through his work he was giving back quite as much as he received in money. His statements are equally true for all the Middle Ages though seldom was there any lavish provision.

"It was a relation of honor, not to be reduced to commercial terms. The money given was not paid for the scholar's services; it was given to secure him the leisure needed for the proper pursuit of his scholarship, not to servile flattery of his patron, nor to any direct furtherance of the patron's ends."[22]

But there was a very desirable and more personal return than mere production of books that poets have confidently promised, even from earliest times. The merest scribbler in the old time

---

[21] *Erasmus*, 31 ff.

[22] Writing to Henry of Bergen, Erasmus says: "I have always received your beneficence as became an honest and grateful client. I have loved you with all my heart, have respected and venerated you, have borne you in mind, and not been silent in your praise. In all my prayers to this day I pray God in whose power alone it lies, to repay with interest all the benefits you have conferred upon me. Beyond this I can do no more." (Epist. 151, Nichols, *Epistles of Erasmus*, I, 325.) Similarly, the same author writing to the Lady de Vere, after commenting upon patrons generally and how he would not trade his patroness for any Maecenas or Caesar, adds: "And as for the return I may make, whatever my poor genius can do shall be exerted to the utmost, that future ages may know that there existed at the extremity of the world one lady, by whose munificence Good Letters, corrupted, . . . ruined, . . . neglected, . . . were encouraged to raise their head." (Ibid., I, 296.)

felt that in him alone rested the conferring of immortality or oblivion, which led Bishop Hurd to liken the dedication of books, as we are told, to the action of the builder of the tower of Pharos, who inscribed his name on the marble and then covered it with a veneer of stucco on which he placed the name of the reigning prince,[23] for often it is the name of the author that has kept alive the name of the patron. Occasionally we do hear in the early dedication, in the midst of extravagant praise, that the glory of the prince will bring immortality upon the writer,[24] and even Spenser, it will be recalled, dedicated his *Faerie Queene* to Elizabeth "to live with the eternitie of her fame." But more often the proposition is reversed, and we hear: "Blessed are they whose memory is enshrined in wise volumes and not in empty images."[25] Long before this time Pliny had spoken contemptuously of Apron the Grammarian, who supposed that every one to whom he inscribed any work would therefore gain immortality.[26]   From this it is but a step to Giraldus Cambrensis in twelfth-century England pointing out that "ad gloriam autem tam poetae quam philosophi tanquam unanimiter omnes invitant,"[27] and quoting Tully, Pliny, Juvenal, Horace, and Martial to make his point. About the same time, Wace was prudently showing the nobility

[23] Wheatley, *Dedication of Books*, 6.

[24] Thus Agathius Scholasticus of Myrina, in the age of Justinian, presenting his collection of epigrams, says, "For I know that the dedication to Theodorus will instill eternal glory into the work of my study." (*Greek Anthology*, ed. Paton, (L. C. L.) Bk. IV, 123.) The idea seems to have persisted side by side with the offer of immortality, to be used when the more ambitious promise might have been a bit indelicate. Thus Erasmus, writing to John Grolier, says frankly that things of little worth are sometimes recommended by the genius of eloquent men. "We authors do ourselves a good turn when we commend our lucubrations to the attraction of a name like yours. It is not you that are a debtor to books, but books that are a debtor to you, when by your means they will have a lasting commendation to posterity. However much the aid of Letters may be needed to secure for Merit an immortal name, in your case there was no need to seek elsewhere what was to be found at home . . ." (Nichols, op. cit., III, 364.)

[25] *Greek Anthology*, ed. Paton, Bk. IV, 125.

[26] Preface to the *Natural History*. Other references in Latin to immortality so obtained are to be found in Ovid, *Tristia*, I, vi, 35-6; III, iii, 77-8; III, vii, 50-2; *Amores*, I, x, 61-2; *Pontic Epistles*, IV, viii, 45-8; *Metamorphoses*, XV, 871 ff; Horace, *Odes*, III, 30; *Virgil, Georgics*, III, 9; Propertius, III, i; and Martial, *Epigrams*, X, xxvi.

[27] *De Principis Instructione, Works*, (R. S.), VIII, 53.

that no matter how great their deeds were, only the poet's pen could immortalize them:

> Bien entend, è cognuis è sai
> Ke tuit murrunt è cler è lai,
> E ke mult a corte durée
> Emprès lur mort lur renumée;
> Se par cler ne est mis en livre,
> Ne pot par el durer ne vivre.[28]

Developing his idea, Wace goes on, showing that those who wrote histories have always been beloved and that barons and noble ladies often gave handsome presents to have their names commemorated:

> Mult seulent estre amé,
> E mult proisié, mult onuré,
> Cil ki les gestes escriveient
> E ki les estoires feseient.
> Sovent aveient des Baruns
> E des nobles dames biax dons.
> Mes ore puis-je lunges penser,
> Livres escrire è translater,
> Fere romanz è sirventoiz,
> Tart truverai, tant seit cortoiz,
> Ki tant me dont, ne tent sa main:
> Donc je aloe un escrivain,
> Ne ki nulle honor autre me face,
> fors tant n'i out, dist Maister Wace.[29]

[28] *Roman de Rou*, ll. 5302 ff., ed. Pluquet, I, 271.

[29] Pluquet, I, 271-2 n. Taking his cue from a similar idea, Randolph Higdon in the preface to his *Polychronicon* does something similar. "I praye who schulde now knowe emperours, wonder of philosofres, oþer folwe þe apostles, but his noble dedes and hir wonder werkes were i-write and so i-kept in mynde? Who schulde knowe Lucilium but Seneca in his pistles hadde i-write his dedes? Writinge of poetes is more worthy to preisynge of emperoures an al þe welþe of þis worlde, and riches þat welde while þey were alyue." (Trevisa's translation, ed. Babington, (R. S.), I, 5.) Passages of similar content and intent are to be found in Giraldus Cambrensis, *De Principis Instructione Liber, Praefatio, Works*, (R. S.), VIII, 5 ff.,, and the *Topographia Hibernica, Introitus, Works*, (R. S.), V, 3 ff.; Jehan de Waurin, *Recueil des Croniques*, ed. Hardy, (R. S.), 1; Gower, *Confessio Amantis*, Prol. 32 ff., *Works*, ed. Macaulay, II, 3; Lydgate, *Troy Book*, Prol. 156 ff., ed. Bergen, E. E. T. S., I, 5, and *Falls of Princes*, General Prologue; Envoy, Book III, ch. xviii; Prologue to Book IV; and Prologue to Book VIII, ed., *The Tragedies, Gathered by Jhon Bochas, of all such Princes as Fell from theyr Estates through the Mutability of Fortune* . . ., printed by John Wayland, 1558; and in the anonymous *Vita Beati Edvardi Regis et Confessoris*, (1455) ed. Luard, *Lives of Edward the Confessor*, (R. S.), II, 361.

Further, William of Malmesbury, dedicating his *History* to Robert of Gloucester, assures him that it is due to princes that men act well or compose anything worthy of remembrance. "Your exertions incite us to make you live forever in our writings."[30] Again in the epilogue of the same work he says that he writes only that Robert's worth might reach posterity,[31] and in the preface of the *Modern History* hints at the same thing.[32] Fired by a similar idea, one of the twelfth century Goliardi threatens total oblivion to the parsimonious as he barters his song for a coat.[33]

Though the idea of immortality through connection with literature is preached in many medieval books, in no place is it done more forcefully, and incidently, because of its wide circulation, more effectively, than in the *Secreta Secretorum*, that old work of advice said to have been presented to Alexander the Great by Aristotle. This work on the governance of a prince existed in all languages,[34] and the number of manuscripts surviving indicates clearly its wide-spread circulation. The matter of rewards is unmistakably settled in the chapter on the advancement of study:

"And take entent to loue hem þat er to be louyd, and to reward hem þat er to be rewardyd; þer-by þou shalt drawe to þe lettryd men to enheye þi louyngℯ, and þy dedys to make ay to last in scripture."[35]

Enough has been said perhaps to show that immortality was held out as a bait throughout the Middle Ages and hence, when we find Renaissance scholars developing the theme to utter ridiculousness, and talking confidently about immortality in their letters to the great, it is to be recognized that the line of reasoning is a traditional one. As early as Dante this confident note is struck. Dedicating his *Divina Commedia* to Can Grande della Scala, he writes:

"Nor does the simple ardour of my affection permit me to pass over in

[30] Tr. Giles, (Bohn Lib.), 1.

[31] Ibid., 478.

[32] Ibid., 480.

[33] *Carmina Burana*, ed. Litt. Vereins in Stuttgart, (1847), 76.

[34] In Middle English and Scots alone there are no less than five different versions surviving, and many works are known to have used it as source.

[35] *Governance of Lordschippes*, cap. 28, ed. Steele, *Three Prose Versions of the Secreta Secretorum*, E. E. T. S., 63   The passage is of similar content in the other versions.

silence the consideration that in this offering there may seem to be greater honor and fame conferred on the patron than on the gift; the rather that in the address I shall appear to such as read with attention to have given utterance to a forecast as to the increase of the glory of your name—and this of set purpose But eagerness for your favour, for which I thirst, heedless of envy, will urge me forward to the goal which was my aim from the first."[36]

Later writers are by no means less sure, but rather have the fullest consciousness that with them lay the power to confer fame, or if they chose, oblivion. Notwithstanding all the idealism in his love for Laura, Petrarch remembers that his sonnets confer immortality on both his beloved and himself.[37] Boccaccio, spurned by his fair one who hoped he might thus go on making her famous by his importunity, hints that he will try the effect of a little blame, and Sannazaro threatens Alfonso of Naples with eternal obscurity for his cowardice before Charles VIII.[38] We find Poliziano urging John of Portugal to be mindful of his immortality and to send him materials to Florence so that he could put them into shape, and that it might not befall him as it had so many others that his deeds "lie hidden in the vast heap of human frailty."[39] Filelfo and Poggio were among the sauciest. Clearly characteristic of the fullest development of this idea is the letter of Beccatelli to Filippo of Milan:

"immortalite, quam non pecunia, non potentii non denique virtute ipsa comparari quis potest absque poetarum auxilio . . . magnam mehercule

---

[36] Epistola X. *Dante's Epistles,* ed. Toynbee, 197 ff.

[37] Sonnet cli. The idea is not absent even in the late Renaissance writers. Spenser, *Amoretti,* lxix, lxxv; Du Bellay, *Ruins of Rome* (tr. by Spenser), xxxii; Drayton, *Idea,* vi, xliv, xlvii; Daniel, *Delia,* xxxviii, lv; Shakespeare, *Sonnets,* xvi, xvii, xviii, lv, lxxxi, are examples of the promise. Jonson, too, has Caesar give the reason for his patronage of letters, thus:

> She [Poetry] can so mould Rome and her monuments,
> Within the liquid marble of her lines,
> That they shall stand fresh and miraculous,
> Even when they mix with innovating dust.
> In her sweet streams shall our brave Roman spirits
> Chase, and swim after death, with their choice deeds
> Shining on their white shoulders.   (*Poetaster,* V, i.)

Cp. Ovid's speech, *Poetaster,* I, i. Further, Sidney in the *Apology for Poetry* speaks of those authors who "tell you they will make you immortal by their verses," (ed. Cook, 57) while Nashe in *Pierce Penniless* informs us that "men of great calling take it of merite to have their names eternized by Poets." (*Works,* ed. McKerrow, I, 159.)

[38] Burckhardt, op. cit., I, 211-2.

[39] Ibid., I, 212.

et admirabilem poetarum vim, sequidem homines ex humo creatos, modo velint, coelo pene dixerim donant."[40]

All these promises would be of little worth if only the humanist believed them, but when we find great princes anxiously corresponding with authors about the immortality of their fame, the matter has real significance.[41]   It is a matter of much doubt if a real and fundamental love of literature was at the bottom of early Renaissance patronage; rather it is apparent that the thirst for posthumous glory was the motive.   To perpetuate a name was a most fervent passion, which manifested itself in the composition of chronicles and panegyrics, in the erection of gorgeous buildings and handsome statues.   But one has only to read the preface to Macchiavelli's *Florentine History* to have the curtain drawn aside with complete disillusionment upon frightful evidence of thirst for fame, utterly unscrupulous as to the means by which it was obtained.

In later times Erasmus, ever self-conscious even to morbidity, carried on the tradition.   Writing to Leo X concerning the dedication of the *Jerome* to him, Erasmus says:

"There is no name more celebrated or more approved than that of Jerome; and yet I see a way by which it may acquire a brighter lustre and a more weighty authority.   The glory of Leo is incomparably brilliant, and yet, if I am not mistaken, no small accession will accrue to it, if so rare, so important, so noble a work shall come to light and be placed in men's hands under the protection of your auspicious name."[42]

But even the conferring of immortality for one's bread became irksome business if one had a big work on hands, and we find Erasmus writing a very vexed letter to his "dear Battus" concerning the importunities of the Lady de Vere:

"May I die if I ever wrote anything so much against the grain.   You would understand and pardon my ill-humor if you knew how hard it is to bring one's mind to the production of a great book, and when one is

---

[40] Quoted by Voigt, *Wiederlebung des Classischen Alterthums*, (3rd edn., 1893), I, 446 n.

[41] There can be no doubt about the sincerity of both writer and patron.   William Nesen, corrector of Froben's press, is overjoyed to hear that Erasmus is going to confer immortality upon him by the dedication of an edition of the *Copia*. (Nichols, II, 372, and 390.)

[42] Epistle 323.   Nichols, II, 203.

on fire with one's subject to be dragged back into these contemptible trivialities. My lady requires to be complimented for her munificence. You say it will not be enough if I make pretty allusions in the work which I am to publish; I must write six hundred private letters besides. The money was promised me a year ago, but you still give me nothing but hopes, and you are as sick as I am of the whole business."[48]

These then are the fundamental social, economic, and intellectual phases of literary patronage in the Middle Ages: first in importance is the almost communal character of medieval society and the gradual awakening or developing of the literary man as he emerged from such a throng and passed from scop to professional writer. Second, under such conditions, it has been shown that literature was not a vocation, but an avocation, and since there was no book-buying public in any real sense, the author sought his readers, not in a large public, but in an individual or a group primarily, with the hope always that through his patron perhaps, he might find other readers or persons so interested as to copy his work. But the medieval author did not always write for a patron; occasionally with no compensation other purposes moved him to write, and he addressed a great variety of readers more specifically. Further, his relationship with his patron when it was an absolutely dependent one, was by no means an unworthy one, binding the writer only to diligence. Finally, the fundamental reason for patronage, or at least the one most preached by the author himself, was the fame and immortality he might confer upon the prince, if the prince would only take some interest in his writings. With these facts as basis, then, it is possible to investigate medieval patronage by certain general manifestations of the relationship as we find it in the literature of the old time.

[48] Froude, *Life and Letters of Erasmus*, 59.

V

COURT WRITINGS

Obviously the first manifestation of a relationship in a patronized poet is the presence of the genre "occasional verse" in his works, for naturally, to gain the ear of his patron, the poet must write about the things that the patron is interested in. Living at court, and steeped in social life, the nobleman likes a poem celebrating the latest wedding, the most flagrant scandal, or the latest coup-d'etat in politics, and, if he be military, a glorification of the deeds of the field. In short, when a poet of the Middle Ages was patronized, even more than in later times, his work had the mark of the coterie, for with conditions of book making as they were, the patronized poet invariably was concerned, not with a large public, but rather with a small group. A considerable portion of the epic writings of the Middle Ages have come to be recognized as courtly. The body of such work is so large and in general so well-known that it may be passed for our purpose with a mention only, as many of these poems and evidences of their patronage will be discussed in other connections. The works of such writers as Marie de France are representative of this type of writing. Marie's lays were undoubtedly intended for the nobility, and Denys Pyramis speaks of her in flattering terms in *La Vie de Saint Edmund le Rey*, saying that her writings were much appreciated by the noblesse, especially the ladies.[1]

Disregarding the matter of patronage in each individual case, beside these more ambitious works there is much medieval poetry which deals definitely with noble characters, or which was clearly prompted by the possibility of finding readers at court. One has but to turn through the works of an author like Eustace Deschamps to find numerous examples. Thus Godfrey of Winchester (d. 1107), though prior of his monastery, wrote a series

[1] ll. 35 ff. *Memorials of St. Edmund's Abbey*, ed. Thos. Arnold, (R. S.), II, 138 ff.

of Latin panegyrical epigrams on various famous people, including the kings Cnut, Edward, William, and Richard; the queens Emma, Edida, and Matilda; various counts, and notable churchmen, including Lanfranc.[2] Almost all of the troubadour and trouvère literature on the continent has such a courtly mark, and in England, Reginald of Canterbury, a native of Fagia, addressed some of his poems to *Domino suo Americo Fagiensi,* and likewise a quantity of hexameters to Anselm.[3] Gace Brulé wrote his *Chansons,* some for the "comtesse de Brie," and some for the "comte Geoffroi," who is perhaps Geoffrey of Brittany, son of Henry II and Eleanor of Acquitaine.[4] Peter of Blois, later archdeacon, first of Bath and then of London, served as Eleanor's secretary, writing perhaps the lost love poems of which he speaks regretfully.[5] Osbert de Clare about the same time actually hails Henry II as Maecenas after the manner of the ancients, which is rare in the Middle Ages. After a long panegyric he adds:

Vir Horatio Maecenas
Amoris laxans habenas,
Suo tempore dilexit
Et in multis hunc provexit;
Et Virgilius, venusto
Carmine gratus Augusto,
Auctus est mercede bona,
Ampla satis sumens dona.
Josephus spe non inani
Filium Vespasiani
Titum colens liberatur
Servitute qua gravatur,
Ergo manum dans Osberto,
Hunc gaudere fine certo,
In afflictione sua
Fac protectione tua,
Ne ecclesia gravetur
Cui praesse se fatetur,
Quam deprimere conantur
Qui perverse malignantur. . . .

---

[2] "Godefridi Prioris Epigrammata Historica," ed. Wright, in *Anglo-Latin Satirical Poets and Epigrammatists of the 12th Century,* (R. S.), II, 148 ff.
[3] *D. N. B.*
[4] Huet, *Chansons de Gace Brulé,* S. A. T. F.
[5] Ten Brink, *History of English Literature,* I, 184.
[6] *Poema ad Regem Henricum Secundum,* Caxton Society, V, 209 ff.

In later times Adam Davy had his five very complimentary Dreams about Edward II,[7] and Laurence Minot wrote his poems in praise of the wars of Edward III.[8] The outstanding example of a poem extolling the virtues of a princely family is *L' Histoire de Guillaume Le Marechal,* count of Striguil and Pembroke and regent of Engand 1216-19.[9] Other such panegyrics will be mentioned in other connections.

At the courts the all-important subjct of love engaged the attention. Guillaume de Machaut, Eustace Deschamps, and writers like them spent much of their time at the courts of princes, and their works are evidence of what was popular in noble circles.[10] Froissart says of himself that he spent his time at the English court, as clerk to Philippa, "serving her with fair ditties and treatises of love."[11] Christine de Pisan addressed many of her epistolary balades, eulogies, and greeting poems to nobles. In France, likewise Margaret of Austria had about her a large number of chroniclers, such as Jacques Lefevre de Saint-Remy, Jacques du Clerq, George Chastellain, and Jean Molinet, and Jehan le Maire, all of whom praise her in the extravagant manner of the time, vying with one another in their fanciful illustrations.[12] Nor was the practice absent in Italy. The court of Beatrice d'Este, to choose only one admirable example, was just

---

[7] *Adam Davy's Five Dreams about Edward II,* ed. Furnivall, E. E. T. S.

[8] *Poems of Laurence Minot,* ed. Hall, (1914):

> þus haue I mater for to make,
> For a nobill prince sake;
> Helpe me, God, my wit es thin,
> Now Laurence Minot will begin.   (pg. 21.)

Ten Brink, (I, 322), thinks that Minot "seems to have been a gleeman who was about to find employment from a nobleman."

[9] Ed. Paul Meyer, La Société de l'Histoire de France, (1891) 3 vols. Lines 19165 ff. are of especial interest. (II, 329.)

[10] In *Le Livre du Voir Dit* Machaut says: "Mo tressoueraine dame, je vous eusse porté mon livre pour vous esbattre, où toutes les choses sont que je fis onques: mais il est en plus de. xx. pièces; car je l'ay fait faire pour aucun de mes seigneurs; si que je le fais noter, & pour ce il convient que il soit par pièces." (ed. Paulin Paris, 69.) Not only does Machaut mention the nobility in his anagrammes, but he accords them a place in his *Jugement dou Roy de Behaingue,* in his *Jugement dou Roy de Navarre,* and in the *Fontaine Amoreuse.*

[11] Hardy, *Philippa of Hainault,* 264.

[12] Thus they do homage to the "Pearl of the World," who combines all virtues, by allowing each letter of the name "Margaret" to stand for the initial of some famous

such a hot-bed of literature. According to her secretary, "l'ele-
gantissimo Calmeta," her court was composed of men of talent
and distinction, most of them poets and musicians who were expected to compose and offer to her the works of their genius.
Her leisure she generally employed by having a certain Antonio
Grifo, or some equally gifted man, read the *Divina Commedia* or
the works of other Italian poets aloud to her. And, adds Calmeta, it was no small relaxation for Lodovico Sforza, when he
was able to escape from the cares and business of state, to come
and listen to these readings in his wife's rooms. She did not content herself with her own court, but sought out the elegant poets
of all Italy, praising and rewarding each according to his merit.[13]
Further, to Poliziano popularity grew so burdensome, that in one
of his letters, he exclaimed:

"Does a man want a motto for his sword's hilt, or a posy for a ring,
an inscription for his bedroom, or a device for his plate, or even for
his pots and pans, he must like all the world to Politian. There is
hardly a wall I have not besmeared like a snail with the effusions of my
brain. One teases me for catches and drinking songs, another for a grave
discourse, a third for a serenade, a fourth for a carnival ballad."[14]

In England there are numerous poems of a semi-political
nature which show court influence or at least interest. There
are numerous elegies,[15] coronation poems,[16] and complimentary

---

lady, of whose virtues a full account is given. M— Marguerite de Danmarck, A—
Artémise de Carie; R— Radégonde de France; G— Gilla de Hongroie; U— Vesta-
Déesse; E— Eriphyle, Sibylle; R— Rachel; I— Ingebergue de Dalmace; T—
Theodolinde de Bavière; E—Eliza de Carthage. ("Christopher Hare," *Marguerite of
Austria*, 317.) Le Maire's long poem, *Le Triomphe de l'Amant Vert*, was at one time
the subject of much speculation, until the simple fact was discovered that this *l'amant
vert* was only a pet parrot, given by Sigismond of Austria to Marie of Burgundy, which
Margaret kept in memory of her mother. (Ibid., 318.)

[13] Cartwright, *Beatrice D'Este*, 142 ff. Isabella d'Este, was equally instatiable for
literary work. From Antonio Tebaldo she was ever begging sonnets, and Niccolo
Corregio constantly promised her his compositions. (Cartwright, *Isabella D'Este*.
I, 81 ff.)

[14] Symonds, *Revival of Learning*, 353.

[15] "Elegy on the Death of Edward I" (c. 1310), in Percy, *Reliques*, Bk IV, No. 2;
"On the Death of Edward III," in Wright, *Political Poems and Songs*, (R. S.), I,
215, 219; "On the Death of Henry IV," by Thomas of Elmham, Ibid., II, 118; "On
the Death of Henry V," Ibid., II, 129.

[16] "To Henry VI on his Coronation," Wright, op. cit., II, 141, and "On the
Coronation of Henry VI," Ibid., II, 146. There is also a poem of joy on the
"Recovery of the Throne by Edward IV," Ibid., II, 271.

pieces,[17] which doubtless were intended for more than popular ears. Among such works, also, is to be mentioned the *Boke of Noblesse,* addressed to Edward IV on his invasion of France in 1475.[18] Hoccleve has numerous welcoming ditties and panegyrics,[19] but it is in Lydgate that we find the complete early fifteenth century court poet. On commission or spontaneously he wrote mummings, balades, and roundels;[20] and both citizen and courtier kept his pen busy. Among his occasional verse are such pieces as the poem in celebration of the marriage of Humphrey of Gloucester and Jacqueline of Hainault,[21] and the *Complaint of the Deserted Duchess,*[22] written when Humphrey had deserted his wife for a mistress, and in which the monk, though apparently then attached to the Duke's household, gives rebuke in guarded terms. Of interest too are the *Balade* and the *Amerous Balade* "made by Lydgate at þe departing of Thomas Chauciers on þe kynges ambassade into ffraunce."[23] The *Temple of Glas* is supposed to have been occasioned by the marriage in 1420 of William Paston and Agnes, daughter of Sir Edmund Berry. About the same time an Austin friar of Stoke Clare, Os-

---

[17] Gower, "De Paçis Commendatione," *Works,* ed. Macaulay, III, 481, and 492. The former has the ending:

This lettre unto thin excellence y sende,
As y which evere unto my lives ende
Wol praie for the stat of thi persone
In worschipe of thi sceptre and of thi throne.

In this connection should be mentioned also the anonymous piece "On the Expected Arrival of the Duke of Lancaster," Wright, op. cit., I, 366. Others are the "Twelve Letters that shall save Merry England," "Edwardus Dei Gratia," and the dramatic bit, "The Receyvyng of Kyng Edward the iiijth at Brystowe," *Political, Religious, and Love Poems,* ed. Furnivall, E. E. T. S., 1, 4, 5.

[18] Ed. Roxburghe Club, 1840.

[19] "Balade . . . au tres noble Roy Henry le Vt . . le jour que les seigneurs de son Roialme lui firent lour homages a Kenyngton (Mar. 21, 1412-3)"; "Balades . . . au tresnoble Roy H. le Quint . . . & au treshonourable compaigne du Jarter"; "Balade . . . at Westmonster (1413)"; and the "Balade to my Gracious Lord of York." *Works,* ed. Furnivall, E. E. T. S., I.

[20] "New Year's Balade at Hertford, with the presentation of an Eagle to the King, 1427," "Roundel for the Coronation, 6 Nov. in Westmonster, 1429"; "Ballade on the Coronation with an Envoy, 1429"; "To My Soverayn Lady"; or "Go Forth King." (doubtfully by Lydgate.)

[21] Printed by Hammond, "Lydgate and the Duchess of Gloucester," *Anglia,* XXVII, 387.

[22] Ibid., 393 ff.

[23] These poems are printed by Furnivall in *N. & Q.,* Ser. IV, ix, 381 ff.

bern Bokenham, who like Lydgate was fond of society, was writing saints legends for a coterie of literary connoiseurs in Suffolk. Writing in the eyes of the court, such poets bent their pens to elegies as a notable evidence of patronage, though an elegy is not necessarily an indication of that relationship. Froissart laments the death of his good friends, though not in an elegy, and Christine de Pisan in 1404, deprived of the Duc de Bourgogne, called upon all France to weep for the nobleman.[24] Further, the court poet often dealt with the political life of the time. Froissart's life, as we shall see, was clearly determined by the favor of his patrons, as were his opinions.

An interesting product of the familiarity of subject and prince is the body of literature entitled *De Regimine Principum*, which becomes commonplace in the late fourteenth and early fifteenth centuries, and which is written by such poets as Scogan, Lydgate, Hoccleve, and others who were known confidents of royalty. The many balades of Eustace Deschamps headed "Conseils" or "Bein Morale pour Princes," and the "moral balade" of Henry Scogan, made for the three young princes, the lords of Clarence, Bedford, and Gloucester, to whom he was tutor, show such wisdom a common thing. Among others are the verses of Gower beginning:

> O recolende, bone, pie rex, Henrice, patrone,
> Ad bona dispone quos eripis a Pharona.[25]

the verses *On the Death of Henry IV* by Thomas of Elmham,[26] and the piece *To King Henry VI on his Coronation*,[27] and the anonymous *De Regimine Principum* of the North.[28] Perhaps the type was set by the various versions of the *Secreta Secretorum*, which incidently, Lydgate and Burgh translated at the royal command, and there can be no doubt that Lydgate's *Story of Thebes*, in which he introduced much proverbial counsel to show his ideal of kingliness, was intended to reach the ear of Henry V, though it is not directly addressed to him. For Henry also, Hoc-

---

[24] "Sur la mort du Duc de Bourgogne (27 Avril, 1404)" *Oeuvres*, I, 255.
[25] *Works*, ed. Macaulay, IV, 345.
[26] Wright, *Political Poems and Songs*, (R. S.) II, 118.
[27] Ibid., II, 141.
[28] *Maitland Folio MS.*, ed. Craigie, S. T. S., 125.

cleve translated the *Regimen of Princes,* and we find him writing
a balade calling upon Henry to rule virtuously and to drive out
heresy.[29]   A similar work is George Ashby's *Active Policy of a
Prince.*[30]

Chaucer's record in respect to such poetical erpressions is interesting. His *Book of the Duchess* was inspired by the death of
a princess, and the inclusion of the tale of Pedro the Cruel, King
of Spain, in the *Monk's Tale,* (when Pedro's daughter was wife
of John of Gaunt), the *Complaint of Mars,* if we assume that he
allegorizes a court scandal, and the *Complaint of Venus,* all are
court subjects. Further, if we interpret the *Parlement of Foules*
and the *Legend of Good Women* as referring to the king and
queen, we find Chaucer definitely writing for courtly readers.
There is some evidence likewise that his work was intended to be
read aloud.[31]

Regarding the *Book of the Duchess,* the elegy written c. 1369
on the death of the Duchess Blanche, it is the basis of much of
the tradition that John of Gaunt was Chaucer's great patron.
The poem is a tribute alike to the chivalrous love of John of
Gaunt for his lady and th affection of the poet for her, and if
we remember that Chaucer might possibly have written it as an
expression of his affection for a beautiful and good lady, (for
some men have done such things), it is not necessary to assume
that he wrote it with the intention of presenting it to her husband
to receive his patronage. He may or may not have done so, but
it is obviously not a necessary sequence,[32] and works have been

---

[29] "Ceste balade ensuyant faite au tres noble Roy H. le V^t (que dieu pardoint!)
le *iour que* les Seigneurs de son Roialame lui firent l*our* homages a Kenyngton."
Minor Poems, ed. Furnivall, I, 39.

[30] *George Ashby's Poems,* ed. Bateson, E. E. T. S., 12 ff.

[31] *Legend of Good Women,* ll. 1554, 2401-2; *Troilus and Cressida,* II, 29-30; 43-4,
also I, 5, 30, 50-2; II, 1751; III, 400; V, 1785. Possibly too, *Anelida and Arcite,*
165-7.

[32] I do not mean to ignore or throw aside completely the likelihood that the poem
was presented to the lady's husband, John of Gaunt. There is no reason why it
should not have been, just as there is no evidence that it was. But to say the following with Samuel Moore, ("Geoffrey Chaucer, Esquire," *M. L. N.,* XXVIII, 191.) seems
to me to overlook the true spirit of the elegy and to carry assumption too far: "Are
we to suppose that Chaucer wrote the *Book of the Duchess* on a venture, not knowing
whether it would be acceptable or not, and that John of Gaunt ignored the work that
was presented to him? To assume this would be, as it seems to me, to beg the ques-

written out of respect when it never occurred to their authors
that their art would put something into their pockets. From
want of evidence, therefore, in regard to patronage of Chaucer in
his writing of the *Book of the Duchess,* we must suspend judgment. Interesting also is the fact that there is no chronicle by
Chaucer that he was moved to poetical expression by the death of
the good queen Philippa, of Lionel, Duke of Clarence, (in whose
service he once was), of the Black Prince, of Edward III; nor for
that matter is there a threnody on the death of Constance of
Castile, second wife of John of Gaunt (d. 1394),[33] nor upon the
Duke of Lancaster himself.[34]

Strangely enough, too, Chaucer is silent on political subjects;
in only one poem[35] can we assume anything like direct reference
to affairs of state, the *Legend of Good Women,* where, indeed,
it is clothed in allegory, readable enough perhaps to contemporaries, but a thing of controversy with us. In the prologue of this
poem (A. 354 ff., B. 374 ff.) there is a kind of *Regimen of Princes*
put into the mouth of Alceste. This passage, if we assume Alceste
to be the queen, has no allegory at all, and Chaucer, assuming the
king and queen as his readers, might be looked upon by them as
intending personal application and knowing what he was about,
but be that as it may, it is the only political passage in Chaucer.
It is remarkable how little connection can be traced between his
writings and the happenings of his time, and obviously he could in
no respect have been a 'poet-laureate.' Of notable people, whom

---

tion, moreover, it is improbable that Chaucer with his facilities for knowing the Duke's
tastes, would have expended his labor on a work that was not likely to be acceptable.
But on any other assumption than the one I have stated, we must admit that John of
Gaunt was with respect to the *Book of the Duchess* Chaucer's literary patron."

[33] It has been suggested that an elegy on Constance could not have breathed the
same evident sincerity as the lament for Blanche, for John of Gaunt's second marriage
was one of political convenience—a thing, by the by, which would hardly have occurred
to a poet who saw the opportunity for largess. It is true that she never identified
herself with England, and from the first had a rival in Katherine Swynford, (probably
Chaucer's sister-in-law) who was openly acknowledged even at state ceremonies at
Westminster and Windsor. (Armitage-Smith, *John of Gaunt,* 357-8.)

[34] An obvious suggestion may be made here, that John, being dead, could not
reward Chaucer for his labor, which may be left without comment.

[35] Hotson suggests that the *Melibeus* was a poetical tract designed to dissuade John
of Gaunt from the invasion of Castile, 1386. ("The Tale of Melibeus and John of
Gaunt," *S. P.,* XVIII, 429 ff.)

he must have known had he lived at court, he writes nothing, and so it is of historical events.   During Chaucer's life, England was in the turmoil of changing opinions and stirring events at home and abroad.   Three plagues with all their horror devastated the land, and in all of Chaucer's thousands of lines there are but two side glances referring to them—the satirical remark about gains "in pestilence" of the doctor of physic in the *Canterbury Tales,* (Prologue 422), and a reference to many deaths (*Pardoner's Tale,* 351).   There is no mention of Tyler's rebellion, and complete disregard of the Wycliffites.[36]   Nor did Chaucer consider himself or his adventures as a soldier in France worth reference in his poems, nor yet even the fortunes of English rule on the continent.   Others of the time found their inspiration just where Chaucer never sought it; Langland in the woes of the people, and Gower, Chaucer's friend, in the many events of the time.   Why did not Chaucer do likewise?   Chaucer the man and Chaucer the poet seem two distinct individuals, and it will not do to say that these events did not interest him, though certainly he did not consider them subject for verse.   More we do not know.

Sometimes too, light pieces of popular subject-matter are addressed to a noble.   In the case of the *envois* appended to the chansons and balades of poets like Gautier d'Épinal and Christine de Pisan and others, the little poem itself is addressed and told where to go and what to do when it gets there:

> Chançons, alez isnelement
> Al conte de priene direz
> Soie merci, qui il vos chant,[37]

or:

> Chançons, di moi a mon seignor Huon:
> Si vain sohait et si espoir breton
> M'ont deceü; car ce est a bon droit.[38]

Sometimes, too, the lord to whom the poem is directed is ad-

---

[36] To assume with Legouis (*Geoffrey Chaucer,* tr. Laelavoix, (1913), 38) that he refrained from mentioning these events, not wishing to displease John of Gaunt, and perhaps unable to approve of his conduct on these occasions, is, while possible, a begging of the question.   There is nothing to tell us one way or the other.

[37] Envoy 2, Chanson VII, *Chansons de Gautier d'Épinal,* ed. Lindelöf and Wallensköld, *Mémoires de la Société Néophilologique a Helsingfors,* III, (1902), 205-320.

[38] Chanson XIII, Ibid.

dressed, and in this case we have something which closely resembles the dedication, though less formal, thus:

> Gui, je bien le sé
> Qu'en Amor tot vostre aé
> Avez esperance eüe;
> S'iert encor guerredoné.[39]

Often, as in the case of many of Christine's balades, the address is at the beginning:

> Prince royal, renommé de sagece
> Hault en valeur, poissant, de grant noblece,
> Duit et apris en honneur et largece,
>   Trés agreable. . . .[40]

or:

> Bon Seneschal de Haynault, preux et sage,
> Vaillant en fais et gentil de lignage,
> Loyal, courtois de fait et de langage.[41]

So Gower addressed an epistle to Thomas of Arundell, Archbishop of Canterbury, beginning:

> Successor Thome, Thomas, humilem tibi do me,
> Hunc et presentem librum tibi scribo sequentem:
> Quod tibi presento scriptum retinere memento,
> Vt contempletur super hoc quo mens stimuletur.[42]

Such work of praise, of course, easily led to flattery, and that very early, and about Athelstan (924-40) William of Malmesbury writes:

"Concerning this king a strong persuasion is prevalent among the English, that one more just or learned never governed the kingdom. That he was versed in literature, I discovered a few days since, in a certain old volume, wherein the writer struggles with the difficulty of the task, unable to express his meaning as he wished. Indeed, I would subjoin his words for brevity's sake, were they not extravagant beyond belief in the praise of the king, and just in that style of writing which Cicero, the prince of Roman eloquence, in his book of Rhetoric denominates "bombast." The

---

[39] Chanson XV, Ibid. Chansons X, IX, XI, and XII have similar envoys.
[40] *Le Debat de Deux Amans, Oeuvres Poètiques de Christine de Pisan*, ed. Roy, S. A. T. F., II, 49.
[41] *Le Livre des Trois Jugemens*, Ibid., II, 111.
[42] *Works*, ed. Macaulay, IV, 1.

custom of the time excuses the diction, and the affection for Athelstan, who was yet living, gave countenance to the excess of praise."[43]

Concerning Queen Matilda, the same writer notes that she

"was thoughtlessly prodigal towards clerks of melodious voice; addressed them kindly, gave to them liberally, and promised still more abundantly. Her generosity becoming universally known, crowds of scholars, equally famed for verse and for singing, came over, and happy did he account himself that could soothe the ears of the queen by the novelty of his song."[44]

Praise abroad was her object, as William says, and in much later times Anne of Bretayne is said to have exclaimed of Jean Marot: "Let me see the oracle that can tell nations I am beautiful." Renaissance scholars used the device to excess, and an Italian patron of letters was always the "wisest man since Solomon," a "demigod," or even "better than the gods," and from a mention in Erasmus' *Praise of Folly*, it is clear that a kind of commerce in this sort of thing was carried on. Folly speaks of the

"general practice of our Nobles and Wise men, who, throwing away all shame, hire some flattering Orator or Lying Poet, from whose mouth they may hear their praises, that is to say meer lyes; and yet composing themselves with a seeming modesty, spread out their Peacock's plumes and erect their Crests, whilse this impudent Flatterer equals a man of nothing to the gods, and proposes him as an absolute pattern of all Virtue that's wholly a stranger to it, sets out a pittiful Jay in other's Feathers, washes the Blackmoor white, and lastly swells a Gnat to an Elephant. In short, I will follow that old Proverb that says, 'He may lawfully praise himself that lives far from Neighbors.'"[45]

Further, the medieval poet took delight in mentioning his benefactors and explaining in whose honor he composed his book, often much after Drayton's principle that:

---

[43] *Chronicle of the Kings of England*, (Bohn Lib.), 130-1.

[44] Ibid., 453.

[45] *Praise of Folly* . . . . *Translated by John Wilson, 1668*, ed. Mrs. P. S. Allen, (1913), 9. In a letter to Paludanus Erasmus writes in a different vein. "People who imagine that panegyrics are sheer flattery seem to be ignorant of the end which men of wisdom proposed themselves when they hit upon this form of oratory. It was their aim so to place before men the beauties of virtue that bad rulers might be converted, the worthy encouraged, the ignorant instructed, the weak strengthened, and even the most reckless led to repentance. . . . In what way could you more sternly rebuke his greed or vehemence or lust than by praising his unselfishness, his gentleness and his self-command? . . . . Even if a prince is far from being what he ought to be, it is highly important that his subjects should picture him to be one of the best of men." (Quoted by Capey, *Erasmus*, 66.)

> Your bounty bids my hand to make it known,[46]

but always in a complimentary and laudatory manner. The mention is sometimes very direct, and in all cases is much less formal than the dedication, though related to it perhaps. Thus Philippe de Thaun begins his *Bestiary:*

> Philippe de Taun en Franceise raisun
> Ad estrait Bestiaire, un livere de gramaire.
> Pour l'onur d'une gemme, ki mult est bele femme,
> Aliz est numeé, reine est corunnée,
> Reine est de Engleterre, sa ame n'ait jà guere!
> En Ebreu en verité est aliz laus de Dé.
> Un livere voil traiter, Des sait al cumencer![47]

So likewise Aymes says he wrote his *Floriment* to please a lady:

> Seigneur oz oies que je di
> Aymes pour l'amour de Meilli,
> Si fist le romans si sagement.[48]

A more fulsome instance is likewise to be found in the old time. At the end of his *Bestiary,* William the Clerk, who flourished in the reign of John, praises his patron, Sir Ralph, extravagantly:

> Guillaume, qui cest livre fist
> En la definaille tant dist
> De sire Raül, son seignuor,
> Por qui il fu en cest labor,
> Qu' il li a ben guerdone,
> . Pramis li a e ben done,
> Ben li a covenant tenu. . . .[49]

Since we do not know who Sir Ralph was, we must take him on William's recommendation. Many other instances of this kind will be touched upon in other connections as we proceed, but the most notable example of such mention is the full catalogue of patrons which Froissart gives in *Le Joli Buisson de Jonece,*

[46] Sonnet to Lady Anne Harrington.
[47] Ed. Wright, *Popular Treatises on Science,* 74. The rubric also contains the same mention. "Bestiarius incipit, quem Philipus Taconensis fecit in laude et memoria reginae Angliae Aaelidis, est nomen vere, quod recte cum uenit ex re, Hebraici dictum est, et quia laus dicitur, a Philippo laudatur."
[48] Ms. Harl, 3983, quoted by Turner, *History of England in the Middle Ages,* IV, 280.
[49] *Bestiaire of William the Clerk,* ll. 4137 ff., ed. Reinsch.

where he devotes about a hundred and sixty lines to their honor.[50]

---

[50] . . . . . Premiers vous example
La bonne, qui pourist en terre,
Qui fu roine d'Engleterre;
Phelippe ot nom la noble dame,
Proposces li soit Diex à l'ame!
J'en sui bien tenus de pryer
Et ses largheces escryer,
Car elle me fist et créa; . . . .
Aussi sa fille de Lancastre . . . .
Elle morut jone et jolie,
Environ de vingt et deux ans;
Gaie, lie, friche, esbatans,
Douce, simple, d'umble samblance;
La bonne dame ot à nom Blanche.
J'ai trop perdu en ces deus dames,
J'en tors mes poins, j'en bac mes palmes.
Encor ot la noble roine
Une fille de bonne orine
Ysabiel, et de Couci dame.
Je doi moult bien proyer pour l'ame;
Car je le trouvai moult courtoise . . . .
Le roy d'Engleterre autant bien,
Son pere, me fist jà grant bien,
Car cent florins, tout d'un arroi,
Reçuc à un seul don dou roy.
Aussi dou conte de Herfort
Pris une fois grant reconfort.
Des dons monseigneur de Mauni . . . .
Et son fils de Pennebruc, ...
—"Et le grant seigneur Espensier,
Qui de larghece est despensier,
Que t'a il fait?". "Quoi?" di je, "assés;
Car il ne fu onques lassés
De moi donner, quel part qu'il fust:
Ce n'estoient cailliel ne fust,
Mès chevaus et florins sans compte;
Entre mes mestres je le compte
Pour seignour, et c'en est li uns.
Et l'autre si m'est moult communs,
C'est le bon seignour de Couci,
Qui m'a souvent le poing fouci
De beaus florins à rouge escaille;
C'est raisons que de li me caille.
Et Beraut, le comte daufins
D'Auvergne, qui tant par est fins, ...
Et son fil, le duc de Bourbon,
Loïs, ai je trouvé moult bon;
Pluisours dons m'ont donné li doi.
Aussi recommander je doi
Charle, le noble roy de France;
Grans biens me fist en mon enfance.

Nor was the custom confined to the early time, as the evidence just cited might lead us to suspect. John Metham, writing his *Amoryas and Cleopas,* praises very highly the knight, "Mylys Stapylton *and* hys lady bothe." He tells us that he has written of his deeds in many places, and he refers his readers to various stories that he had formerly written, where they may read the more complete praise of his patron. He names a work on *King Cassyon,* and others on *Alexander Macedo, Josue, Josepus,* and *Crysaunt,* all of which apparently have perished.[51]

The Italian painters of the Renaissance had a very clever scheme which nothing prevents from being carried also into literature, that of introducing their patrons, often as characters,

---

> Le duc et la ducoise aussi
> De Braibant moult je regrasci,
> Car il m'ont toutdis este tel
> Que euls, le leur et leur hostel
> Ai je trouvé large et courtois
> Le duc Aubert premierement . . . .
> Et aussi mes seigneurs de Blois,
> Loïs, Jehan, et Gui, des trois.
> Moult acointés ja un temps fui,
> Et especialement de Gui, ...
> C'est le bon seigneur de Beaumont, ...
> Et le senescal, Dieux li vaille!
> Car c'est un seigneur de grant vaille
> Et qui m'a donné volentiers; . . . .
> Et le seigneur de Moriaumés, ...
> Car il sont jone et à venir;
> Se m'en pora bien souvenir.
> Quant je ferai un aultre livre.
> Mes tous ceulz qu'à present vous livre,
> M'ont largement donné et fait . . . .
>   "Amé, le conte de Savoie, ...
> Me donna de .xx. florins d'or; . . . .
> Et c'est raisons que je renomme,
> De Cippre le noble roy pere,
> Et que de ses bienfais me pere . . . .
> Haro, que fai! je me bescoce;
> J'ai oublié le roy d'Escoce,
> Et le bon conte de Duglas,
> Avec qui j'ai mené grant glas.
> Bel me reçurent en leur marce
> Cils de Mare et cils de la Marce,
> Cils de Surlant et cils re Fi; . . . .

—(ll. 230 ff. *Poésies de Froissart,* ed. Scheler, *Académie Royal de Belguique,* Brussels, 1871, II, 8.)

[51] *Works of John Metham,* ed. Craig, E. E. T. S., 78 ff.

sometimes as extra figures, into their pictures,[52] and a like practice prevailed in writing. Hartman von Aue went to the archives of his feudal lord at Aue for the subject of his finest romance, *Der Arme Heinrich;* the romance of *Melusine* had a similar basis; and Peter Luder, at the court of the Palsgrave Frederick, dedicated to him an elegy in which the Palsgrave himself is introduced under the name of Panphila and two Heidelberg doctors as Yopas and Cinthius.[53] Among Chaucer's works it is a recognized fact that the poet did something of the sort in the *Legend,* though opinions differ slightly as to who is meant by the various characters. Professor Brandl[54] on worthless evidnce suggested that he cast historical personages into allegorical guise in the *Squire's Tale,* which he believed written to celebrate the deeds of John of Gaunt in Spain, and to a certain extent, the exploits of Edward III and the Black Prince. Cambalo in this scheme is John of Gaunt; Algarsyf, the Black Prince; Cambyskan, Edward III; Canacee, Constance de Padella, eldest daughter of Pedro the Cruel and second wife of John of Gaunt; the heart-broken falcon is Elizabeth, daughter of John of Gaunt and Blanche; the unfaithful tercelet is John de Hastings, Earl of Pembroke, and the kite is Philippa Mortimer. The idea is ingenious and utterly indefensible, and Professor Kittredge, disproving it conclusively, notes among other inconsistencies that it is hardly probable that John of Gaunt, the haughtiest noble in England, would at any time have been pleased with a poetic tribute that represented his daughter as a heart-broken divorced wife.[55] Likewise Hotson would have us

[52] Thus in the *La Beata Osanna* of F. Bonsignori, Isabella d'Este is represented: in the *Madonna della Vittoria* of Andrea Mantezna, the Marquis Francescoo Gonzago and his brothers kneel before the Virgin and child, and the town of Mantua forms the background of Andreas' *Death of the Virgin.*

[53] Voigt, *Wiederlebung des Classischen Alterthums,* II, 297.

[54] *Englische Studien.* XII, 161 ff.

[55] Brandl likewise finds historical persons in the so-called *Chaucer's Dreme,* which he insists is not a love poem, but a mendicant epistle. But he confuses two distinct characters, the "ancient lady" and the young and blooming mistress of the dreamer, and assumes them to be the same person whom he thinks Margaret, duchess of Clarence. Further, as Professor Kittredge notes, surely no poet ever before begged money of a duchess by telling her he dreamed she was his wife. (*Englische Studien,* XIII, 24.)

believe that in the *Tale of Melibeus* John of Gaunt "could not fail to see, as in a mirror, himself as Melibeus and his own better sense (or perhaps that of Katherine Swynford) as the allegorical *dame Prudence.*"[56] Enough has been said of such pieces, for making every allowance, one must judge by what one sees and not by what may be deeply hidden, so that such possibilities, while interesting, are too deep to be taken seriously for our discussion.

[56] "The Tale of Melibeus and John of Gaunt," *S. P.*, XVIII, 437.

VI

WORKS WRITTEN AT REQUEST

One of the earliest manifestations óf patronage of letters, after the advantages of literature were recognized, is the matter of writing at request. The relationship between author and noble in this case is very obviously patronage in that it was an encouraging interest whether it ever became anything else or not. Nobles often requested or commanded poets to write for them; in early times it probably was a matter of obligation on the part of the poet, but as the literary man became more independent through a recognition of his worth, it is more probable that the lord solicited his protégé for favors. Whether poets were rewarded for such works is not always clear; certain known cases will be treated in their proper places, but it is clear that there is no reason why they could not be, just as it is evident that the person who requested the work might be no more than an interested friend. The custom began early. Among the Semitic peoples books were written at the command of princes and commanders, and when we find it evident again in the Middle Ages, it is to be recognized that such a proceeding is not new. In England we find the custom even among the Anglo-Saxons. The Venerable Bede wrote much of his work at request. He tells us that his *Commentaria* on the Old and New Testaments, as well as other of his works, was done at the request of Bishop Acca of Hexham, and the *Ecclesiastical History,* if not written at the request of Ceolwulf, King of Northumberland, at least was sent to him by request for reading and correction.[1] At the request of the same Acca of Hexham, Eddius Stephanus wrote his *Life of Wilfrid,* the man who had invited him from Kent to teach in Northumbria the Gregorian

---

[1] Preface and dedication to Ceolwulf.

method of chanting.[2] Aelfric, dedicating his *Lives of the Saints* to the alderman Aethelwerd, says:

"I have now collected in this book such Passions of the Saints as I have had leisure to translate into English, because that thou, beloved, and Aethelmaer earnestly prayed me for such writings and received them at my hands for the confirmation of your faith,"[3]

and in his general preface he excuses his translations of sacred narrative into our own tongue because of the request of the faithful, especially Aethelwerd and Aethelmaer, "who most highly honor my translations by their perusal of them."[4] Further, in his address of the *Homily on Chastity* to Sigefryth, he notes that he was requested to write it,[5] as he does to Wulfgeat in the *Homily* addressed to him[6] and the same is true of the address of the *Genesis* to Sigwerd.[7]

These instances are enough to show that the custom existed in England before the Conquest and in Norman England it persisted as well. Adelaide de Brabant, wife of Henry I, engaged a trouvère, probably Herman of Valenciennes, to compose the *Voyage of St. Brandon to Paradise*,[8] and at her order, the trouvère David wrote down a metrical history of the reign of her husband, which was probably set to music.[9] Geoffroi Gaimar ascribes the existence of his *Lestoire des Engles* to an Anglo-Norman lady, "dame Custance le gentil,"[10] Sanson de Nanteuil's translation into Anglo-Norman of the *Proverbs of Solomon* was done at the request of another lady, Aeliz de Condè,

[2] Bede, *Ecclesiastical History*, tr. Giles, (Bohn Lib.) 173.

[3] *Aelfric's Lives of Saints*, ed. Skeat, 4-5. Aethelmaer was the son of Aethelwerd and the patron of the monastery of Eÿnsham in Oxfordshire of which Aelfric was made abbot in 1005. Aethelmaer, during his later life lived in the vicinity, and it is through him that Aelfric probably made the acquaintance of the men of note in that neighborhood who encouraged his writings. (Ten Brink, *History of English Literature*, I, 109.)

[4] Ibid., 4-5.

[5] White, *Aelfric; a New Study of his Life and Writings*, 175, (Yale Studies in English), (1898), Chapter XII, where the prefaces are reprinted.

[6] Ibid., 175.

[7] Ibid., 177.

[8] Ed. Suchier, *Romanische Studien*, I, 567 ff.

[9] *Lestoire des Engles of Geoffrey Gaimar*, ll. 6484 ff., ed. Hardy and Martin. (R. S.) I, 276.

[10] Ibid., ll. 6436 ff., I, 275.

to whose household he was attached,[11] and Wace and Benoit de Sainte-Maure both wrote at the request of King Henry II. Similarly, Gervase of Tilbury wrote for the amusement of the young prince Henry, son of Henry II, a lost *Liber Facetiarum,* and for the amusement of the Emperor Otto IV, the *Otia Imperialia* (c. 1211) which is dedicated to Otto.[12]   Just a little earlier Ethelred of Rievaux wrote his *Vita et Miracula S. Edwardi Regis et Confessoris* at the request of Laurence, Abbot of Westminster, and addressed it to Henry.[13] Geoffrey of Monmouth explains he was obliged to publish the *Prophecies of Merlin* "at the request of my acquaintances, but especially of Alexander, bishop of Lincoln" to whom he sent them with a dedicatory letter.[14] William of Malmesbury, having acquired credit as a scholar, wrote his *Vita S. Patricii, Miracula S. Benigni, Passio S. Indracti,* and the *De Vita S. Dunstani* at the request of the monks of Glastonbury.[15]   Walter Mapes is said to have written several romances of the Round Table, one of which, the *Percival,* is reported to have been dedicated to Henry II, and the two others, the *Mort d'Artur* and the *Lancelot du Lak,* written at his bidding.   Likewise, Mapes' *De Nugis Curialium* appears to have grown out of a request of a friend called Geoffrey, and he elsewhere implies that he wrote at the wish of Henry.[16] Finally, Giraldus Cambrensis tells us that Archbishop Baldwin so admired his *Topographia Hibernica* that he fixed upon him the injunction of writing, in collaboration with Joseph of Exeter, the archbishop's nephew, a history of the Crusade for which the world was just then preparing. Giraldus was to write the prose and Joseph the verse.[17]

On the continent about the same time Gautier d'Arras wrote his *Eracle* for Thiebaut V of Blois and Marie the countess;[18] and Marie de France wrote "pour amour le cumte Willaume"

---

[11] Quoted by Sharon Turner, *History of England during the Middle Ages,* IV, 280, from Ms. Harl., 4388. The lady was probably the wife of Osbert de Condé, lord of Horncastle in Lincolnshire during the reigns of Henry I and Stephan.

[12] *D. N. B.*

[13] *D. N. B.*

[14] Bk. VII, Giles, *Six Old English Chronicles,* (Bohn Lib.) 194-5.

[15] Giles, *William of Malmesbury's Chronicles of the Kings of England,* (Bohn Lib.) ix.

[16] *De Nuglis Curialium,* ed. Wright, (Camden Society) 140.

[17] *De Rebus a se Gestis, Works,* (R. S.) I, 79.

[18] Prologue and Epilogue, Löseth, *Oeuvres de Gautier d'Arras,* I, 1-4 and 339.

and for the "flourz de chevalrie," King Henry.[19] Hue de Rote-
lande, having finished his romance *Ipomedon,* wrote a sequel,
Prothesilaus, addressed to Gilbert Fitz-Baderon, fourth Earl of
Monmouth, (d. c. 1190-1)[20] and Girard de Cambray (or Amiens)
in the thirteenth century wrote his *Enfances Charlemagne,*

> Par le commandement le frere au roy de France
> Le comte de Valois, . . .[21]

and his *Escanor* was written at the command of a great princess
of Spanish origin, wife of a king of England, who was none other
than Eleanore of Castile, (d. 1290), wife of Edward I.[22] Egidio
Colonna, tutor to Philip the Fair, wrote for the instruction of
that prince and at his request his *De Regimine Principum,* which
was ordered translated into the vernacular soon after Philip's
accession in 1268.[23] Many other instances might be cited.[24]

[19] Prologue and conclusion to *Fables,* Roquefort, *Poésies de Marie de France,*
II, 61; II, 401-2. The "cumte Willaume" is generally accepted as being William
Long-epee, earl of Salisbury, natural son of Henry II and fair Rosamond. Perhaps
the success of the *Fables* caused Henry II to request the Lais which she duly dedicated to him. Dinaux, questioning whether the count is Guillaume de Dampierre,
mentions the anonymous *Renard Couronné,* and *Judas Machabee* of Gautier de Belle-
perch, both addressed to him. (*Trouvères,* . . . . II, 67 ff.)

[20] Epilogue, Ms. Egerton 2515, quoted by Ward, *Catalogue of Romances,* I, 753-4.
The command, he says, is one he cannot disobey or disregard.

[21] Quoted by Dinaux, op. cit., I, 15. The passage occurs at the end of the third
book. The Count of Valois is Charles de Valois, brother of Philippe le Bel and
grandson of St. Louis. (d. 1325.)

[22] *Roman von Escanor von Girard von Amiens,* ed. Michelant, Bibliothek des Litt.
Vereins in Stuttgart, CLXXVIII, 1886. Prologue ll. 1 ff. A part of the prologue
which proceeds this is missing. Though Girard says the queen gave him the subject,
it is a great deal to admit that a southern princess should know so much about the
legends of a court in North Britain, and Girard's familiarity with English topography
warrants the supposition that he resided at the English court, especially since he says:

> Girardins d'Amiens qui envie
> n'a d'ajouter el conte fables
> ne mos qui ne soit veritables
> ne vous en set avant retraire,
> fors que Giffles se prist a traire,
> si tost qu'il perdist sa`compaingne,
> en la cort au roi de Bretaingne
> ou il fu puis tout son eage;
> mais lonc tans ot au cuer grant rage
> de la mort de sa douce amie. (ll. 25898 ff.)

[23] Ed. Molenaer, *Li Livres du Governement des Rois, a XIIIth Century Version
of Egidio Colonna's Treatise De Regimine Principum,* (1899), 2. The work is dedicated "a son especial seigneur, né de ligne roial et sainte, mon seigneur Phelippe,
ainz né fiz et oir mon seigneur Phelippe tres noble roi de France," and the initial
letter represents the presentation of the book.

[24] The famous romance of family tradition, *Melusine,* was compiled in 1387 by

In England and Scotland, too, many authors carefully tell us in their works on whose commission they write,[25] but enough

---

Jean d'Arras, secretary to the Duc de Berri, from records in the castle of Lusignan and chronicles obtained from the Earl of Salisbury in England, for the amusement of the duke's sister. A metrical version was later composed by La Coudrette at the request of William, Duke of Parthenay, "that men might know who made the castle and town of Lusignan." When La Coudrette had partly finished his work, his good lord died and his son, John, who ought to be named Alexander, he is so noble and generous, is unwilling to leave the work unfinished. Both pieces were translated into English (*Melusine*, ed. Donald, E. E. T. S., (1898); *Romans of Parthenay*, ed. Skeat, E, E. T. S., Prologue and ll. 6308 ff.) The circumstances of writing are fully explained in both cases; in addition the latter romance was also translated into English at the request of an unknown lord. Folio 1 of the Ms. which may have contained the name of the patron is missing.

Jean de Meung translated Vegetius' *Art of Chivalry* at the instance of "Jehans, contes de Eu" (ed. Robert, S. A. T. F.) and Christine de Pisan was besought to write her *Book of the Duke of True Lovers* "by one who, instead of making request, has the right to give command to one even more worthy than I" (tr. Kemp-Welch, (King's Classics), 1.) The same authoress wrote her *Histoire de Charles V Roy de France* for Philip of Burgundy who died before it was finished and for whom at the beginning of Book II there is a prologue of lament (Le Beuf, *Dissertations sur L'Histoire Ecclesiastique* . . . . (1743) III, 105.) This famous duke of Burgundy and equally famous patron of letters was responsible for many books. For him David Aubert, his librarian, revised among other works, Perceforest's *Anciennes Chroniques d'Angleterre*, (Prologue, Ward, *Catalogue of Romances*, I, 378) and "couchie en cler françois" *Les Conquestes de Charlemaine*. (Colophon, reprinted by Paris, *Histoire Poètique de Charlemagne*, 96.)

[25] Trevisa translated for Thomas Barclay and in Caxton's edition of Higdon's *Polychronicon* there is a "Dialogue on Translation between a lord and a clerk" which goes over the whole matter, while the *Epistle* again refers to Barclay's request. (*Polychronicon Ranulphi Higdon Monachi Cestrensis*, ed. Babington (R. S.) I, lxi.) Capgrave wrote his *Life of St. Norbert* at the command of the abbot of Durham (*Capgrave's Lives of St. Augustine and St. Gilbert*, ed. Munro, E. E. T. S., xiii.) John Metham wrote his *Physiognomy* at the request of the "rygh[t] notabyl knygh[t], Syre Mylys Stapyltun." (*Works of John Metham*, ed. Craig, E. E. T. S., 120.) The English *William of Palerne* was written for Sir Humphrey de Bohun, earl of Hereford, "in ese of englysch men." (ed. Skeat, E. E. T. S. ll. 161 ff. and 5526 ff.) William of Worcester wrote his *Verificatio Omnium Stellarum fixarum pro anno 1440* "ad instantiam J. Fastolfi militis," whose secretary he was, (Gairdner, *Paston Letters*, (1872), 1, cxiv n.) and the *Dicta et Opiniones Diversorum Philosophorum* was translated from French for the same knight by Stephan Scrope, his son-in-law. (*Cat. Lib. Mss. Bib. Harl.*, II, 633.) The translator of the *De Re Rustica* of Palladius, while he makes no formal address, after exclaiming:

A lord to plese, how suete is to laboure

leaves no doubt as to his lord's identity:

My blissid lord, mene I the duc homfrey.

(Bod. Ms. Arch. F. d. 1, quoted by Vickers, *Humphrey of Gloucester*, 394.) Benedict Burgh, taking up Lydgate's incomplete *Secrees of Old Philosoffres* complains of three things that cause his hand to quake: the difficulty of the task, the command of the "persone of magnificence Royal," and the detraction of rivals. (ed. Steele, E. E. T. S., 50.) The *Governance of Prynces*, translated by James Yonge, 1422, is the result of

instances have been cited to indicate clearly that the custom was a universal one. It now seems well to center upon a few well-known English authors and to note the circumstances attending their writing at request. Among Chaucer's works there exist only three such pieces, and these are only said to be so by later editors. Tradition has it that his *A. B. C.* poem was translated at the command of the Duchess Blanche of Lancaster; the rubric of the *Compleynt of Mars* "made by Geoffrey Chaucier, at þe comandement of the þe renomed and excellent Prynce, my lord

---

the command of his "nobyll and gracious lord, Iames de Botiller*e*, Erle of Ormond, etc." (ed. Steele, *Three Prose Versions of the Secreta Secretorum*, E. E. T. S., 121 ff.) Atkynson's version of the *De Imitatio Christi* was written "at ye speciall request & commaundement" of the Lady Margaret of Richmond and Derby, (*The Earliest English Translation . . . . of the De Imitatio Christi*, . . .ed. Ingram, E. E. T. S., 153) for whom probably Skelton in the *Garlande of Laurell* speaks of translating a French work *Of Mannes Lyfe the Peregrynacioun*, (ll. 1219 ff., *Works*, ed. Dyce, I, 410) and on whose death he wrote a Latin elegy. (Ibid., I, 195.) The anonymous cleric who translated the *Orlogium Sapientiae, or the Seven Poyntes of Trewe Wisdom*, addresses his "moste worschipful lady . . . . and derrest loued goostly dou3hter," but interesting to note, it develops that he is actually writing at the desire of a group, "for goostlye comfort of 3owe spec. iallye *and* oþer deuowte persones þat desyrene hit." (ed. Hortsmann, *Anglia*, X, (1888) 325-6.)

In Scotland, Henryson wrote his *Moral Fables of Esope* "be request and presept of ane Lord," whose name he does not mention. (*Works*, ed. Metcalfe, 4.) Richard de Holland composed his *Buke of the Howlat* for Elizabeth Dunbar, countess of Moray, (ed. Amours, *Scottish Alliterative Poetry*, S. T. S., 81) and Sir David Lindesay wrote his *Complaint . . . . of the Kingis Auld Hound callit Bagasche* at the command of James V. (ed. Murray, *Minor Poems of Lyndesay*, 556.) Sir Gilbert the Haye made his prose translation of the *Buik of Alexander* for Lord Erskine, (ed. Stevenson, S. T. S., xxix) and *Buke of the Law of Armys* for William, earl of Orkney. (Ibid., Prol. 2.) Finally, Andrew Wyntoun's *Chronicle* was written at the instance of "Schir Iohne of Wemys" in whose service he was. (ed. Amours, S. T. S., ll. 55 ff.) Andrew's reasoning about the responsibility of the work is interesting:

> He mone of neid be personer
> Off quhat kin blame so euer I beir*e*;
> Syne throuch his bidding and çounsaill
> Off det I spendit my travale;
> For all honest det suld be
> Qwyt with possibilite,
> And bowsumnes, that as þe wice
> Sayis, is better þan sacrifice;
> For in þe sacrifice þe slayne,
> And nocht þe slaar*e*, tholis þe pane.
> So þat þe slaar*e* haif þe neid,
> The pane is soft he tholis in deid,
> Than suld with rycht þe meid be maire
> That sufferis in him self þe saire. (ll. 61ff.)

Other examples of these and other authors receive treatment in other places in this essay.

þe Duc John of Lancastre," suggests another; and of a third Lydgate says:

> This poete (Chaucer) wrot at Request of the quene;
> A legende of parfight hoolynesse
> Off goode women to fynden out nyntene
> That did excelle in bountee and fayrnesse.[26]

But Chaucer himself never makes a definite statement as to who inspired his work, though it was a common practice to do so. Gower has been named as the encourager of the *Canterbury Tales*, though evidence is lacking.

Hoccleve, who wrote much at request, is of especial interest. He wrote one of his virgin poems at the request of T. Marlburgh, another at the command of "mon meistre Robert Chicele,"[27] and the third at the command of "madame de Hereford,"[28] who were either patrons or merely friends. It is his *Complaint*, however, that is most important for our study. First in the Hocclevian manner there is a bit of self-pity. Then at the beginning of the *Dialog* with his friend, speaking of his translation of the treatise *Learn to Die*, the poet says he undertakes it:

> . . . at the exitynge/and monicion
> Of a devout man. (ll. 234 ff.)

A little later in the same piece the friend who is urging him to desist from working because of his health happens to mention:

> Thou seidist/of a book thow wer in dette
> 'Vn-to my lord/þat now is lieutenant,
> My lord of Gloucestre/is it nat so?' (ll. 532 ff.)

and Hoccleve answers:

> Yis soothly, freend/and as by couenant
> He sholde han had it many a day ago;
> But seeknesse and vnlust/and othir mo
> Han be the causes of impediment. . . .
> ffor him it is/þat I this book shal make. (ll. 535 ff.)

As soon as he heard of his coming from France, Hoccleve says,

[26] *Falls of Princes*, Prologue.
[27] *Hoccleve's Minor Poems*, ed. Furnivall, I, 67.
[28] Ibid., I, 8.

he took pen and ink; he'd like to write something to please him,
for:

> Next our lord lige, our kyng victorious (Henry V)
> In al this wyde world/lord is ther noon
> Vn-to me so good ne so gracious,
> And haath been swich/yeeres ful many oon. (ll. 554 ff.)

He'd like to translate Vegetius on *Chivalry,* but such a work
would be superfluous in Humphrey's case; he knows it too well.
It would be a good deed, says Hoccleve in the midst of his
praises, to chronicle his feats:

> ffor they ensaumple mighte, and encorage
> fful many a man. (ll. 604 ff.)

He begs his friend to advise him, and he reminds him that
Humphrey cares only for proper things; he must write on a
worthy topic, why not, says the friend, since it is Lent, repent
his sinfulness, especially for having written so in blame of women,
and now write in praise of them. The duke likes "with ladyes to
haue daliance," and he'll show them the book and "syn he thy good
lord is" he'll get him forgiveness. Thomas therefore decides to
English a tale from the *Gesta Romanorum;* as second part of
this treatise he introduces the *How to Learn to Die;* and after a
short prose piece on the *Joys of Heaven,* he tells us he intended
to stop his work. His friend, however, presses him to translate
another tale of warning to young men, and after some misgiv-
ing, Hoccleve translates the *Gesta* tale of Jonathas and Felliculus.
Finally, the whole is brought to a close by an address to Lady
Westmorland:

> Go, smal book/to the noble excellence
> Of my lady/of Westmerland/ and seye,
> Hir humble seruant/with all reuerence
> Him recommandith vn-to hir nobleye;
> And byseeche hire/on my behalue, & preye,
> Thee to receyue/for hire owne right;
> And looke thow/in al manere weye
> To plese hir wommanhede/do thy might.
>
>> Humble seruant
>> To your gracious
>> noblesse
>>> T: Hoccleue.

These circumstances have been put forth at such length because they are interesting as illustrating what hight have occurred in the case of many books written at request. First, this treatise on *How to Learn to Die* is a work undertaken at the instance of a devout man, then it is a book owed to Duke Humphrey (or really not owed exactly, but undertaken to please him) and finally, since a work commending the ladies will be most pleasing, the treatise is sandwiched between two tales from the *Gesta Romanorum* and the whole commended, not to Duke Humphrey, but to Lady Westmorland. Sly Thomas Hoccleve!

It is in Lydgate's work, however, that one finds such pieces most abundantly, for Lydgate among these medieval writers had perhaps widest popularity, and those who commanded his pen ranged from England's sovereign to a "citesyn of London." At the command of Henry V Lydgate undertook much of his important work. The *Troy Book* was done

> For to obeie with-oute variaunce
> My lordes byddyng fully and plesaunce.[29]

and the prologue further makes clear what Henry liked:

> Whiche hath desire, sothly for to seyn,
> Of verray knyȝhthod to remembre ageyn
> The worthynes, ȝif I schal nat lye,
> And the prowesse of olde chiualrie,
> By-cause he hath Ioye and gret deynte
> To rede in bokys of antiquite,
> To fyn only, vertu for to see,
> Be example of hem, and also for to eschewe
> The cursyd vice of slouthe and ydelnesse.[30]

The rubric of every manuscript, as well as Caxton's printed edition, states that the *Life of Our Lady* was written "at the excitation and styryng of the noble and victorious prynce Kyng harry the fyfthe"[31] and though there is no evidence outside of the

---

[29] Prologue. ll. 73 ff., *Lydgate's Troy Book*, ed. Bergen, E. E. T. S., I, 3. Lydgate gives us the same information several times in the poem.

[30] ll. 75 ff. The reason for this translating Lydgate says was:
> By-cause he wolde that to hyȝe and lowe
> The noble story openly wer knowe,
> In oure tonge. (ll. 11 ff.)

[31] Blades, *Biography and Typography of William Caxton*, 299.

rubrics there is no reason for rejecting the assertion. On commission of Humphrey, Duke of Gloucester, Lydgate wrote his
Falls of Princes, (of which more later in another connection),
and sometime in the first year of Henry VI's reign, Lydgate
wrote for some great lord, Humphrey perhaps, the *Serpent of
Division,* a tract showing what harm is caused by division in a
realm. It is in prose, due probably to the haste in which it was
written, for possibly Humphrey wanted to use it at once to deter
any possible rebellion on the death of Henry V.[32] Thus work is
interesting to us as a work done at request to serve the ends of
the patron in his political schemes, and there is at least one other
such work in Lydgate's writings. For Richard Beauchamp, Earl
of Warwick, Lydgate wrote in heroic couplets a defence of
Henry VI's title to the crown of France.[33] This was intended
by Warwick to please his superior the Duke of Bedford, who
had ordered the French original to be written by Laurence Colet.[34]
The third great translation of Lydgate, the *Pilgrimage of the*

[32] MacCracken, *Studies in the Life and Writings of John Lydgate,* (Manuscript
Thesis preserved in the Harvard Archives), 68.

[33] "Here begynneth a remembraunce of a peedeugre how that the kyng of Englond,
Henry the sext, is truly borne heir unto the corone of Fraunce by lynyalle succession,
als wele on his ffader side, Henry the fifth, whom God assoile, as by Kateryne quene
of Englond, his modir, whom God assoile, made by Lydgate Johan the monke of Bury,
at Parys, by the instaunce of my lord of Warrewyk." (Wright, *Political Poems and
Songs,* (R. S.), II, 131.) The command is referred to again in the text.

[34] MacCracken, (op. cit., 69) thinks it was probably distributed as a handbill to
accompany a genealogical tree, but this is hardly probable. Another interesting example of what appears to be a political work is a Middle English translation from
Claudian. It appears to be a treatise of encouragement, and the "auctour spekith to
this tretyse" in this wise. He counsels his work to pray God be his guide that through
its impudence the lord who is named the defence of all England be not misled:

> Marke stilicoes life. whom peoplis preysed
> with what labouris, of the regions wide
> And Rome hir selfe; the consulat he vpreised
> ffor now the parlement pierys. wher thei goo or ryde
> Seyen the duke of yorke hath god vpon his side
> Amen. Amen. blessed Ihesu make this rumour trewe.
> And aftir feele peryles. this prince with Ioie endewe.

At the end he prays:

> My lord off yorke most tendurly graunt good ihesu thys
> Preeude in hys herte, how euyr honor merces est virtutis.

("Eine Mittelenglische Claudian-Uebersetzung," ed. Flügel, *Anglia,* XXVIII, 256, and
299.)

Life of Man, was begun in 1426 and finished two or three years
later for Thomas Montecute, Earl of Salisbury:

> Wych gaff me ffyrst in comavndement
> Thys seyde book in Englysshe for to make.[35]

From 1427 to 1430 Lydgate seems to have been busy at court
writing mummings for the king and balades for the queen, which
are too numerous to mention individually.[36]   By the court ladies
he was equally employed.   For Anne, Countess of Stafford, he
wrote an *Invocation* to and perhaps a *Life of St. Anne.*[37]   His
Life of St. Margaret was written at the command of the
Countess of Marche, later Countess of Huntingdon.[38]   Of his
Life of St. Giles he tells us:

> There was to me brought a litil bille
> Of gret devocioun by a creature,
> Requeryng me to do my best care
> Affter the tenour oonly for Giles sake
> Out of latyn translate that scripture,
> Folwyng the copie this labour vndertake.
>   To whos requeste I lowly did obeye,
>   Briefly this stoory to put in remembraunce.[39]

For Alice, Countess of Suffolk, daughter of Thomas Chaucer,
Lydgate wrote his *Interpretation* or *Virtues of the Mass,*[40] and
for Isabella, Countess of Warwick and wife of the Richard

[35] Prologue, ll. 132 ff., ed. Furnivall, E. E. T. S.   Montecute was killed at the
siege of Orleans in 1428, and as there is no mention of him or envoy to him in the
finished poem, MacCracken (op. cit., 68) suggests that the poet is silent because his
patron is dead and cannot reward him.

[36] To the queen seems to be addressed the admonitory "ditey agayne Hornes"
called *Bewte will shewe, thow Hornys be Away;* (*Political, Religious, and Love
Poems,* ed. Furnivall, E. E. T. S., 45 ff.) to her is dedicated the *Valentine to her that
Excelleth all* (MacCracken, *Minor Poems,* I, 309), and the rubrics of several manuscripts of the balade *That now is hay sometyme was grasse* state that it is "a balade
whych John Lydgate the monke of bery wrott and made at the commaundement of
the quene Kateryn, as in here sportes she walkyd by the medowes that were late
mowen in the month of July." (MacCracken, *Thesis,* 162.)

[37] *Minor Poems of Lydgate,* ed. MacCracken, I, 130.

[38] Ibid., I, 176.

[39] ll. 27 ff., Horstmann, *Altenglische Legenden, Neue Folge,* 371.   The envoy is
addressed:

> Noble princesses and ladyes of estate,
> And gentilwomen lower of degre,
> Lefte vp your hertes, calle to youre aduocate.   (ll. 520 ff.)

[40] MacCracken, *Minor Poems,* I, 87.

Beauchamp referred to above, he translated from the French the *Fifteen Ooes of Our Lady,* [41] and for the eldest daughter of Richard and Isabella, between 1442 and 1468 he composed his *Guy of Warwick.* [42] From these indications of Lydgate's patronage we may conclude that much of his religious poetry was written primarily for the lords and ladies of court and for the services of court chapels, perhaps as MacCracken suggests, to bind the ruling power of England more closely to the church.

In this connection Lydgate's *St. Edmund and Fremund* gives interesting information. With the end in view of binding the cloister of St. Edmund still closer to the king,[43] William Curteis, the abbot, dedicated to him an elegantly miniatured life of the patron saint, the text of which Lydgate was commissioned to write.[44] This presentation copy is preserved as Harleian Ms. 2278, and contains matter which is omitted in other manuscripts of the work. After a prayer to Edmund to preserve Henry VI,

> As iust enheritour off Ingelond and France,

there is one envoy, containing the author's apologies and bidding the little book be fearful in so high a presence, and another headed *Regi* which states succinctly the purpose of the poem:

> Souereyn lord, plese to your goodly-heed
> And to your gracious Royal magnificence
> To take this tretys, which a-twen hope and dreed
> Presentyd ys to your hyh excellence!
> And for kyng Edmundis notable reuerence
> Beth to his chyrche dyffence and Champioun,
> Be-cause yt ys off your ffundacioun!

Thus, proceeding just as the author might to gain the favor of his lord, the Abbot of Bury St. Edmunds besought the royal patronage for his monastery.

[41] Ibid., I, 260.

[42] *Harvard Studies and Notes,* V.

[43] The priests at Bury St. Edmunds, Lydgate says in his prologue, sing ever for Henry and pray St. Edmund to be his protector:

> Hopyng ageynward, the kyng shal for his sake
> Been to that chirch diffence and protectour
> And unto his handis al her quarel take.   (ll. 165 ff. Horstmann,

Altenglische Legenden, Neue Folge, 380.)

[44] ll. 186 ff.

The success of the *Edmund* perhaps stirred John Wethsam-
stede, Abbot of St. Albans, to wish for a similar work, for he
applied to Lydgate in 1439 and the monk undertook the *Albon
and Amphabell.*[45]   Finally, for his own abbot, William Curteis,
Lydgate wrote a version of the *De Profundis* of which he
says he was:

> Lat charchyd in myn oold dayes
>   By William Curtys, which gaf Comaundment
> That I shoulde graunte myn assent
> Offe that kynrede make a memorial
> With *De Profundis* whan so that it be sent.
> At his chirche to hang it on the wal.[46]

Nor was Lydgate's activity confined to court and ecclesiastical
circles.   He was in fashion, and to be in fashion in fifteenth
century England was in principle not much different from being
in fashion to-day.   Worthy and wealthy citizens *must* have Dan
John do work for their parlors, the guildhalls, and city chronicles,
and thus Lydgate translated from the French for a "worthy
citesyn of London" the *Bicorne and Chichevache,* the tale of two
beasts, one of which grew fat on patient husbands, while the other
grew lean on meek wives.[47]   For the walls of the hall of the
Armourers' Company he wrote the *Lyf of St. George,*[48] and for
the vestibule of the same hall perhaps the room in which business
was transacted, he may have written his *Measure is Treasure.*[49]
For a guild of Corpus Christi celebrators he wrote an account of
the procession;[50] according to Shirley's rubric he wrote two dis-
guisings for William Estfeld, Mayor of London in 1429;[51] for
"great estates of the land" he wrote the *Mumming of Fortune
and the Four Virtues,*[52] and the *Mumming at Hertford* was
"devysed by Lydgate at þe Request of þe Countre Roullour

---

[45] Ms. Trin. Coll. Oxf. 38, quoted by Horstmann, op. cit., 378 n.

[46] Ed. MacCracken, *Minor Poems,* I, 84. The *Gloriosa Dicta Sunt De Te* was done
at the instance of the Bishop of Exeter. (Ibid., I, 315.)

[47] Halliwell, *Minor Poems of Lydgate,* Percy Society, II, 270.

[48] MacCracken, *Minor Poems,* I, 145.

[49] MacCracken, *Thesis,* 74.

[50] Chambers, *Medieval Stage,* II, 161-2 and Note.

[51] The *Mumming of David* for the Goldsmiths' at Candlemas and the *Mumming of
Jupiter's Messengers* for the Mercers at Twelfth Night. (MacCracken, *Thesis,* 74
and 94-5.)

[52] Ibid., 74.

[Brys slayne at Loviers]."[53] For London also was composed a poem celebrating the magnificent reception to Henry VI on his return from his coronation in France,[54] but greater yet is the translation of the French *Dance of Death,* which he tells us he found at Paris in St. Innocent's and which at the suggestion of a friend "a French clerk" he sent to London. According to Stow the pictures of the *Daunce of Macabree,* together with Lydgate's stanzas were painted on the wall of the north cloister of St. Paul's at the expense of John Carpenter, town clerk of London,[55] probably the same man with whom Hoccleve was acquainted.

In short, Lydgate is about as near the professional poet as is found in the Middle Ages and on account of his vogue he ever found new commissioners. He not only wrote such ambitious works as the *Troy Book* and the *Life of Our Lady* for his sovereign, saints' legends and interpretations of the mass for the good court ladies and monasteries, but he ministered also to the wants of the court by penning light mummings, and to the general public as well in the verses for painted cloths, for the walls of guildhalls and even St. Paul's, for verses to be put in the city chronicles or to be scattered as broadsides. The fact also that he did this by request and not by his own initiative, makes him, as MacCracken suggests, a reflector of the temper and taste of his time in every walk of society, for in the old time there is no poet who was asked by so many people to write upon so many subjects.

But Lydgate was not alone in vogue. In southwestern Suffolk Osbern Bokenham was writing his saints' legends for his circle of friends.* Most interesting among these for our purpose is

---

[53] Hammond, "Lydgate's Mumming at Hertford," *Anglia,* XXII, 367.

[54] MacCracken, *Thesis,* 75.

[55] Ibid., 76 note.

* His *Legend of St. Margaret,* while primarily a work to excite men to the service of this saint, was written also at the instance of a dear friend, who is Thomas Burgh (ll. 175 ff. Horstmann, *Osbern Bokenham's Legenden,* (1883), 5.) The *Legend of St. Anne* was written for his friends, John and Katherine Denston,

> As they a dowghter han, yung & fayre of face,
> Wyche is Anne clepyd is worship. lady, of þe. (ll. 697 ff.)

Ibid., 54.) For the same Katherine Denston and another lady of the same name, Katherine Howard, Bokenham wrote the *Legend of St. Katherine* (ll. 50 ff. and 1052 ff. Ibid., 161 and 185.) His *Legend of St. Dorothy* was written for John and Isabel Hunt, (ll. 239 ff. Ibid., 126.) and in the prologue and epilogue to the *Legend of St. Elizabeth* he prays for Elizabeth Vere, Countess of Oxford, who wished the

the *Legend of St. Mary Magdelen,* for from what he informs us of it, we may infer the circumstances of the writing of many of his tales. Epiphany Eve, 1445, he tells us he was present at a festival at which the Lady Bourchier, Countess of Hugh, also was present. As the others danced, he and the countess walked and talked, and the lady chanced to make mention:

> Of dyuers legendys wych my rudnesse
> From latyn had turnyd in-to our language
> Of hooly wummen now in my last age.

For a long while she has had a "syngulèr deuocyoun" for Saint Mary Magdelen, she says:

> Whos lyf in englysshe I desyre sothly
> To han maad, & for my sake
> If ye lykyd, þe labour to take,
> & for reuerence of hyr, I wold you preye. (ll. 92 ff.)

Bokenham is a little doubtful, but the command is not to be disobeyed, and he promises to perform her wish when he has returned from a pilgrimage he has vowed to make. What is of interest to us is that it was through the knowledge of the work Bokenham had done for others that his new patroness, Lady Bourchier, asked him to undertake another life.[56] Other legends also came from the pen of Bokenham, for he speaks of the "englishe boke in whiche y haue compiled of legenda aurea and of oþer famous legendes at the instaunce of my specialle frendis and for edifica-

---

life of that saint. (ll. 75 ff. and 1155 ff. Ibid., 240, and 266.) He mentions the latter again in the prologue to the *Legend of St. Mary Magdelen* in connection. with the *Elizabeth,* which he newly had begun to rhyme. (ll. 71 ff. Ibid., 128.) Finally, in the prologue to the *St. Agatha,* Bokenham asks a blessing upon "Agas Fleg" for whom the work was doubtless written. (ll. 56 ff. Ibid., 210.)

[56] Another such case is to be noted in Capgrave's *Life of St. Gilbert.* Dedicating that work to the "maystir of þe order of Sempyngham," an order patronized by St. Gilbert, Capgrave says: "Now with-inne fewe days was notified on-to me þat þe lyf of our fader Seynt Augustyn, whech þat I translat in-to our tunge at instauns of a certeyn woman, was browt to jour presens, whech lykyd jou wel, as it is told, saue je wold I schul adde þerto alle þoo relygyous þat lyue vndyr his reule. . . . Than aftir je had red þis lyf of Seynt Augustyn je sayde to on of my frendes þat je desired gretly þe lyf of Seyne Gilbert schuld be translat in þe same forme." (*Capgrave's Lives of St. Augustine and St. Gilbert,* ed. Munro, E. E. T. S., 61.) Capgrave lists in a*Sermon* other works of his own and the persons for whom he wrote them. (Ibid., 146-7.)

cioun and comfort of alle tho þe whiche shulde redene hit and here hit,"[57]

but these seem to have been lost.

It is in Caxton also that we have a most interesting follower of the practice. As first printer in England, naturally much of his work was done to satisfy persons who for one reason or another desired particular books, and he was continuously being sent books for translation. There is not space to name all of his works so undertaken, so a few must suffice. His first book, *Recuyell of the Histories of Troy*, was done at the command of Margaret of Burgundy, and we have every reason to believe she patronized the printer munificently. In his Prologue to the works he tells us how, discouraged by the "simplenes and vnperfightnes" that he had in language, he had put aside his book after having written only five or six quairs, and "fyll in dispayr of thys werke and proposid nomore to haue contynuyd therin." But one day in conversation with his "right redoughted lady" Margaret, sister to the King of England, he happened to mention his neglected work, whereupon she asked to see it.

"anone she fonde a defaut in myn englissh whiche sche comāded me to amende ād more ouer comanded me straytli to contynue and make an ende of the resydue than not translated. whos dredefull comādment y durst in no wyse disobey because y am a seruāt vnto her sayde grace and resseiue of her yerly ffee and other many goode and grete benefetes. and also hope many moo to resseyne of her hyenes but forth wyth went and labouryde in the sayde translacion aftyr my symple and pour connyng."

The finished work he then desires his lady to accept and take in gree, beseeching her and all others that read it to excuse his rude and simple translation.[58] In his prologue to the *Golden Legend* he tells us to avoid being idle, he had

"parfourmed & accomplisshed dyuers werkys & hystoryes translated out of frensshe in to englysshe at the requeste of certeyn lordes/ladyes and gentylmen/as thystorye of the recuyel of Troye/the book of the chesse/the hystorye of Jason/ The hystorye of the myrrour of the world/the xv bookes of Metampheseos in whyche ben conteyned the

[57] *"Mappula Angliae* von Osbern Bokenham," ed. Horstmann, *Englische Studien*, X, 6.

[58] Blades, *Life and Typography of William Caxton*, I. 131 ff.

fables of ouyde/and the hystorye of godefroy of boloyn in the conqueste
of Iherusalem wyth other dyuers werkys & books/"

and in the epilogue he says that this work is done at the command
of the "noble and puyssaunte erle/ and my special good lord
Wyllyam erle of arondel/"[59]   His *Knight of the Tower* is produced because "a noble lady which hath brouʒt forth many noble
and fayr douʒters which ben vertuously nourisshed & lerned"
brought him a book asking it to be translated into our vulgar
English. He begs this good lady to pardon his "symple and
rude reducynge" and humbly beseeches her to "receyue this lytel
book in gree & thanke/ & I shalle praye to almyghty god for her
long and good lyf."[60] The *Order of Chivalry* was translated from
the French "at a requeste of a gentyl and nobyl esquyer" from
copy that he brought, and *King Arthur* is the result of the request
of "many noble and dyuers gentylmen of thys royame of Englond."[61]   The *Curial* was translated at the instance of a "noble
and vertuous Erle" from a copy furnished by him,[62] and the translation of Christine de Pisan's *Fayts of Arms* was made at Henry
VII's "desire whiche to me I repute a comandemēt / & verili glad
to obeye/" and with his good wishes Caxton beseeches to be
pardoned his simple and rude translation.[63]

Occasionally Caxton was requested only to print books that
had already been translated or compiled. Among such were the
Chronicles of England,[64] the *Fifteen Oes and other Prayers*, [65]
and the *Dictes and Sayings of the Philosophers*, translated by
Anthony, Earl of Rivers, found good by Caxton, who commended the Earl's work and was commanded to print the book.[66]
So also is the case of the *Cordyale*, translated by the same lord,
who commanded it to be printed and so multiplied to "goo

[59] Ibid., I, 165 ff.
[60] Ibid., I, 171.
[61] Ibid., I, 177.
[62] Ibid., I, 177.
[63] Ibid., I, 186.
[64] "Atte requeste of dyuerce gentilmen." (Blades, *Biog. and Typog.*, 247.)
[65] "By the comaudementes of the moste hye & vertuous pryncesse our leige ladi
Elizabeth by the grace of god Quene of Englonde & of Frauce. & also of the right
hyhe & most noble pryncess Margarete Moder vnto our souerayn lorde the kyng."
(Ibid., 352.)
[66] Blades, *Life and Typography*, I, 141.

abrood emong the peple." "In whiche" says Caxton, "I am bounden so to do for the manifolde benefetes and large rewardes of hym had and receyued of me vndeseruid." [67] Nor is nobility altogether responsible for the printer's work. His *Lyf of Charles the Grete* was written more directly at the request of "the venerable man, messire henry bolomyer chaonne of laussanne," and "a good and synguler frend of myn, Maister wylliam daubeny, one of the tresorers of the Jewellys of . . . Kyng Edward the fourth," [68] though Caxton tells us also of the request of "somme persones of noble estate and degree." *Boethius* was done "atte request of a singuler frende and gossib of myne";[69] the *Royal Book,* originally "made in frensshe atte requeste of Phelip le bele kyng of frauce," was translated into English "at the request & specyal desyre of a synguler frende of myn a mercer of lodon,"[70] and the *Good Manners,* at the desire of "an honest man & a specyal frence of myn a Mercer of london named wylliä praat which late departed out of this lyf," from copy furnished by him.[71]

The later printers likewise did much of their work for noble patrons, though the custom of mentioning the fact gradually fell into disuse. Wynken de Worde, in his edition of Walter Hylton's *Scala Perfectionis* says that he printed it at the request of the Lady Margaret,[72] and he reprinted Higden's *Polychronicon* and the *De Proprietatibus Rerum* of Bartholomaeus Anglicus at the request of Roger Thornye, mercer.[73] Alcock's *Mons Perfec-*

---

[67] Ibid., I, 149-50.
[68] Ed. E. E. T. S., 1 ff. and 251.
[69] Blades, *Life and Typography,* I, 151.
[70] Ibid., I, 185.
[71] Ibid., I, 183.
[72] This heuenly boke more precyous than golde
was late direct wyth gret humylyte
For godly plesur. theron to beholde
Vnto the right noble Margaret as ye see
The kyngis moder of excellent bounte
Herry the seuenth that Jhu hym preserue
This mighty pryncesse hath comaunded me
Temprynt this boke her grace for to deserue.   (Duff, *Fifteenth Century English Books,* 53.)
[73] Lathrop, "Early English Printers and their Patrons," *The Library,* 4th Series, III, No. 2, 91.

tionis was "enprynted . . . at the Instaunce of the ryght reverende relygyous fader Thomas Pryor of ye house of saynt Anne the ordre of Chartouse,"[74] the *Contemplation of Sinners* was undertaken" at the deuoute and dylygent request of the right reuerende fader in god and lord Rycharde [Fox] bysshop of Dureham and lorde pryueseall of Englond."[75]   Henry Watson, at the request of Wynken, who was moved thereto by the Lady Margaret, translated Brandt's *Ship of Fools* into English prose from the French,[76] and the *Imitation of Christ* likewise was done for her,[77] but after Margaret's death, there is only one patronized work from Wynken's press, Katherine of Siena's *Orchard of Sion,* which Richard Sutton, prior of the monastery of Sion, caused to be printed "at his great cost." [78]   Pynson printed the *Breviarum Sariburiense* at Margaret's expense; [79] "two venerable doctours of the faculte of theologye at Parys" caused him to print *The chirche of euyl men and women,* [80] and as "prynter unto his most noble grace," Pynson put out an edition of Lydgate's *Troy Book* for Henry VIII.[81] The edition of the first part of Froissart is also said to have been done at the commandment of this sovereign.[82] Richard Fox in 1516 again was patron by desiring the *Rule of Saint Benet,* and in 1521 Pipewell's *Boke of the Cyte of Ladyes* was printed at the "exortation of the gentylle erle of Kent."[83]

Thus, throughout the Middle Ages, authors continued to record the fact that they wrote their works at the request of certain noblemen. But they did even more; in their miniatures they represented themselves as visited in their studies by royalty and

---

[74] Ibid., 91.

[75] Ibid., 91.

[76] Axon, "The Lady Margaret as a Lover of Literature," *Library,* VIII, 37.

[77] In the colophon to the *Parlyament of Devils,* the *Gospel of Nicodemus* and Hawes' *Conversion of Swearers,* Wynken styles himself "Prynter vnto the mooste excellent Pryncesse my lady the kynges mother." (Axon, op. cit., 37, and Lathrop, op. cit., 92) which probably implied some sort of fee or retainer, and after her death he appropriately changed the title in Fisher's *Sermons* to "sometime printer to the king's grandam."

[78] Lathrop, op. cit., 92.

[79] Axon, op. cit., 94.

[80] Lathrop, op. cit., 94.

[81] Ibid., 94.

[82] Ibid., 94.

[83] Ibid., 95.

commanded to perform the task.[84] Perhaps a statement of the commission in the prologue or epilogue lent weight to the work, gave it protection, and recommended it to readers, but it is to be recognized also that such a mention usually calls from the author a high compliment upon his inimitable prince, and hence may be his expression of gratitude for patronage, either material or not. Thus in the *Vita Eduuardi Regis qui apud Westmonasterium Requiescat*,[85] written shortly after the Conquest, the subject is the glory of King Edward and the queen. In grateful terms the author alludes to the relief of poverty by the queen and her kindness to him,[86] and states that his work is undertaken for her:

> Si tamen ad laudes attineat dominae,
> Cui me vovisti specialus. . . . (ll. 30 ff.)

Finally, says he, what he has written is for her honor,[87] and he dedicates it to her.

It is clear also that not all works written at request were patronized works. Peter of Blois, archdeacon of Bath, vice-chancellor of England, and Protonotary of the whole kingdom, was requested by Henry de Longchamp, Abbot of Croyland, to write a life of Guthlac from the works of St. Felix, Bishop of the East Angles, promising him what materials he needed. Peter, however, discovering that Felix had not written a life of Guthlac because he had lived before him, decided to continue the annals begun by Ingulph.[88] It is not likely that a man of Peter's position would be beholden to the patronage of an abbot. Further, Boccaccio wrote his *Decameron* at the request and for the amusement of Maria, daughter of King Robert, celebrated in his writings as Fiammetta, where patronage again does not enter in. Nor would

[84] Two notable examples are to be found in a single manuscript of Vincent de Beauvais' *Speculum Historiale*. In one Vincent is represented as seated writing, while St. Louis, King of France, with his attendants stands before him and is apparently giving instructions. The other, just beside it, shows Queen Jeanne de Bourgogne with her attendants, visiting Jean de Vignay, probably to give orders for the translation of Vincent's work. (Martin, *Les Miniaturistes Françaises*, Fig. 26, 124.)

[85] Ed. Luard, *Lives of Edward the Confessor*, (R. S.), 389 ff.

[86] ll. 33, 1331.

[87] Ejus honore fuit quod, quae supra titulantur,
Dicere malebas, cumque velit repetes. (ll. 1333 ff.)

[88] *Ingulph's Chronicle*, tr. Riley, (Bohn Lib.), 224-7.

one suspect that the author of the *Luue Ron* was patronized in
his work, though he tells us:

> A Mayde cristis me bit yorne.
> Þat ich hire wurche a luue ron.[89]

But there are cases where rewards were paid for such works.
Giraldus Cambrensis whom we have found writing his *Topographia Hibernica* for Henry II and his *Expugnatio* for Richard,
we find in another work complaining that his labors were unrewarded,[90] which indicates that a reward was expected. Ethel-
wold, almost two centuries before, had translated his *Regularis
Concordia* into English in obedience to the command of Eadgar,
and for his task had received an estate from the king, which he
gave to the monastery of Ely.[91] Similarly, Gautier d'Arras, in
his *Eracle* alludes to a reciprocal promise whereby the prince for
whom he wrote it was to accord certain favors and the trouvère
was to compose a new poem in two or three years, which is
doubtless the *Ille et Galeron*.[92] A most interesting instance is
to be found in the preface to the *Meliadus* written by Hélie de
Borron. The author thanks the three persons of the Trinity for
giving him the liesure to complete the work of the *Brut*, and for
enabling him to win through it the good favor of King Henry,

[89] *Old English Miscellany*, ed. Morris, E. E. T. S., 93. The rubric likewise records
that it was a piece "quem composuit frater Thomas de hales . . . . ad instanciam
cuiusdam puelle deo dicate."

[90] *Praefatio Prima*, ed. Dimock, (R. S.) *Works*, VI, . "Sed quia principalibus
parum literatis et multum occupatis *Hibernicam* Anglorum regi Henrico secundo
Topographiam, eiusdemque filio, et utinam vitiorum non succedaneo, Pictavensium
comiti Ricardo *Vaticinalem Historiam*, vacuo quondam quoad accessorium illud et
infructuoso labore peregi . . "

[91] *D. N. B.*

[92] Quens Bauduins, a vous l'otroi;
Ainz que passent dui au ou troi,
Metrai ailleurs, espoir, m'entente.
Sire, je sui de bone atente;
Mais gardez que n'i ait enjan,
Se me pramesse n'est ouan,
Dont gardez qu'ele soit en tens;
Vous savez assez que je pens.
Deus me doinst gré de men signeur
De çou et d'el adès grigneur. (ll. 6586 ff., Löseth, *Oeuvres de
Gautier d'Arras*, Bibliothèque Française du Moyen Âge, (1890), I, 341.)

who has now ordered him to write another which shall contain
all that was omitted in the *Brut*. This he had undertaken at the
request of an old companion in arms, "mon seignor robert de
boron." After the completion of the *Brut,* he says the king saw
that there still remained much Grail material untranslated, so he
desired Hélie to continue his work. He is happy to think that
his former works are so popular that "en touz les leux ou
cheualier o langue francoyse repairent sunt li mien dit chery,
et honore sor touz autres diz francoys." In addition he boasts
that King Henry has already given him two castles.[93] The
Estorie des Engles which we found Geoffrai Gaimar compiling
at the instance of his lady Custance le gentil, was indebted to her
for more than its suggestion. Geoffrai says he could not have
finished but for her aid, for she sent to Hemsley to borrow a
book from one Walter Espec for him, a work translated from
the Welsh at Robert of Gloucester's command.[94] He adds that
she prized the volume of the trouvère David's so highly when it
was finished, that she paid him a marc of silver, burnt and
weighed, for a copy.[95] His contemporary Wace, who likewise
wrote much at request, states expressly:

> Je parole à la riche gent
> Ki ont les rentes è l'argent,
> Quer por els sunt li livres fez,
> E bien dités, è bien retrez.
> Mort est ki jadiz fist noblece,
> E perie est od lie largesce.[96]

In later years Wace began, at the request of his king, a History
of the Normans called the *Roman de Rou,* which after some
interruptions he put aside in 1170 because he had lost favor with
his lord and another had been appointed historiographer in his

[93] Ms. Adds. 12,228, quoted by Ward, *Catalogue of Romances,* I, 365 ff.
[94] ll. 6436. *Lestorie des Engles of Geoffrai Gaimar,* ed. Hardy and Martin, (R. S.)
I, 275.

> [95] Dame Custance en ad lescut,
> En sa chambre souent li lit;
> E ad pur lescrire done
> Vn mare dargent, ars et pese.   (ll. 6496 ff.)

[96] *Roman de Rou,* ed. Pluquet, I, 272 n.

place. Before he stopped writing, however, he had had his say about his parsimonious lord:

> Li Reis jadis maint bien me fist,
> Mult me donna, plus me pramist;
> E es il tot duné m'eust
> Ço k'il me pramist, mielx me fust:
> Nel' poiz avier, ne plout al Rei,
> Maiz n'est mie remez en mei.   (ll. 16532 ff.)

and he puts down his pen with:

> Ci faul le liure Maistre Wace;
> Qu'en velt avant fere, s'un face.

His successor was Beneoit de Sainte-Maure who wrote his *Roman de Normandie* at his sovereign's request.[97]

In later times also, a writer might look for some reward for a work done on commission, and Sir Richard Ros, translating *La Belle Dame Sanz Mercy*, says in the *Verba translatoris* to his work:

> I can no more, but axe of hem socoures
> at whos requeste thou made was in þis wise.[98]

So, too, Capgrave, in the prologue to the *Life of St. Augustine*, tells us that the cause of his writing is the ardent desire of "a noble creatur, or gentill woman," who selected him rather than another for the work because "sche supposed veryly þat I wold do it with þe bettir wil." Therefore he writes for her "plesans and consolation," "þat hath so willed me with sundry [r]etributione[s] þat I coude not disobeye hir desir."[99] Finally, from Caxton we gain a bit of information upon this matter also. To translate the *Golden Legend* he tells us "was grete & ouer chargeable to me

---

[97] De lui est l'estoire fenie
U merveilles aveit à dire,
Al translater e al escrire.
Ore dunge Deus par as duçor
Qu'al plasir seit de mun seignor,
Del bon rei Henri fiz Maheut;
Qui si benigne cum il seut
        Seit al oïr e al entendre! (*Chronique des Ducs de Normandie par Beneoit*, ll. 26515 ff., ed. Michel, (1836-44), II, 383.) Wace also records the fact. (*Roman de Rou*, ll. 16526 ff.)

[98] ll. 845 ff., ed. Furnivall, *Political, Religious, and Love Poems*, E. E. T. S., 80.

[99] *Capgrave's Augustine and St. Gilbert*, ed. Munro, E. E. T. S., 1.

taccomplisshe," as we may well guess, so he laid it aside, and so it would have remained had it not been for

"thynstaunce & requeste of the puyssant noble & vertuous erle my lord wyllyam erle of arondel/whiche desyred me to procede & contynue the said worke/& promysed me to take a resonable quātyte of them when they were achyeued & accomplisshed/and sente to me a worshypful gentylman a seruaunte of his named John Stanney whych solycyted me in my Lordes name that I shold in no wyse leue it but accomplisshe it promysyng that my sayd lord shold duryng my lyf veue & graunte to me a yerely fee/that is to wete a bucke in sommer/& a doo in wynter/with whiche fee I holde me wel contente/. Thenne atte contemplacion & reuerence of my sayd lord/J haue endeuoyred me to make an ende & fynysshe thys sayd translacion/and also haue enprynted it in the moost best Wyse that I haue coude or myght/and presente this sayd boook to his good & noble lordshyp/as chyef causer of the achyeuyng of hit/prayeng hym to take it in gree of me Wyllyam caxton hys poure seruaunte/& that it lyke hym to remembre my fee/& I shal praye vnto almyghty god for his longe lyfe and welfare. . . ."[100]

Such then is the fairly complete history of the *Golden Legend,* and we may hope that the Earl of Arondel did not forget his promises. Further, the *Mirrour of the World,* originally translated into French from Latin, by the "ordynaunce of the noble duc Johan of Berry and Auuergne" was

"rudely translated out of ffrensshe in to Englissh by me symple psone william Caxton/at the request. desire. coste and dispense of the honourable & worshipful mā Hugh Bryce Alderman & Cytezeyn of London/entendyng to present the same vnto the vertuous noble and puissant lord/wylliam lord hastynges lord Chamberlayn. . . . whom he humbly besecheth to resseyue in gree & thanke."[101]

Finally, the reward may not have been expressly agreed upon beforehand; such is the faith of men, that they will not be put down. When Caxton translated the *Four Sonnes of Aymon* at the request of Robert, Earl of Oxford, for whom he had done other works, he expresses his faith that he will not be made to lose by the bargain:

"Whyche booke, accordynge to hys request, I have endevorde me to accomplysshe/and to reduce it into our englyske, to my great coste/and charges, as in the translatinge/as in the enprynting of the same, hopyng/&

---

[100] Second Prologue, Blades, *Life and Typography,* I, 167.
[101] *Prologue declaryng to whom this book appertayneth,* Blades, op. cit., I, 153. The same words are carefully repeated in the Epilogue. (I, 156.)

not doubtyng/but that hys good grace/shall rewarde me in suche wise that I shall have cause to pray for his good and prosperous welfare."[102]

Hence, it may be assumed that works written at request may be considered as evidence of patronage in the encouraging sense in any case, but often in a more substantial sense and our view has shown us that the writing of works under such circumstances was far from an uncommon thing in the Middle Ages, and well bespeaks praise for those who commanded and encouraged writing.

But this phase of literary patronage gives us something more than an indication of interest in literature; it tells us a great deal about the taste of the time.   The matter has been touched slightly in the case of poets like Lydgate, but is worthy of more emphasis. Epics of marvellous tales and histories, either new of in translation, perhaps form the greater number of works done by request, with books on chivalry and general conduct finding a less important place with saints' legends and devotional pieces, but so much of medieval literature has been lost that conclusions drawn from such evidence is of no more worth in regard to the taste of the age than are conclusions drawn more largely from the fact that manuscripts survived at all.   From a poet like Lydgate or Bokenham who wrote for a coterie some facts may be drawn, but it is from Caxton that one gets the greatest information.   In the article referred to above, read before the Bibliographical Society,[103] Professor H. B. Lathrop, basing his conclusions upon numerous works of the early printers in England which are mentioned as written by 'request,' 'desire,' or 'command' or a noble, shows that especially Caxton, and to a less degree his immediate successors, were not leading or guiding taste, but gratefully, though boldly, obeying an insistent demand.   Following Mr. Duff's classification of Caxton's productions, out of twelve books of private devotion, four are supported or requested by patrons; of thirteen ethical or moral works, six are so supported; of three treatises on practical matters, two are at request, and the third, the *Doctrinal of Health*, a 'boke of Physike,' was sure to be in

---

[102] *Caxton's Four Sonnes of Aymon*, E. E. T. S., 4.

[103] "The First English Printers and their Patrons," *The Library*, 4th Series, III, No. 2, 69 ff.

demand. Of six books of information, three were patronized, and of the eight romances, five were printed at request. Hence, out of a total of seventy-seven titles of first editions, twenty were done at request. Of this number nine were official and legal works; and including liturgical books, elementary text-books, and official publications, there are twenty-one titles about which there could be practically no question of preference or of judgment. Caxton learned the art of printing for the purpose of making a living from it, [104] and his prefaces show that he took no step without careful assurance of support and patronage.[105] Though his personal preferences were for romances, he seems to have rather printed books of accepted popularity in order to make the work of his press known. Professor Lathrop's conclusions, then, show him to have been

"a conservative man of business, sounding his way continually. . . . He was indeed in a real sense a man of letters by profession and not a mere printer, and he purveyed to his aristocratic English public a selection of the books, French and English, from a former generation which time and public preference had winnowed from the mass."

Finally,

"his position was like that of a modern dealer in costly bibliographical rarities, or pictures, or *objets d'art,* who knows in advance where he can place a purchase, who owes a great part of his business success to his talent in forming friendly connexions with wealthy customers, and who does not simply manufacture for a quantity public."

After Caxton a more mechanical and impersonal view of the art of printing set in, and though Wynkyn de Worde and his successors still printed at the request of patrons, what had been a real fact in the business of Caxton gradually dwindled in importance and the later printer courted his new patron, the general public.

[104] He himself says so in the prologue to *Charles the Grete.* He humbly thanks God and is "bounden to praye for my fader and moders soules that in my youthe sette me to scole, by whyche, by the suffraunce of god, I gete my lyuyng I hope truly." He hopes for a continuance of grace that he "may come out of dette & dedely synne." (ed. Herrtage, E. E. T. S., 3.)

[105] The Prologue to the *Recuyell of the Histories of Troy* shows us his method.

VII

THE EPILOGUE EXCUSATORY AND THE "GO, LITTLE BOOK" FORMULA

Very often, as our discussion has proceeded, quotations have been noted which contain the author's address of humility in which he says his book is finished, and as it goes forth, he begs his readers or his patron, to forgive his rudeness, to correct his work where it is erring, or at least to overlook it, for he means well. Such addresses are to be found generally in dedications or in the epilogue appended to a work, and are a recognized medieval formula.

Examples of such pleas are to be found in Philip de Thaun's *Li Livre des Creatures*[1] and John the Chaplain's translation of *Boethius,* the latter addressing the patron:

> Beseching to your noble excellence,
> Þat be your help it may amended be.[2]

Chaucer likewise employed it in the address to Gower and Strode appended to the *Troilus:*

> To vouchen sauf, ther nede is, to correcte,
> Of your benignities and zeles gode.[3]

Lydgate and Burgh in the address to the *Secrees of Old Philosoffres* develop the theme:

> Excellent prynce/this process to Compyle
> Takith at gre/the Rudnesse of my style.[4]

Lydgate's Envoy to the *Guy of Warwick* contains the same matter:

---

[1] Wright, *Popular Treatises on Science,* 20.
[2] Ed. Schümmer, "John Walton's metrische Überstezung der Consolatio Philosophiae," *Bonner Studien zur Englischen Philologie,* VI, (1914), 1.
[3] ll. 1858 ff. The Franklin's *Headlink* is likewise an illustration in point.
[4] ll. 20 ff. ed. Steele, E. E. T. S., 1.

Mekely tranlatid vnder coreceyoun
Settynge a syde pryde & presumpcyoun,
And pray iche oon þat shall off hit take hede,
Ffavor & support whan þey hit rede.[5]

At the beginning of the *Amoryas and Cleopas* of John Metham, the "sympyl wryter" asks suffrance for his rude workmanship, for he realizes it is hard to please people.[6] Sir David Lyndesay in the 'Epistil' to his *Dreme,* concludes:

Bot humblie I beseik thyne Excellence,
With ornate termes thocht I can nocht expres
This sempyll mater, for laik of Eloquence,
3it nocht withstandyng all my besynes,
With hart and hand my mynd I shall addres,
As I best can, and most compendious
Now to begin: The mater hapnit thus.[7]

Sometimes too, the excusatory epilogue indicates a larger public than the single lord to whom it is addressed as is to be noted in the final chapter to Bokenham's *Mappula Angliae,* where the author muses:

"Me semythe þat hit is my parte, aftir þes lytulle & shorte treteys drawyn & abstract out anoþur mannys longe and laboryous werke, to preyen and lowly to besechyn yche man þat schalle be redere or herere þer-of of III þyngis yn aspecialle,"

whereupon he makes his abject apologies.[8] Further, in the short "Apologetik of þis englisshe compyloure" appended to the Douce *Life of St. Katherine,* the author beseeches "lowely and mekely" all men and women

"Þat in happe rediþ or heriþ þis englishe, . . . þat þey wol be fauorabil and benigne reders or herers. . . . and forgif hym alle defautes, . . . raþer arretynge his lewdnesse to symple ignorauns and obedyens þanne to pryde or presympcyone. For wite alle men þat he þe whiche drewe þis englische, so as (it) is, oute of latyne, knowynge his owne sympilnesse and vnkonynge durst not haue presumed to take siche a

[5] *Harvard Studies and Notes,* V, 213.
[6] *Works of John Metham,* ed. Craig, E. E. T. S., 3.
[7] ll. 50 ff., *Monarche and other Poems,* ed. Hall, E. E. T. S., 263.
[8] "*Mappula Angliae* von Osbern Bokenham," ed. Horstmann, *Englische Studien,* X, 33.

labour on hand, but if his sovereyn hadde bidden hym, whome he myghte not ageyne-seye."[9]

There are numerous excusatory addresses in Caxton's prologues and epilogues. Hence, such humble petitions were in accord with a universal custom when addressing the great.

From this there developed the more highly formalized and sophisticated address to the book itself which generally began "Go, little book," and contained directions for the little book as to where to go and how to conduct itself after it got there. Such verses are a bit of delightful modesty and abject humility on the author's part, and usually of exaggerated compliment to the lord to whom the little quair is venturing, and it is clear that the custom is due in large measure to the audiences for which men were writing. The "Go, little book" formula is significant because of its relation to the dedication.

Such addresses to the book are as old at least as the Romans. Catullus and Martial each have one in which the debate is settled as to who shall be patron to their little books,[10] and Horace, more nearly in the spirit of the times of which we deal, warns his innocent but restless little offspring of its possible reception in the broad bad world:

> For mart and street you seem to pine
> With restless glances, Book of Mine!
> Still craving on stone wall to stand
> Fresh pumiced from the binder's hand.
> You chafe at locks, and burn to quit
> Your modest haunt and audience fit,
> For hearers less discriminate.
> I reared you up to no such fate.
> Still, if you *must* be published, go;
> But mind, you can't come back, you know![11]

This device has already been noted in the *chansons* of such writers as Christine de Pisan and Gautier d'Epinal, and Thibaut de Champagne, addressing the Virgin, counsels his poem:

[9] Horstmann, "Prosalegenden," *Anglia*, VIII, 195-6.
[10] Catullus, I, i; Martial, III, ii.
[11] Epist. I, 20. The translation is from Lang's *Ballads of Books*, 2.

A la Dame qui tous les biens avance
T'en va, chançon s'el te vielt escouter
Onques ne fu nus de millor chaunce.[12]

On the whole examples of the form are very rare in early medieval literature. In the fifteenth century, however, we find the device in use frequently. Metrical love letters sometimes have such an address as the piece ventures forth; so the little bit *To My Heart's Joy* concludes:

go, litil bill, and say thoue were *with* me
this same day at myne vp-Ryssinge,
where that y be-sought god of merci
tho to haue my souerein in his kepeing
    As wyssely god me save
    As y am onely yours
    what payne so eu*er* y haue,
    And will be at al owres.[13]

Likewise, the epistle addressed *Unto my Lady, the flower of Womanhood* has such an envoy,[14] and in the *Parliament of Love,* the poet notices one lady especially who is so very attractive that he withdraws into a corner and composes a little song of praise to her which he directs:

Go, thow litle songe, thow hast a blisful day;
For sche þat is the floure of wo*m*manhede
At her oown leyser schall the syng and rede.[15]

Similarly, the *Amerous balade by Lydgate that hathe lost his thanke of wymmen* is bid:

Go forthe in hast þow lytel songe and no lenger tarye!
Now vyon þe first day/of þis Januarye
And to conferme fully vp my choyse/ay frome yere to yere.[16]

---

[12] Quoted by Adams, *Mont St. Michel and Chartres,* 229.
[13] ll. 21 ff. *Political, Religious, and Love Poems,* ed. Furnivall, 40.
[14] Go littil*e* bille, with all humblis
vnto my lady, of womanhede þe floure,
and saie hire howe newe troiles tileth in distreȝ
All onely for hire sake, and in mortall*e* langoure;
And if sche wot nat whoo it is, bute stonde in erore,
Say it is hir*e* olde lou*er* þat loueth hir*e* so trewe,
hir louynge a-lone, not schanginge for no newe. (ll. 36ff. Ibid., 44.)
[15] ll. 106 ff. Ibid., 51.
[16] ll. 69 ff. Hammond, "Lydgate's New Year's Valentine," *Anglia,* XXXII, 196.

The *Amerous Balade . . . at the departing of Thomas Chauciers*
likewise has an envoy:

> Go lytel bille in lowly wise
> Vn-to myn hertes souereyne
> And prey to hir for to devyse
> Summe relees of my mortel peyne.[17]

These are interesting as belonging to pieces that were probably
intended to be sent from one person to another, and hence assumed
this conventional ending.   But billets-doux were not the only
form which took on this address.   Lydgate's *Churl and the Bird*
ends with an envoy addressed to Chaucer:

> Goo litell quayer and recomande me
> Vnto my maister with humble affection.
> Beseke hym lowly of mercy and pite
> Of thy rude makyng to haue compassion. . . .
> Alle thing is said vnder correction
> With supportacion of his benygnyte.[18]

The *Temple of Glas* has a similar petition[19] as has the *Falls of
Princes,* and he translated De Deguileville's *Pilgrimage of the
Life of Man* which contains a prologue beginning: "Go fforth
thow dreme!"[20]   So likewise Hoccleve's *Complaint,* as we have
seen, has such an address to the Lady Westmorland, and in a
balade to his work sent to the Duke of Bedford with the *Regiment
of Princes,* he pleads:

> For rethorik hath hid fro me the keye
> Of his tresor/nay deyneth hir nobleye
> Dede with noon so ignorant as me!
> **Cest tout.**[21]

[17] *N. & Q.,* IV, ix, 383.
[18] Duff, *Fifteenth Century English Books,* 76.
>[19] Now go thy way thou litil rude boke
>To her presence as I the comande . . . .
>And pray to hir hit be non offence
>Yf ony word in the be myssaid
>Besechyng her she be not euyl a paid
>For as her list I will the eft correcte
>Whan that her liketh ageinward the directe
>I mene that benygne and goodly of face
>Now go thy way and put the in her grace.   (Duff, op. cit., 76.)
[20] Ed. Furnivall, E. E. T. S., 8.
[21] *Minor Poems,* ed. Furnivall, I, 5-7.

Capgrave's *Life of Norbert* also has the command:

> Go litel book, to him Þat wil ye rede;
> Say you were made to Þe Abbot of Derham.[22]

Caxton's *Dictes and Sayings of the Philosophers,* which we found him printing for Anthony Earl of Rivers, has such an address to that lord;[23] Stephan Hawes' "Excusation of the Author" to his *Pastime of Pleasure* is such a poem; and there are several in Skelton's works.[24]

Often the little book is upbraided for its brazenness in approaching so high a personage, or warned to be seemly in its behavior and not be forward or arrogant. Thus, Lydgate's *Nightingale,* addressed to the Duchess of Buckingham, is to offer itself "wyth humble reuerence,"[25] and the *St. Edmund is* told:

> Go litel book! be ferffull, quaak for drede
> For tappere in so hyh presence![26]

The *Troy Book,* addressed to Henry V, is admonished:

> And be nat hardy to apperen in no place
> With-oute support of his magnificence:
> And who-so-euere in Þe fynde offence,
> Be nat to bold for no presumpcioun—
> Þi silfe enarme ay in pacience,
> And Þe submitte to her correcioun. . . .
>
> And whan Þou art most likely to go wrack,
> Agen[e]s hem Þin errour nat diffende,
> But humblely with-drawe & go a-bak,
> Requerynge hem al Þat is mys to amende.[27]

---

[22] *Capgrave's Life of St. Katherine,* ed. Horstmann, E. E. T. S., xliv. The Ms. also has an illuminated letter in which the author is represented delivering his book to his patron whom he addresses in a most humble manner. (Ibid., xlv.)

[23] Blades, *Life and Typography,* I, 149.

[24] They are appended to the *Garland of Laurell,* and *Hawe the Douty duke of Albany* etc., and there is one in Latin beginning:
I, liber, et propera, regem, tu pronus adora.
(*Works,* ed. Dyce, I, 14, 424; II, 83.)

[25] *Nightingale Poems of Lydgate,* ed. Glauning, E. E. T. S., 2.

[26] Horstmann, *Altenglische Legenden, Neue Folge,* 440.

[27] "Verba Translatoris ad librum suum," III, 879.

Of similar nature also is the address of the *Interpretation of the Mass* made for the countess of Suffolk:

> Be nat to bolde to appere in no place.
> Of malapertnesse nor presumpcion.[28]

Occasionally, too, the address indicates that the author has more than one reader in mind, and Lydgate's *St. Austin* is sent:

> In many shire and many Cite toold,
> To echon to whom I it directe.[29]

Sometimes the address avows its point, that of gaining protection, and Hoccleve in the Balade sent with the *Regimen of Princes* to Henry V, first is horrified and then becomes philosophical:

> O litel book/who gaf thee hardynesse
> Thy wordes to pronounce in the presence
> Of kynges ympe and Princes worthynesse,
> Syn thow all nakid art of eloquence? . . .
> I am right seur, his humble pacience
> The yeueth hardynesse to do so.

> But o thyng woot I wel; go wher thow go,
> I am so pryuee vn-to thy sentence,
> Thow haast, and art/and wilt been eueremo,
> To his hynesse of swich beneuolence![30]

Metham in such an address to his *Amoryas and Cleopas* bids his little book go to those for whom it was made:

> Enfformyng *th*em how feythful*l*y I hem beseke
> Off supportation of *th*e rude endytyng oute of Greke.[31]

Poor Sir David Lyndesay's *Monarche* will be scorned by the worldly:

> We haue no kyng the to present allace!

[28] *Minor Poems*, ed. MacCracken, I, 115. The *Exortacion to Prestys* also has such a stanza (Ibid., I, 86), as has the spurious version of the *Valentine to Her that Excelleth All.* (Raw. Poet, 36, Ibid., I, 310.)

[29] MacCracken, *Minor Poems*, I, 206. Others are addressed more largely to a public. The *Fifteen Joys and Sorrows of Mary* has a message:
> To alle tho that shal the seen or reede!
(Ibid., I, 279), and the "lytel bylle" of *Cristes Passioun* is told to hang before Jesus and bid people think of him (Ibid., I, 221), as is the prayer *To St. Thomas* (II), (Ibid., I, 143.)

[30] *Minor Poems*, I, 61.

[31] *Works of John Metham*, ed. Craig, E. E. T. S., 80.

Its simplicity will bar its acceptance; nevertheless:

> Go first tyl Iames, our Prince and Protectour,
> And his Brother, our Spirituall Gouernour,

let them correct you, and if they admit you:

> Than go thy waye quhare euer thou plesis best.[32]

But the writer is not always so humble; sometimes his subject makes him more certain of himself. At the end of the *Schir William Wallace* the poet addresses his work:

> Go nobill buk, fulfillyt off gud sentens,
> Suppos thow be baren off eloquens
> Go worthy buk, fulfillit of suthfast deid;
> Bot in langage off help thow has gret neid.
> Quhen gud makaris sang weill in to Scotland,
> Gret harm was it than nane off thaim ye fand.[33]

Sometimes, too, such a piece has absolutely no point, as seems to be the case with Hoccleve's *Balade to my Gracious Lord of York*. It begins:

> Go, little pamfilet, and streight thee dresse
> Vn-to the noble rootid gentilnesse,

and is simply a poem of compliment. Don't let your wife see it, Hoccleve begs; I have none to send her; ask prince Edward not to let Mr. Picard see it; oh well, let him see it anyway; I'll correct anything he doesn't like. God bless the Duke and Duchess and give them prosperity.[34]

For our purposes in a study of patronage, the "Go, little book" poems are interesting because they form part of the evidence that there was connection between the nobility and the author in the Middle Ages, and their tone prepares us for the sycophancy and slavishness which we find evident sometimes in dedications. This attitude, generally, begins to show itself in the writers of the fifteenth century, but it is more marked in the Elizabethan and later ages in England.

---

[32] Ed. Hall, E. E. T. S., ll. 10 ff.
[33] ll. 1451 ff. Moir, S. T. S., 377.
[34] *Minor Poems*, I, 49 ff.

VIII

DEDICATIONS

Aristides, 400 B. C., reminds us that temples should be dedicated to the gods and books to great men,[1] and there can be no doubt, as Edmund Gosse tells us, that "to compose a dedication was one of the primitive instincts of scribbling man."[2] Indeed, nothing could be more universal than the custom of book dedication. Not only does it exist among the Greeks and Romans from whom modern Europe might be supposed to acquire such a custom, but the earliest authentic connected literary production in the Tauranian languages, the *Ko-ji-ki*, which precedes by at least a century the most ancient extant composition of non-Aryan India, dating 712 A. D., bears a preface which is virtually a dedication. Yasamaro, the author, presenting his book written at request of the Empress, adds: "I, Yasamaro, with true trembling and true fear, bow my head, bow my head."[3] It is of interest to note too that two of the books of the *Bible* bear dedicatory addresses. Luke addresses his *Gospel* and the *Book of Acts* to most excellent Theophilus, probably a Roman of equestrian rank.[4] The dedication of books, then, may be looked upon as a universal custom.

Even the most retiring of authors hopes he may have at least one reader and determines in his own mind who that reader is to

[1] Orat. I, *Sacrorum Sermonum*, V.

[2] "Elizabethan Dedication of Books." *Harper's*, CV, 165.

[3] Ed. Chamberlain, *Trans. Asiatic Society of Japan*, (1885), Suppl. to Vol. X.

[4] "Forasmuch as many have taken in hand to set forth in order a declaration of those things which are most sincerely believed among us, even as they delivered them unto us, which from the beginning were eyewitnesses, and ministers of the word; it seemed good to me also, having had perfect understanding of all things from the very first, to write unto thee in order, most excellent Theophilus, that thou mightest know the certainty of those things, wherein thou hast been instructed." (*Luke*, I, 1-4.)

"The former treatise have I made, O Theophilus, of all that Jesus began both to do and teach." (*Acts*, I, 1.)

be. The dedication in reality is the choosing of the right one—
the one from whom the author has nothing to fear and the one
who will read the book as he would have it read and be the all
sympathetic, all indulgent critic. Nor is there anything to prevent
the author choosing his reader any more than there is to prevent
the reader choosing his author. In short, the sympathizer must
undoubtedly have preceded the patron, who is really the growth
of a comparatively elaborate civilization, and the dedicated book
is nothing more than a rather long friendly letter. To believe
that no one dedicated a book until it occurred to him that the
dedicatee might put something into his pocket, is absurd. In
fact, dedications may be said to have passed through three distinct phases of development,[5] if one can speak of such a custom
as developing. In the first stage dedications arise from the
spontaneous expression of love or respect for a friend or perhaps a patron and of trust that he will read the book as the author
would have it read; in the second stage all sense of shame is
lost to the author and he sells his dedication and his praise to
whoever is likely to pay or will pay highest; finally, in the third
stage, and the present one, there is a return to the first stage
with the disappearance of the patron, and the dedication is used
now only as a means of showing esteem or of associating the
book with a friend, the older epistolary form being often reduced
to the initials of the person so honored.

Among the Romans the artist who consecrated his work to
a deity and the author who dedicated his book to his friend,
belonged fundamentally to the same class as far as sentiment
was concerned.[6] Simply, to dedicate was to speak and to ex-

---

[5] Wheatley, *The Dedication of Books to Patron and Friend,* (1887), v. This work,
however, does not touch our period.

[6] In his *Praefatio to Liber de Die Natali ad Q. Cerellium,* Censorinus says: "Also
before using for life the fruits of their harvest, they offer the first fruits to the gods,
and because they possess both cities and country, do not fail to raise to them temples
and chapels which are dedicated to them. Some likewise, in order to thank the
heavens for their health consecrate their hair to a divinity. For the same reason,
I who have received much from your literary treasurers, offer to-day this feeble homage
of my gratitude." How closely connected the two forms of dedication were in the
old time is seen in the following dedication from the *Greek Anthology,* (ed. Paton,
Bk. VI, 80.) "I am the nine books of Agathias Daphniad, and he who composed me
dedicated me to thee, Aphrodite. For I am not so dear to the Muses as to Love,

press one's feelings by a gift, and the word *dedicare,* first a technical term of religious life, passed into the language of literature.[7]   Cicero's letters to Atticus throw much light upon the Roman custom.   To Cicero, who needed no patron, the dedication was not a hastily compiled affair, written as a speculation and attached to a work merely for the possibility of gain, but it was a sacred expression of feeling and sentiment,[8] with some sense of the propriety of address.[9]   The first copy of a work, beautifully written and carefully corrected, went to the person whose name it bore,[10] and prefixed to this copy was a dedicatory epistle of private character and apparently not intended for publication, in which the author, addressing his dedicatee, stated plainly why he had been selected.[11]   Occasionally also, the tract was intended as a bit of instruction,[12] and where patronage entered into the matter, as in the case of Maecenas and Virgil, the dedication was often an expression of gratitude.[13] Our earlier mention of Martial and the later Roman writers

---

since I treat of the mysteries of so many loves.   In return for his pains he begs thee to grant him either not to love, or to love one who soon consents."

[7] Haenny, Louis, *Schriftsteller und Buchhändler in Alten Rom,* (1885), 115.

[8] The name of the Roman dedicatee was inseparably connected with the work, as: Quintillian, *Institutionis Oratorae ad Vitorum Marcellum;* Cicero, *De Finibus bonorum et Malorum ad M. Brutum; Cato Major de Senectute ad T. Pomponium Atticum, De Officiis ad Marcum filium,* etc.   An address of some sort usually preceded each book of a work.

[9] The debate concerning the propriety of the dedication of the *Academia* to Varro is interesting in this connection.   (*Cicero's Letters to Atticus,* ed. Winstedt, L. C. L., xiii, 12.)   Cicero, further, tried to respect the wishes of his publisher in his dedications.   (xiii, 12, 3.)   Interesting, too, is his confession to Atticus of having a volume of prefaces ready made from which he selected one as need arose, and he did the very human thing of using one twice.   (xvi, 6.)   It leads one to question whether the same thing may not have been true about dedications, though the care which attended dedicating, on the whole, would scout such a question.

[10] Cicero was vexed that Balbus secured the *De Finibus* before Brutus, his dedicatee. (xiii, 21.)

[11] The very familiar character of such dedications as Pliny's to the *Natural History* to his friend Titus Vespasian, leads one to such an assumption.   So Catullus, dedicating to Cornelius, sends his book because he used to think his trifles worth something.

[12] Thus Quintillan, dedicating to Marcellus Vitorius his *Institutionis Oratoriae* hopes it will be helpful to his son.

[13] Thus Vitruvius Pollio, dedicating his work on Architecture to Caesar says: "As through your kindness, I have been thus placed beyond the reach of poverty, I think it right to address this treatise to you. . . . It is proper to deliver down to posterity as a memorial, some account of these your magnificent works."   (tr. Gwilt, 2.)

shows us by contrast how ideal this early use of the dedication was. Hence, enough has been said, perhaps, to justify the formation of a few general principles to be borne in mind in our view of medieval dedications. It is clear that they may be viewed doubtfully as absolute evidence of patronage, though it is to be recognized they are an indication of it and have ever been a sporadic means of getting it, even if the aid so gained were only temporary. Further, it is well to note the temporary character of the reward of dedications. A man could live by them as he could by book sales, but his living was dependent in such a case, not only upon the patron, but upon his own output, while with a regular Maecenas he was sure in most cases of a living whether he worked or not.

In the Middle Ages we have represented to some extent the first stage of the dedication mentioned above. Like the Romans, the medieval writers in many respects seem to have looked upon the dedicated book much as if it were a kind of long letter, an idea thoroughly in keeping with the conditions of literary prodution in the Middle Ages, when books were written in most cases for a small group of readers or even for an individual instead of for a larger public. Such a long epistle is the *Ancren Riwle,* which not only has an introduction addressed to three "leoue sustren" who "habbe moni dai iremd on me efter riwle," but which is addressed to them throughout.[14] Another example is the *Omulum,* addressed to "Wallterr, broþerr min" in the flesh, in the faiṫh, and in God's house of the order of St. Austin, to whom the author says:

> Icc hafe don swa summ þu badd,
> *Annd* forþedd to þin wille.[15]

Further, the Douce *Life of St. Katherine* was translated from such a letter written in Latin by "Dan Stephan of Senys" to "Frere Thomas Antonij of Senys," October 26, 1411, "vnder þe open hande of two notaryes, in presens of many witnesses,

---

[14] Ed. Morton, Camden Society, XLVII, (1853), 2. At the end the author makes the simple plea: "Ase ofte ase ȝe redeð out o þisse boc, greteð þe lefi mid one Aue Marie, uor him þat maked þeos riwle, and for him þet hire wrote and swonc her abuten. Inouh meðful ich am, þet bidde so lutel." (pg. 430.)

[15] Ed. White, (1852), I, 1. It was not intended for his reading specifically.

and with appensyon*e* of oure grete couente-seel to þe testymon*e* or trewþe and atte I shulde fulfill ȝou*re* askynge."[16]   In none of these works obviously, though all three are written at request and addressed to the author's friends or relatives, are there any evidences of material patronage.

Quite rapidly, however, other possibilities were apparent,[17] and the dedication was put to less ideal uses. As a rule, when a book is addressed in glowing terms to a prince or noble, the work is connected with him in some commercial or tutelary way.

There is prodigious uniformity in the Middle Ages and the same is true of dedications. Nothing is more like a dedication than another dedication; in fact, a dedicatory epistle of the earliest times is not at all different in essentials from that of the most recent. Whether in prose or verse, the dedicatory address usually begins with superlative praise, then passes on to a few explanations with good wishes at the end. The early English dedications of Bede and Aelfric, when compared with the later medieval dedications of a time when the author had warmed to his work are simplicity itself. In the *Praefatio* to the *Ecclesiastical History* to Ceolwulf, who is represented as a lover of literature and possibly a patron, Bede begins:

"I, Bede, servant of Christ and priest, send greeting to the well beloved King Ceolwulf. And I send you the history, which I lately wrote about the Angles and Saxons, for yourself to read and examine at leisure, and also to copy out and impart to others more at large; and I have confidence in your zeal, because you are very diligent and inquisitive as to the sayings and doings of men of old, and above all of the famous men among our people. . . . I have written this for your profit and for your people; as God chose you out to be king, it behoves you to instruct your people. . . . "[18]

So likewise Aelfric, dedicating his *Genesis,* is very simple in his address to his patron, Aethelweard the alderman:

[16] Horstmann, "Prosalegenden," *Anglia,* VIII, (1885), 184, 195.

[17] Early medieval examples indicate a relationship of poet and patron. John Erigina, known to have been patronized by Charles the Bald, whom he often visited, dedicated to him a Latin translation of the Greek treatises of Dionysius the Areopagite, c. 860, (Warton, I, 205-6), and Hucbald, pupil of Milo, dedicated his master's *De Sobrietate* to the same emperor, c. 82. (*British Museum Catalogue of Western MSS. in the Old Royal and King's Collections,* I, 98.)

[18] *Ecclesiastical History,* ed. Millar, E. E. T. S., 3-4.

"Aelfric the monk humbly greeteth Aethelweard the ealdorman. Thou dist pray me, friend, to translate the Book of Genesis from Latin into English. Then it seemed to me wearisome to accede to thee in this matter, and thou saidst that I need only translate the book as far as the account of Isaac, son of Abraham, because some other man had already translated the book for thee from that point to the end."[19]

In the Latin preface to Volume II of the *Catholic Homilies,* Aelfric records his indebtedness to his patron, Archbishop Sigeric:

"Aelfric, a humble little servant of Jesus Christ, wishes to the honourable and loveable Archbishop Sigeric perpetual well-being in the Lord. I confess to thy Bountifullness, Venerable Lord, that I think myself altogether unworthy and presuming, in that I have taken upon myself to address thee by religious discourses, namely, in the little book which I have lately set forth under thine authority; but inasmuch as thou hast only too amply praised the result of my study, and hast willingly accepted that translation, I have hastened to form this following book, according as the grace of God has guided me. . . . And though I was much shaken by the incursions of injurious pirates, after I had sent the previous little book to thy Holiness, yet being unwilling to be found false to my promises, with a suffering mind I have carried through the present work. . . . This work I commit to thine authority, to be corrected, as I did the former, earnestly praying thee not to refrain from wiping out any stains of evil heresies that may be found therein, for I would rather receive blame from thy Benignity, than praise from the ignorant for attractions, which are not well founded. I beg thy Benignity to read through this translation, as thou didst the previous one, and to judge whether it should be given to the faithful, or cast aside. The blame of the envious will not disturb me if the granting of this favour is not displeasing to thy gracious authority. Fare thee well always in Christ. Amen."[20]

This dedication is of extreme interest not only as a dedication of the early time, but because of the light it throws upon the production of books. There can be no doubt that the archbishop was Aelfric's patron, and that being the case, we may make some conjectures as to the patron's duties. Aelfric is sending his treatise, asking that it be looked over and be judged whether it should be given to the faithful or cast aside, a clear indication that the archbishop was probably censor. Further,

---

[19] Reprinted by Gem, *An Anglo Saxon Abbot, Aelfric of Eynsham: A Study,* 52.
[20] Ibid., 198.

Aelfric mentions a former work, presented just as this one is, for which he was "shaken by the incursions of injurious pirates," though Aelfric says he didn't mind much since he had the sanction of the good bishop, the implication being that he felt sure of the archbishop's protection. Throughout, however, Aelfric speaks as a man writing because of an urge within, encouraged by his superior, and not as a mere servant obeying a command. Felix, author of *St. Guthlac*, however, speaks with more of the ring of the employee in his address to his patron:

"To the truly believing in our Lord for ever and ever, to my dearest lord above all other men, earthly kings:—Alfwold, king of the East Angles, rightly and worthily holding the kingdom:—I, Felix, have set forth the true belief, and the blessing of eternal salvation for all God's faithful people, and send greeting. Thy words and command I have obeyed; the book which thou bespakest I have composed, concerning the life of Guthlac, of venerable memory, with clear words and testimonies. I therefore beg and beseech the learned and the faithful, if he here find any ridiculous phrase, that he blame us not therefore. . . . let him not blame us who have but obeyed compulsion and command, and fulfilled an order. . . . as thou didst require of me that I should write and relate concerning the conversion of Guthlac and the example of his life. . . . I accordingly have obeyed thy commands, and have fulfilled thy word and will, and I have composed the text of this present work as I best might, with the wisdom of my predecessors and their elders. . . ."[21]

These early English dedications have been quoted thus extensively because of their interest if their simplicity of form is compared with the form of address later. How much more warm is the address of William of Malmesbury to Robert Earl of Gloucester:

"*To my respected Lord, the renowned Earl Robert, son of the King, health, and so far as he is able, his prayers, from William, Monk of Malmesbury.*

The virtue of celebrated men holds forth as its greatest excellence, its tendency to excite the love of persons even far removed from it; hence the lower classes make the virtues of their superiors their own, by venerating those great actions, to the practice of which they cannot themselves aspire. Moreover, it redounds altogether to the glory of exalted characters, both that they do good, and that they gain the

[21] Ed. Goodwin, 3-5.

affection of their inferiors. To you, Princes, therefore, it is owing, that we act well; to you, indeed, that we compose anything worthy of remembrance; your exertions incite us to make you live forever in our writings, in return for the dangers you undergo to secure our tranquility. For this reason I have deemed it proper to dedicate the History of the Kings of England, which I have lately published, more especially to you, my respected and truly amiable Lord."

William then praises his patronage of the arts and his especial patronage of the obscure literary men of the time, for:

"Indeed, the greatness of your fortune has made no difference in you, except that your beneficence now almost keeps pace with your inclination.

Accept, then, most illustrious Sir, a work in which you may contemplate yourself as in a glass, where your Highness's sagacity will discover that you have imitated the actions of the most exalted characters, even before you could have heard their names."[22]

The same author, writing of events in his own times at request of the same duke, wishes

"To his most loving lord, Robert, son of King Henry, and earl of Gloucester. . . . after completing his victorious course on earth, eternal triumph in heaven."[23]

When the dedication took verse form it changed but little, at least no more than the verse required, and Geoffrey de Vinsauf, dedicating his *Poetria Nova* to Pope Innocent, and finding the name *Innocent* in its Latinized form could not be placed in hexameter verse without hurting the prosody, after a bit of deliberation imagined it two words, and thus wrenched matter for the sake of compliment.[24] In his epilogue to the

---

[22] *Chronicles of the Kings of England,* tr. Giles, (Bohn Lib.), 1-2.

[23] Ibid., 480. Nor does the English form differ from the French. Illustrative examples are Jean de Meung's dedication of his *Boethius* to Philip IV, (Langlois, "Traduction de Boece par Jean de Meung," *Romania,* XLII, (1913), 336), Laurent de Premierfait's dedication of his translation of Boccaccio's *De Casibus Virorum Illustrium* and *Decameron* to Jean, duc de Berry, (Hortis, *Studj sulle Opere del Boccaccio,* 731 and 743), or Christine de Pisan's address of her *Livre de la Paix* to Prince Louis, and *Le Livre des Trois Vertus or Trésor de la Cite des Dames* to Margarite de Bourgogne. (Thomassy, *Essai sur les Escrits Politiques Christine de Pisan,* 159 and 186.)

The Latin dedication is likewise similar. Compare the address of Giraldus Cambrensis *De Jure et Statu Menevensis Ecclesiae Dialogus* to Archbishop Stephan, (*Works,* ed. Brewer, (R. S.) III, 101) and Thomas Walsingham's dedication of the *Ypodigma Neustriae* to King Henry. (ed. Riley, (R. S.) 3.)

[24] *Histoire Littéraire de la France,* XVIII, 308.

same work, a magnificent eulogy addressed as much to Chancellor William as to the pope, Geoffrey says:

Quod Papae scripsi munus speciali libelli
Occipe, flos regni, Primo potians honore
Hujus secreti. Nec id unum sume, sed una
Do tibi me totum, Guilleme, vir auree, totus
Sum tuus ad votum.[25]

Marie de France, in the prologue to her *Lais,* after explaining that because she feared to be idle she set to work, says that she found the market for translated tales overcrowded, and calling to mind lays she had heard minstrels sing, decided to put them into writing. Then she goes on:

En l'honur de vos, nobles Reis,
Ki tant estes prus è curteis,
A ki tute joie s'encline,
E en ki quoer tuz biens racine;
M'entremis de Lais assembler
Por rime faire è reconter.
E mun quoer penseie è diseie,
Sire, ke vus presentereie;
Si vus les plaist a recevoir,
Mult me ferez grant joie aveir.
A-tuz-jurs-mais en serai lie.
Ne me tenez à surquidiè,
Si vos os faire icest présent
Ore oez le comencement.[26]

[25] Ibid., XVIII, 308.
[26] *Poésies de Marie de France,* ed. Roquefort, I, 44 ff. *L'Estoire de Seint Aedward le Rei,* translated from Latin bears the following inscription to Eleanor, queen of Henry III:

Under your protection I place
This book, which for you I have made,
Noble lady of high descent,
Eleanor, rich queen
Of England, who art the flower
Of dames in virtues and honours;
No man is there who does not love you and prize
Your goodness and intelligence, and frankness:
But that I should be called a flatterer
I would willingly speak of your virtues;
But in a word everything surrounds you.
Since it befits me and I venture to say it.
As a carbuncle is among other gems
A flower are you among other women;
    Who are the fountain of perfection,
To you I make this little present. . . .

(ed. Luard, *Lives of Edward the Confessor,* (R. S.), ll. 49 ff, 180 ff.)

Li Rois Adenes, one of the most celebrated trouvères of the thirteenth century, dedicated his *Cleomades* to Robert of Artois, thus:

> A noble conte preu et sage
> D'Artois, qui a mis son usage
> En Dieu honnorer et servir,
> Envoi mon livre, por oyr
> Conment il est fais et dités.
> Or veuille Diex que il soit tés
> Que li quens li reçoive en gré,
> Et li doinst par sa grent bouté
> Honnour d'armes, et d'amor joie!
> Si m'ait Diex! je le verroie.
> Ainsi soit il que je l'ai dit,
> Amen, amen, *et explicit.*[27]

Finally, to mention no more, Christine de Pisan could also use the poetical form as is shown by her dedication to *Le Livre du Chemin de Long Estude:*

> Tres excellent Majesté redoubtee,
> Illustre honneur en dignité montee,
> Par la grace de Dieu royauté digne,
> Puissant valeur, ou tout le monde encline,
> Tres digne lis hault et magnifié,
> Pur et devot, de Dieu saintifié,
> Cil glorieux de qui vient toute grace.
> Vous tiengne en pris et croisse vostre attrace.
> A vous, bon roy de France redoubtable,
> La VIᵉ Charles du nom notable,
> Que Dieux maintiengne en joie et en santé,
> Mon petit dit soit premier presenté. . . .[28]

This treatment of the form of the dedication has indicated among other things that there was present a flattering address which might well be used for purposes of stirring patronage. In fairness, it may be said that in the Middle Ages at least, dedications were perhaps no more flowery on the whole than other letters of supplication,[29] though sometimes, when the dedi-

[27] ll. 18677, ed. Van Hasselt.
[28] Ed. Püschel, 1.
[29] The addresses of Dante's *Epistles,* which have nothing to do with patronage of letters, but are supplications for aid, nevertheless are very similar. "To the most glorious and most fortunate Conqueror, and sole Lord, the Lord Henry, by Divine

cator warmed to his work, his praise was limitless.[30]   Hence, as the *Guardian* was later to remind us, "even truth itself in a dedication is like an honest man in disguise, or visor mask, and will appear a cheat by being dressed like one."[31]   In Elizabethan times, however, when obtaining patronage and holding it was a matter of considerable tact and moment, we find flattery and abjectness with sickening frequency.   Superlative is heaped upon superlative applied both to real and imaginary virtues, and making all allowances for the grandeur, flower, and general elaborateness of an age of ruffs, farthingales, and puffed trousers, much that is not always worthy must be recognized.   This is due, of course, not to any basic insincerity in the authors themselves, but to the economic conditions facing the literary profession.

Much was made often in early times, as has been indicated, of the appropriateness of address, and when Lord de Joinville, seneschal of France, looked about for a prince worthy enough to be addressed in his *Memoirs of Louis IX,* though he perhaps needed no patron, he dedicated it :

"*To the most noble, most excellent, and most potent prince, Louis, son to the King St. Louis, of most renowned and holy memory, by the grace of*

Providence King of the Romans, and ever Augustus, his most devoted servant, Dante Alighieri, a Florentine undeservedly in exile, and all the Tuscans everywhere who desire peace, offer a kiss on the ground before his feet." (Toynbee, *Dante's Epistles,* 100. Epist. VII.) So likewise are the other letters of Dante and those written in the name of the Countess of Battifolle. (Ibid., 110 ff.)

[30] There need be no doubt about the existence of fulsome dedications in the Middle Ages, though they are not the rule. Philip of Paris, the translator of the original of the early fifteenth century English *Gouernance of Lordschipes,* a version of the *Secreta Secretorum,* dedicating to Guy de Vere of Valence, says. "As michel as þe mone ys more shinyng þan þe oþer sterrys, and as þe bem of þe sunne ys moor bryght þan þe light of the mone, As mekyl as þe clernesse of ȝoure wyt & þe depnesse of ȝoure conynge passys all men þat now er on any syde of þe see, as wel Barbarys as Latyns yn litterure." He then goes on to praise him for "all þe graces of halowes, þe clennesse of Noe, þe strength of abraham, þe faith of ysaak, þe longe lastynge of Jacob, þe sofferynge of Moyse, þe stabilnesse of Josue, þe deuocioun of hely, þe perfeccioun of helise, þe Benignite of dauid, þe wit of Salamon, þe pacience of Iob, þe chastite of daniel, þe facconde of ysae, þe perseuerance of Ieremi with all oþer vertuȝ of halowes in þi halynes most fully dwelles; ȝit yn all fre conynges þou ys best lettridd, yn decretals of haly chirche & lawes wysest, In diuinite & moralite beste taught." (Steele, *Three Prose Versions of the Secreta Secretorum,* E. E. T. S., 41.) The same original was translated by Lydgate and Burgh, where the panegyric is turned into verse. (ed. E. E. T. S., 11-2.)

[31] No. 4. March 16, 1713.

God, King of France and Navarre, and Count Palatine of Champagne and
Brie, John Lord of Joinville, Seneschal of Champagne, sends health,
wishing that, at his prayer, Jesus may anoint him with holy love."

He adds that he had been requested to write by the wife of
Louis the Pious:

"This I very humbly promised to execute to the best of my power; and
because you, my most excellent and potent lord, are his eldest son and
heir, and have succeeded to the crown and kingdom of our late lord and
king, St. Louis, I send this book to you, not knowing any one living to
whom it can more properly belong, in order that you and all others who
may read it, or hear it read, may profit by imitating the example and deeds
which it contains, and may God our Father and Creator be worshipped
and honored by it."[32]

William of Malmesbury, likewise, at the end of his *Chronicle*
of the Kings of England, says:

"For when I had finished this work, after contemplating many characters,
I determined that it might more especially. to be dedicated to you; as,
when I examine others, I observe nobility in one; in another military
science, in a third learning; justice in a fourth, but munificence in few
indeed. Thus I admire some things in one, some in another, but in you
the aggregate of all."[33]

Finally, Petrarch set a noble example by promising Charles IV
the dedication of his *Lives of Illustrious Men,* when the Emperor
should have proved himself worthy of it by noble deeds.[34]

But what evidences of patronage may be drawn from dedications? It has been indicated that dedications in many cases were
the means of expressing respect or esteem and had little connection with the patron, but it is evident also that when the book is
addressed to a prince or noble in a position to become a patron of
letters or who is addressed as one, patronage undoubtedly exists,
and dedications, therefore, in all ages have been generally recognized as an indication of this relationship. At least a certain
amount of encouragement must have been given. George Nev-

---

[32] *Chronicles of the Crusades,* (Bohn Lib.), 350. A manuscript of the work in the
Bibliothèque Nationale, contains an illumination of Joinville offering his book to
Louis le Hutin. It is reproduced in Aubrey, Audric, and Crouzet, *Hist. Ill. de la Litt.*
Française, 21.
[33] Tr. Giles, 477.
[34] Jerrold, *Petrarch,* 192.

ille, Archbishop of York in the fifteenth century and a believer in alchemy, is often the dedicatee of alchemical treatises,[35] and it is not to be doubted that he gave his protection.

The approbation of a great man, as evidenced by a dedication, had an effect more indirect, but no less important, than pleasing the patron, for the effect upon the author's readers was perhaps equally important. In classical times, Atticus, Cicero's book-seller, advised him whom to select as his dedicatee, probably with an eye to currency, and in medieval literature there are numerous evidences, indirect generally, that the patron lent currency to a literary work. In Anglo-Saxon times, Adamnan took his *De Situ Terrae Sanctae* to Aldfrith, and through him it came to be read by others.[36]

In later times, Boccaccio, dedicating his *De Casibus Virorum Illustrium* to Maghinardo dei Cavalcanti, says that he had carefully selected his dedicatee,

"that so adorned, it might add something to its reputation, and that supported by his protection it might, under better auspices that I could give it, go forth to the public."[37]

In England, the author of the Lambeth *S. Hieronymus,* addressing his "right nobill and worthy lady" says that he writes:

"That not only ye shuld knowe hit the more clerely to your gostely profecte, but also hit shuld mow abyde and turne to edificacion of othir that wold rede hit and do to copy hit, for youre selffe, and sithe to lat other rede hit and copy hit, who so will. For ther is ther-in nedefull to be had and know and had in mynd of all ffolke."[38]

Martin Le Franc, dedicating his *Champion des Dames* to Phillippe le Bon, duke of Burgundy, states the case most clearly.

"Ce n'est pas . . . chose nouvelle que ceulx qui livres batissent et composent volontiers, présentent leurs ouvrages et labours aux grands seigneurs, adfin de leur monstrer et offrir la très entière affection qu'ilz

[35] George Ripley, canon of Bridlington, dedicated to him his *Medulla Alchemia*, and Thomas Norton of Bristoll dedicated and presented his *Ordinall of Alchimy* to him. Ripley also dedicated another work, his *Compound of Alchymie*, to Edward IV. These pieces are collected by Elias Ashmole in his *Theatrum Chemicum Brittanicum*. (Corser, *Collectanea Anglo-Poetica*. Chetham Society, Pt. I, 63 ff.)

[36] Bede, *Ecclesiastical History*, Ch. xv., tr. Giles, (Bohn Lib.) 263.

[37] Quoted by Root, *P. M. L. A.*, XXVIII, 418.

[38] "Prosalegenden," ed. Horstmann, *Anglia*, (1880), III, 328-9.

ont à eulz, et que soubz leur nom leurs livres prennent quelque auctorité et cours, laquelle chose se je fais, prince très excellent, avecques ce que les sages m'en ont donné l'example et le chemin ouvert, vostre très doulce humanité singulierement m'y semont et attrait et de bien loing appelle."[39]

Further, there are numerous appeals by the author to the reader to correct the work and hold him blameless for his errors.[40] References to the benefits of protection granted by the dedicatee's name also abound. We have seen Aelfric in his *Catholic Homilies* unmindful of critics so long as he pleased Archbishop Sigeric. Geoffrey of Monmouth in his dedicatory epistle to the *Prophecies of Merlin,* to Alexander, Bishop of Lincoln, states quite definitely as he reflects upon his many faults :

"Notwithstanding, since the deference which is paid to your penetrating judgement will screen me from censure, I have employed my rude pen, and in a coarse style present you with a translation out of a language with which you are unacquainted."[41]

Saxo Grammaticus, dedicating his *History* to Andrew, successor of Absalon, who had commanded the book, says :

"I entreat thee chiefly, Andrew, who wast chosen by a most wholesome and accordant vote to be successor to the same office and to headship of spiritual things, to direct and inspire my theme; that I may baulk by the defense of so great an advocate that spiteful detraction which èver reviles what is most conspicuous."[42]

Finally, Gower, very specifically says that in having the royal protection :

> . . eek my fere is wel the lasse
> That non envoye schal compasse
> Withoute a resonable wite
> To feyne and blame that I write.[43]

But the author gained something more material than currency and protection from his work. Oftentimes he mentions in his epistle his obligation to the lord he is addressing, and his

[39] Quoted by Doutrepont, *La Littérature Française à la Cour des Ducs de Bourgogne,* Bibliothèque du XVe Siècle, (1909), 303.

[40] The matter became commonplace.

[41] Giles, *Six Old English Chronicles,* (Bohn Lib.), 195.

[42] Ed. Elton, 77.

[43] *Confessio Amantis,* Prol. 57 ff.

feeble attempt to give return by dedicating his book. Several cases of this kind have already been noted, and another such is Dante's dedication of the last cantica of the *Divine Comedy:*

"To the magnificent and most victorious Lord, the Lord Can Grande della Scala, Vicar-General of the most holy principality of Caesar in the city of Verona, and town of Vicenza, his most devoted servant, Dante Alighieri, a Florentine by birth, not by disposition, prayeth long and happy life, and perpetual increase of the glory of his name."

Dante speaks of the fame of his friend which drew poets to him to view his splendor and become his friend. He then defends himself against the charge of presumption in claiming friendship, for there are many friendships between persons of superior station and their inferiors, and the disparity of God and man in no wise impedes their friendship.

"Esteeming, then, your friendship as a most precious treasure, I desire to preserve it with assiduous forethought and anxious care. Therefore, since it is a doctrine of ethics that friendship is equalized and preserved by reciprocity, it is my wish to preserve due reciprocity in making a return for the bounty more than once conferred upon me. For which reason I have often and long examined such poor gifts as I can offer, and have set them out separately, and scrutinized each in turn, in order to decide which would be the most worthy and the most acceptable to you. And I have found nothing more suitable even for your exalted station than the sublime cantica of the *Comedy* which is adorned with the title of *Paradise;* this then, dedicated to yourself, with the present letter to serve as its superscription, I inscribe, offer, and in fine, commend to you."[44]

So also Petrarch, in his *Epistle to Posterity,* speaking of Robert of Naples as "the only monarch of our age who was the friend at once of learning and of virtue," says that when he showed him the *Africa,* the king

"asked that it might be dedicated to him in consideration of a handsome reward. This was a request that I could not well refuse, nor, indeed, would I have wished to refuse it, had it been in my power."[45]

Similarly, Lydgate, in his Epistle dedicating his *Troy Book* to Henry the Fifth after a panegyric in which he finds him equal

---

[44] Toynbee, *Dante's Epistles,* Epistola X, 195 ff.

[45] Robinson and Rolfe, *Petrarch,* 81-2. The Latin, *ut cum sibi inscribi magna pro munere posceret,* may mean only that the book was to be dedicated to Robert as a great favor.

to the nine worthies, begs him "disdeyne nat benyng[e]ly to se vpon þis boke":

> And [eke] in þi knyʒtly aduertence
> Considre & se, my sovereyn lord most dere,
> Of þi Innate famous sapience,
> Þat Crist Iesus received with good chere
> Þe twey Mynutes ʒoue of herte intere
> Be Þe wydowe, whiche if will & þouʒt
> Gaf all hir good, & kept hir silf riʒt nouʒt.
>
> By whiche ensample, so þat it nat offende
> Þoruʒ my vnkonnyng to þin hiʒw noblesse,
> Late good wil my litel gift amende,
> And of þi mercy & renomed goodnesse
> Haue no disdeyn of my baryn rudnesse,
> And, in makyng þouʒ I haue no mvse,
> Late trewe menyng þe surplus [al] excuse.[46]

In later times Erasmus dedicating his *Lucian* to Archbishop Warham, speaks of his obligation to Warham's transcendant liberality, and:

"In these circumstances I have thought it the best thing I could do, to beg you to accept a small literary keep-sake—a flower culled from the garden of the Muses—in evidence of a grateful and loving heart. I therefore send you the *Saturnalia* of Lucian, an amusing book, which I have not inscribed to any other patron, and which you may seasonally take up when you are inclined to laugh."[47]

Further, Boccaccio quite frankly dedicated his *Ameta* to Nicola de Bartolo del Bruno, his "only friend in time of trouble."[48]

Though praise is the usual thing in a dedication as a matter of course, complaints, which are so common in the later ages, are met with even in medieval times. There are a few general complaints of the decadence of the times as far as literature is concerned, and the dedicatee is told that princes no longer are interested in poetic works as a rule, the implication being, since the work is dedicated to one, that this particular noble has a much finer grace. In fact, Boccaccio leads us to suppose that

---

[46] ll. 64 ff., ed. Bergen, E. E. T. S., III, 878.
[47] Nichols, *Epistles of Erasmus*, II, 134.
[48] Hutton, *Boccaccio*, 87.

for this reason Dante sought the public as his patron by writing in the vernacular, when he says:

"Seeing that liberal studies were utterly abandoned, and especially by princes and other great men, to whom poetic toils were wont to be dedicated, wherefore the divine works of Virgil and other illustrious poets had not only sunk into small esteem, but were well nigh despised by the most. . . . he conceived it was a vain thing to put crusts into the mouths such as were still sucking milk; wherefore he began his work again in a style suited to modern senses and followed it up in the vernacular."[49]

But it could become much more personal than this, and Giraldus Cambrensis, after having tried dedications upon several English princes, addressed a version of his *Itinerary of Archbishop Baldwin through Wales* to Stephan Langton, Archbishop of Canterbury, in which he records his disappointment:

"I had formerly completed with vain and fruitless labor the Topography of Ireland for King Henry the Second and its companion, the Vaticinal History, for Richard of Poitou, his son, and I wish I were not compelled to add, his successor in vice; princes little skilled in letters, and much engaged in business. To you, illustrious Stephan, archbishop of Canterbury, equally commendable for your learning and your religion, I now dedicate the account of our meritorious journey through the rugged provinces of Cambria, written in a scholastic style."

He promises him the dedication of his treatise on the *Instruction of a Prince* and praises Stephan for not partially distributing his bounties to his family and friends, but to letters and merit, among other things.

"It is not, however, by bearing a cap, placing a cushion, by shielding off the rain, or by wiping the dust, even if there should be none, in the midst of a herd of flatterers, that I attempt to conciliate your favour, but by my writings."

To him he dedicates, and if he fails to find favor, says Gerald, he will consider the art of letters as vanished, "and in hope of its revival I shall inscribe my writings to posterity."[50] Poor Gerald! He carried out his threat in this very *Liber de Principis Instructione:*

"Sed quonium opuscula nostra quae iuvenales olim anni ambitu plini

---

[49] Quoted by Toynbee, *Dante Alighieri*, (Oxford Biographies), 217.
[50] Wright, *Historical Works of Giraldus Cambrensis*, 328 ff. To Langton also is addressed the *De Jure et Statu Menevensis Ecclesiae, Works*, (R. S.), III, 101.

laboriose produxerant, alia principibus edita fuerant, alia praelatis et infructuose scriptis hodie novis, quankuam egregiis, innata finalis temporis hujus malitia odium auctoribus invidiam pariter et offensam, non praemium aut gratiam comparantibus."

Hence, quoting, as he says, Cicero: "Praesentes frustus contemmnamus posteritatis gloriae servimus," and "Vitae brevis est cursus, gloriae sempiternus," he dedicates in a cynical vein to Posterity, or if to any prince, then to Louis of France, who is interested in letters. Gerald then shows that the greatest princes were great

"quia liberalitate conspicuus. . . . quanquam tamen in nobis jam aetas infirmior, et metae finalis cursus affindior, liberales et largos ad remunerandum litterati labores non illaudibiles nec expectat retributiones."[51]

In later times the expectation of a reward for dedications continued. Renaissance Italy was notorious for its shamelessness in this matter,[52] and an interesting example occurs in England. Erasmus dedicated his *Copia* to Colet, as it appears, because of a bargain between them. He expected fifteen angels, and appears to have written a lively letter (lost) to remind the Dean of St. Paul's of his debt, to which Colet evidently replied in a serious tone, for we find Erasmus replying, assuring him how much he regretted his poverty and recounting the whole affair. Among other things Erasmus says: "I answered with a smile that your school was not rich, and that I wanted some one who would put a little cash into my hand." [53]

[51] *Works*, ed. Warner, (R. S.), VIII, 6 ff. Gerald had many troubles with his dedications as is noted below.

[52] Poggio's speculation concerning his dedications may be taken as typical. He wished to dedicate a book to Ghismondo Malatesta, so he sent it to Roberto Valturia, a favorite at court, asking him to examine it to see if it will be acceptible, and to feel about to see if the Prince is desirous of fame. If so, then he is to write a fulsome preface promising immortality after the approved fashion. If Ghismond is indifferent, he is to send the book back. (Voigt, op. cit., I, 333.) Poggio's anger is shown in another case. He translated Xenophon's *Cyropedia* and looked to Alfonso of Naples as dedicatee. Wishing to be sure of a good reception he felt about, and finally decided to send the book in a beautiful binding with a glowing dedication to the king. Alfonso did not respond, and Poggio began calumny, removing the dedication from those copies issued. Alfonso soon sent 600 ducats, and Poggio assured him that they were again friends. He hadn't minded the omission of reward so much, but some envious person had told him Alfonso was not pleased by the work! (Ibid., I, 334 f.)

[53] Nichols, *Epistles of Erasmus*, II, 70-1.

Occasionally the author with no regard for patronage at all might for his facetious purpose append a satirical dedication to his work, addressed as to a patron, as in the case of Richardus Divisiensis *De Rebus Gestis Richardi Primi*. This mocking letter addressed to Robert, his former prior who had changed orders, is one of the most amusing things of the early Middle Age. It begins beautifully:

> "*To the Venerable Father Robert, his very good Lord, formerly Prior of the Church of Winchester, health to persevere in the good work he has begun, his faithful servant, Richard, surnamed of Devizes, sends greeting.*"

Then after much else, he professes that Robert wished to see a copy of the book, and closes his dedication, but what an ending:

> "Oh, what delight! if that holy spirit, if the angel of the Lord, if the deified man who is become already of the number of the gods, should deign to remember me before the great God, me, who am scarcely worthy to be accounted a man. I have done that which you desired, do that which you have promised."[54]

But dedicating was at best a poor paying business, and we find even the medieval author using his wits to remedy the evil by trying the plan of multiple dedication so profitable in Renaissance Italy and Elizabethan England. In the *Libell of English Policye,* 1436, we have in one manuscript the address:

> Go forth, libelle, and meekly shew thy face
> Appering ever with humble countenance,
> And pray my lordes thee to take in grace
> In opposaille and cherishing th' avaunce
> In hardiness, if that not variaunce
> Thou hast fro trouble by ful experience,
> Autors and reson; if ought faille in substaunce
> Remit to hem that yaf thee this science;
>
> Sithen that it is soth in verray fayth
> That the wise lord baron of Hungerforde
> Hath thee overseen, and verrily he sayth,
> That thow art trew, and thus he doth recorde,
> Next the gospel, God wot, it was his worde,
> Whan he thee redde alle over in a night
> Go forth trew boke and Christ defend thy right.

[54] *Chronicles of the Crusades*, (Bohn Lib.), 1 ff. The original is to be found in the Rolls Series, ed. Howlett, *Chronicles of Stephan, Henry II, and Richard I*, III, 381 ff.

In Ms. Harleian 4011 the following lines form the conclusion
instead of the last stanza quoted above:

> To the greet prelat, heighest confessour,
> The grete mayster of the gretest house,
> Chef tresourere of the grete socour,
> Bishop and yerle and baroun plentivous;
> Of highe wittes lordes three famous,
> To examine thy doubled venditee
> I offer thee hem, to be gracious
> To myn excuse; farewel, myn own tretee.[55]

This may or may not be multiple dedication, but about the
following there can be no doubt. Thomas Hoccleve's *Balade to
my Maister Carpenter*, beginning:

> See heer, my mais*ter* Carpenter, I yow preye,
> How many chalenges ageyn me be;
> And I may not deliure hem by no weye,

apparently has no special point, but it has this interesting fact
concerning it. The name "Carpenter," probably that of the
famous town clerk, member of parliament, and benefactor of early
fifteenth century London, is in the manuscript written over an
erasure, the original probably having the name of another
person to whom Hoccleve may have sent it, as he perhaps later
did to other moneyful folk. The marginal note at the beginning
of the poem "ceste balade feust tendrement considre, & bone-
ment execute," seems to indicate, as Furnivall suggests, that
Hoccleve intended it to stand hard usage.[56]

But sometimes the author dedicated his work, for one reason
or another, to the wrong man; such happenings are as old as
classical times. Cicero's predicament with the *Academia* has
already been mentioned. This originally was in two books, one
addressed to Catullus, the other to Lucullus, and a copy was sent
to Atticus. Upon second consideration, Cicero decided that
though these were learned men, they were not suitable dedicatees, so he accordingly substituted Cato and Brutus in their
places, only to receive a letter from Atticus saying that Varro

---

[55] Ed. Hertzberg, 64 ff. and note.
[56] *Hoccleve's Minor Poems*, ed. Furnivall, I, 63, and note.

was much offended at being slighted. Therefore, snatching at
the idea thus sugested, Cicero recast the whole piece, and under
the old title put out a new edition in four books instead of two,
dedicating the whole to Varro but the other edition had been
copied, and passed into circulation. In England a most interesting early case occurs with poor Giraldus Cambrensis' *Itinerarium Kambriae,* mentioned above in another connection. Several editions are known to exist, each dedicated to a different
patron. The first (c. 1191) is dedicated to William de Longchamp, Bishop of Ely and Regent of England during Richard's
absence in Palestine, who was the most powerful man in England up to October 1191, when he was ignominiously driven
from the land. We may be sure Gerald would not have dedicated to him after his downfall, as sure at least as we may be
that he would not have the face, after his invective against him
in the last chapter of his life of Archbishop Geoffrey of York,
to dedicate to Longchamp after he was brought back to England
and restored by Richard. This first edition, with hopes of
patronage perhaps, dates, therefore, about the middle of 1191.
Indications are that Gerald, after the Chancellor's downfall,
did all he could to suppress this panegyrical dedication and to
counteract it by the vilest abuse in the chapter in the life of
Geoffrey, for the dedication exists in only three manuscripts,
and one of these contains only the first part, the latter and
highly flattering section, being blotted out. Then in the dedication to the first edition of the *Descriptio Cambriae* to Archbishop Hubert, Giraldus speaks of having addressed him in the
Itinerary also, and since this could not have been before 1193
when Hubert was promoted from Salisbury to Canterbury, it
may have been a new edition, or more probably merely a presentation copy to a possibly more worthy patron, of the first edition from which the epistle to Longchamp was removed. No copy
exists, but it was not like Gerald to allow a new archbishop to
come to his seat without some word from him, and we may
accept his own statement as true. A very distinct new edition,
dedicated this time to Hugh of Lincoln, was published after
1194, and still another dedicated to Stephan Langton, c. 1214.

Giraldus would hardly have dedicated to Langton while he was in exile and disgrace, for then he was not yet Archbishop of Canterbury and a prospect for patronage, and Giraldus in his dedication speaks significantly of Langton's righteous disposal of benefices. Interesting also is the fact that this later dedication is a repetition, word for word, of the dedication to Hugh of Lincoln.[57]

With the *Descriptio Cambriae* Girald appears to have done much the same thing. What appears to be the first edition must date about 1194, about three years after the *Itinerary,* and is dedicated to Archbishop Hubert of Canterbury, to whom Gerald had previously presented a copy of the *Itinerary.* A copy was also addresed to Bishop Hugh of Lincoln, and though no manuscript now exists, a preface so addressed is preserved in Girald's collection of prefaces in the *Symbolum Electorum.*[58] The lost Westminster manuscript, used by Warton, was also dedicated to Hugh. This may have been a new edition, altered little, if at all. A very definite second edition does exist, dedicated to Archbishop Langton, and that after the third edition of the *Itinerary,* dating probably c. 1215. All three of these prefaces addressed to Hubert, Hugh, and Stephan, interestingly enough, agree all but exactly, except, of course, when the patron is named.[59]

Politics often had something to do with the change of dedication and with change of heart, as is notable in the case of the troubadour Perdigon, who turned against his old patrons in time of trouble,[60] and likewise of Capgrave and his *Histories of the Henries,* dedicated to Henry VI. In this work his primary object was the praise of his king, and in order to do it better, to publish what he could collect out of previous writings the praises of those who had borne the name of Henry. A comparison of the two histories of Capgrave, the *De Illustribus*

---

[57] A fuller account with full description of the various manuscripts is to be found in the edition of the *Itinerarium Kambriae* by Dimock, *Works,* (R. S.), VI, xxv ff. and 3 ff.

[58] *Works,* (R. S.), VI, 3 ff.

[59] See the introduction by Dimock, *Works,* (R. S.) VI, xxix.

[60] Farnell, op. cit., 251 ff.

Henricis and the *Chronicle,* throws no little light upon Capgrave's character as a politician or as a fair and impartial historian. The chronicle, dedicated to Edward IV, in its vehemence of praise of him, not only implies adverse feelings to the fallen Lancastrian House, but exhibits them boldly. When Henry again came to the throne, his tone is all praise for the first Henry of Lancaster, for after all, Capgrave was interested not so much in the quarrels of Lancaster and York, as in the "benigne Lord" who should "receyve his book, thouȝ it were simpil." [61]

As an example of the man determined both in life and opinions by the favor of his patrons stands Froissart, and in no place is this indicated more than in the dedications to the *Chronicle.* To Froissart's attachment to the English party in early life through the favors and protection of Queen Philippa and Robert of Namur, are due the English accounts of Crecy and Poitiers. At Philippa's death in 1369 Froissart was drawn more and more closely to Brabant and Wincelas of Bohemia, whose father fell at Crecy and who had different sympathies from Froissart's. Another patron, Gui de Chatillon, Count of Blois, whose father likewise had died at Crecy, and who himself was captured at Poitiers, was then maintaining his right in Brittany against English rivals. It is natural, therefore, that the last books of the *Chronicle* and the revision of the early ones undertaken for Gui should have a different sound.[62] It is to be hoped it pleased its patron, but for spirit and color one prefers to read the earlier version. But Gui was not able to keep friends with Froissart; his wealth had shrunk, and when Froissart wished to go to England in 1394 he sought elsewhere for patronage, from Albert of Bavaria, William of Ostrevant, the Duchess of Brabant, and the Lords of Couci and Gommegines. These were no new friends to Froissart, nor is there anything exactly disloyal in his change, but it meant a change again of sympathies and a remembrance of an older obligation than that owed to Chatillon, the old relation to England and Phillippa and her folk.

---

[61] *Capgrave's Histories of the Henries,* ed. Hingeston, (R. S.), xiii ff. 1 ff. and 98 ff.
[62] Lettenhove, *Oeuvres,* XIV, 1.

But perhaps the most notable case of double dedication in England at least, in the early time, is the change of heart experienced by John Gower in his *Confessio Amantis*. The earliest form of the work, bearing date of 1390, in his prologue Gower tells us, was:

> A bok for king Richardis sake
> To whom belongeth my ligeance.

Richard, meeting him on the Thames, had requested that he should book some new thing, and Gower before closing his prologue praises Richard greatly. Toward the end of the work he prays for the king, commends him highly, and dedicates his book:

> But thogh me lacke to purchace
> Mi kinges thonk as by decerte,
> Yit the Simplesce of my poverte
> Unto the love of my ligance
> Desireth forto do plesance:
> And for this cause in my entente
> This povere bok heer I presente
> Unto his hihe worthinesse,
> Write of my simpl besinesse,
> So is seknesse it suffre wolde. . . .
> I have it mad, as thilke same
> Whiche axe forto ben excused,
> That no Rethoriqe have used
> Upon the forme of eloquence. . . .[63]

But this same redaction contains another dedication in Latin at the end, this time to John, Count of Derby:

> Explicit iste liber, qui transeat, obsecro liber,
> Vt sine liuore vigeat lectoris in ore.
> Qui sedit in scannis celi dit vt ista Iohannis
> Perpetuis annis stet pagina grata Britannis.
> Derbeie Comite, recolunt quem laude periti,
> Vade liber purus, sub eo requiesce futurus.

Apparently this volume has a double dedication, but the book has a still further history. Versions of the poem exist which omit the ardent praise of Richard, and evidences show that in some copies at least this change took place shortly after its com-

[63] Bk. VIII, 3044* ff.

pletion.[64] Finally, there is a third redaction which alters the passages under discussion in several ways. It is now:

> A bok for Englondes sake
> The yer sextenthe of kyng Richard,[65]

and all further mention of Richard is omitted. A passage upon the worth of books and clerks and fame through writings is substituted for the panegyric of the king, and then a dedication to Henry of Lancaster is introduced into the text of the poem;

> Bot for my wittes ben to smale
> To tellen every man his tale,
> This bok, upon amendment
> To stonde at his commandement,
> With whom myn herte is of accord,
> I sende unto myn oghne lord,
> Which of Lancastre is Henri named:
> The hyhe god him hath proclamed
> Ful of knythode and alle grace.
> So woll I now this werk embrace
> With hol trust and with hol believe;
> God grante I mot it wel achieve. (ll. 81 ff.)

Further, in the eighth book, instead of praying for the king, the author prays for the state of England, speaks of the evil of divisions in the land, and discusses the duty of a king.[66] If we are to assume that the Latin dedication was in the original version and not added matter, it is hardly accurate to say that the dedication was changed in the later version; rather it was made more prominent and personal mention of the king suppressed. Doubly dedicated in this case the early version certainly was.[67] Why this change was made is mere conjecture; we are only imperfectly informed of the circumstances, though the presence of both dedications disposes of the idea of disloyalty on Gower's part to Richard, a suggestion which would have been rather

---

[64] This matter is treated by Macaulay in his edition of Gower, II, xxii, and need not be entered into here.

[65] ll. 24 ff. This dates the version 1392-3 and not later than June, 1393.

[66] Versions occur also in which the epilogue is rewritten and the preface left in its original state. (II, xxii.)

[67] The copy presented to Richard doubtless omitted the Latin inscription.

premature even in 1393.[68] The change was probably gradual; Macaulay suggests that Gower's faith in Richard was shaken, and that he removed the lines of praise in the epilogue and substituted the more general ones on the state of the kingdom; later in 1392-3 when the Earl of Derby had become a model of chivalry, mention of Richard was removed and the name of Henry substituted.

Before leaving the matter of multiple dedications in the Middle Ages, it is necessary to note at least its prevalence among the early humanists. Lionardo d'Arrezzo received a call to England from Humphrey, Duke of Gloucester, [69] who apparently had Aristotle's *Ethics* and wanted the *Politics,* commissioning Bruni to translate the work. Bruni accepted and dedicated the book to Humphrey. There was some delay, however, in acknowledging this tribute, which to the haughty Lionardo seemed to indicate that he did not have sufficient respect for so glorious a work, and he transferred the dedication to Pope Eugene IV, cancelling the first preface and substituting a new, probably receiving the praise and thanks he sought.[70] Verily, the Middle Ages believed in proper response. Candido Decembrio, who apparently wanted to be acquainted with Humphrey, availed himself of the opportunity thus offered, and extended to Humphrey instead a translation of Plato's *Republic.* He first sent him the fifth book, and the duke in acknowledging it expressed surprise that it was not dedicated to him. Decembrio assured him, however, that the single works were dedicated to different individuals (the fifth to Giovanni Amedei, the sixth to Alfonso, Bishop of Burgos, and the tenth to Francesco Picolpasso, Archbishop of Milan), but that the entire work should bear Humphrey's name.[71] The translation of the *Republic* took Decembrio

---

[68] II, xxii. Gower was no prophet, and there is no reason for supposing that he discriminatingly selected a more worthy candidate to the throne.

[69] Vespasiano says *Worcester,* though *Gloucester* seems to be correct. Lionardo's dedication of the work to Humphrey is preserved in two manuscripts in the Bodleian Library. They are described by Macray, "Early Dedications to Englishmen by Foreign Authors and Editors," *Bibliographica,* I, 328.

[70] Vespasiano, "Lionardo d'Arrezzo," ed. Schubring, 238. Humphrey had apparently been somewhat importunate, for in his dedication to the Duke, Bruni says that Humphrey had feared that he would not fulfill his promise and send only words instead of his work, a thing altogether foreign to his character. (Macray, op. cit., 328.)

[71] Letter to Humphrey to Decembrio and the reply, Borsa, "Correspondence of Humphrey, Duke of Gloucester," *English Historical Review,* XIX, 514 ff.

three years, as we learn from another letter, and its dedication
contains the hint that so immortal a work as the *Republic* will
render Humphrey immortal. After this introduction, Decembrio
was given a commission by Humphrey to purchase books for
him in Italy, as a reward for which Humphrey offered a stipend
of 100 ducats, unless the Humanist preferred that the recompense
take some other form, with the provision, of course, that there
was no objection from Duke Filippo Maria Visconti to his
secretary receiving pay from a foreign prince.[72] There is no
evidence that the salary was ever paid, but the greedy humanist
seems to have been too importunate. Decembrio had a rival for
the favor of the Duke of Milan in Filelfo, who had received a
house in Milan as reward for his literary labors,[73] and it appears
that Decembrio felt that if Humphrey purchased for him the
villa *olim Francisci Petrarcae* he could eclipse his rival in splendor.
The tone of Humphrey's letter made him bold, and in an evil
hour he asked for the villa.[74] This letter appears to have been
left unanswered by the duke, and in March 1444 we find him
writing, not to answer his petition, but to ask why Decembrio had
sent no books or letters for nearly a year, assuring him that he
need not fear that he would be unrecompensed, for the duke
never allowed service to go without renumeration.[75]

So great a figure is Humphrey of Gloucester, in fact, that
more than brief mention must be made of him. That he was a
patron of letters and more than a dilettante is amply attested,
and of his taste there can be no doubt. Nor was his patronage
a pose adopted for the popularity it would bring. In England
among those who dedicated to him is Capgrave, who apparently
got acquainted through his dedication of the *Commentary on
Genesis* to him, for he speaks of the duke's love of learning as a

---

[72] Letter xviii, pg. 524. Compare Letter xv, 522.

[73] Voigt, op. cit., I, 513.

[74] Letter xiv, pg. 521.

[75] Concerning the whole matter see another article on the "Correspondence of
Humphrey Duke of Gloucester" by Newman, *English Historical Review*, XX. Peter
de Monte also bought books for Humphrey. (See [Creighton], "Some Literary
Correspondence of Humphrey Duke of Gloucester," *English Historical Review*, X,
99 ff.)

matter of report and not of personal knowledge. Capgrave commends this work to Humphrey interestingly enough, because in it, he says, is to be found the science of judging literature.[76] It is significant that such a science should be expounded in a theological treatise, and equally significant that it is Humphrey who is addressed, a circumstance which clearly shows his position in the thought of his age.[77] It is generally conceded that at his instance, too, Capgrave wrote in the vernacular his *Chronicle* which is dedicated to the king, and if this is true, Humphrey, as Vickers points out,[78] occupies an interesting position in the Renaissance movement and the development of the nationalities of Europe, which is mirrored by the adoption of the vernacular languages for scholarly purposes.

Among others, Nicholas Upton dedicated to him his *De Studio Militari*,[79] Lydgate wrote on commission for him, and about him were a number of secretaries, now quite forgotten men, such as John Homme, Richard Wyot, John Everton, and Henry Abingdon, all of whom copied books and found reward in his employ.[80] But Humphrey's fame as a patron was not confined to England, Italian scholars in Rome, Florence, Naples, and Milan looked upon him as a Maecenas, and judging from his correspondence with Decembrio, it is clear that his interest was more than superficial. In his household were several Italian scholars, among them Tito Livio, described as "poet and orator of the Duke of Gloucester," who at Humphrey's suggestion compiled his *Vita Henrici Quinti*, dedicated to Henry V, a work of distinctive influence in English historical literature.[81] Humphrey owed his popularity in Italy to the eulogy of a learned clergyman, Zanol Castiglione, who was commissioned to buy books when he visited the continent, and through him several humanists entered into

---

[76] Ed. R. S. 229-32.
[77] Vickers, *Humphrey of Gloucester*, 386-7.
[78] Op. cit., 385.
[79] Vickers, op. cit., 388.
[80] Ibid., 386. Reginald Pecock, the famous heretical bishop of St. Asaph, is also said to have been a protégé of Humphrey's, and since his heterodoxy did not begin until after Humphrey's death, Vickers suggests that the Duke's orthodoxy may have served as a restraint. (Ibid., 289.)
[81] Kingsford, *English Historical Literature in the Fifteenth Century*, 52.

relations with the English duke and dedicated their works to him. Besides Decembrio and Leonardo Bruni, Antonius Pacinus dedicated to him his translation of Plutarch's *Life of Marius*.[82] Perhaps, no better summary of Humphrey's importance as a patron could be found than a letter addressed to him in 1441 by the University of Oxford authorities:

"Nullus enim inter principes Christianos, apud Ytalos Grecosve scriptores celebrior, nullus clarior, nullus omnium ore personancior habetur. Quanta industria tot indies libri vestro sacratissimo nomini consecrati de grecorum fontibus in Latinam linguarum scaturint! Quantis insuper lugubracionibus et vigiliis, non modo ut ceteri ex Grecis traducant, sed et contemplacioni magnitudinis vestre nova in nostram linguam excudant opera, non nostrates solum sed ipsi etiam eloquentissimi et doctissimi de Italia viri insudaverunt! Quot preterea non de Grecia, Latia, Ytaliave, sed de omnibus tocius orbis partibus volumnia ad vos cotidie confluxerint satis superque satis pulcrum et delectabile est intueri."[83]

Two English authors are of particular interest in the matter of dedications and their relation to patronage: Chaucer, who apparently did not dedicate,[84] and Caxton, who almost invariably did. Though given to prologues Chaucer seems not to have indulged in dedications; there are only two cases in his works outside of his *Complaint to his Empty Purse* which may be looked upon as such. The treatise on the *Astrolabe* is addressed to 'litel Lowis,' and really not dedicated at all, while his *Troilus* is addressed in an envoy not to patrons, but to two friends:

> O moral gower, this boke I directe
> To thee, and to the philosophical Strode,
> To vouchen sauf, ther nede is to correct,
> Of youre benignites and zeles goode.

Who the little Lewis of the *Astrolabe* is, is uncertain; perhaps

---

[82] Macray, op. cit. Several books inscribed to Henry VII are mentioned by Macray as well as foreign dedications to princes of a later period than that with which our study deals.

[83] Anstey, *Epistolae Academicae*, I, 203.

[84] But he did apparently write poetic epistles; the *Balade of Truth* is addressed to "thou vache"; the *Lenvoy de Chaucer a Scogan* is addressed to his 'frend,' while most interesting of all is the *Lenuoy a Bukton*, the envoy of which reads:
> This litil writ, proverbes, or figure
> I sende you, tak kepe of hit, I rede:
> Unwys is he that can no wele endure.

his son, or possibly as Professor Kittredge suggests,[85] a son of
Sir Lewis Clifford, which is not unlikely when we remember that
the *Balade of Truth* is addressed to Clifford's son-in-law, Sir
Philip la Vache.[86]   Shirley speaks of another.   In the rubic of
the *Lak of Steadfastness* he says:

> "This Balade made Geffrey Chauncier's the Laureall Poete of Albion,
> and sent it to his souerain lorde kynge Richarde the Secounde þane being
> in his Castell of Windesore."[87]

But Chaucer himself is silent, and if we ask the cause, the only
reason appears to be that he intended no others.   If the poet
wanted to honor anyone with his works, and especially if he
wanted to gain favor by it, it lies in the nature of the case that
he would make no secret of it, or leave it entirely unspoken,
but would publish the person's fame abroad.   A reticent or
silent dedication is absolutely none, and Chaucer knew it, and
his one formal dedication is significant—to his friends and
brothers in Apollo.[88]

Caxton's dedications and prefaces are famous and valuable
for the light they shed upon the life of the man and upon the
development of printing in England.   From then we learn the
circumstances under which books were written, at whose request
they were compiled, to whom they were to be presented, and
generally why.   Sometimes we hear of a work being made
"vnder the hope and shadowe of your noble protection,"[89] and
often of particular patronage to the printer in a particular work
or in a general way.   An excellent example of Caxton's dedication is the prologue to *Blanchardine and Eglantine:*

> "Unto the right noble puyssaũt & excellẽt prycesse my redoubted lady

[85] *M. P.* XIV, 131.

[86] *M. P.* IX, 209 ff.

[87] The envoy of Chaucer's poem is a bit of advice addressed sure enough: "O
prince."

[88] Kuhl, (*P. M. L. A.*, XXIX, 275) points out that Strode was standing council
for the city in which office he had to plead for orphans etc., and suggests that to him
Chaucer may have owed—indirectly to be sure—his appointment as guardian of the
heirs of Edmund Staplegate of Canterbury and John de Solys of Kent, guardianship
being then a desirable and profitable office.

[89] Prologue to the *Play and Game of Chess*, addressed to George, Duke of Clarence,
(Blades, op. cit., I, 135); *Jason*, I, 139; *The Mirrour of the World*, I, 156; and the
Tully of Old Age, I, 160.

my lady Margarete duchesse of Somercete/Moder vnto our naturel & souerayn lord and most Crysten kynge henry yᵉ seuenth by the grace of god kynge of englonde of ffraûce lorde of yrelonde &c. I wyllyam caxton his most Indygne humble subgette and lytil seruaût presente this lytyl book vnto the noble grace of my sayd lady whiche boke I late receyued in frenshe from her good grace and her cōmaudement wyth all/For to reduce & translate it in to our maternal & englyssh tonge/whyche boke I had longe to fore solde to my sayd lady and knewe wel that the story of hit was honeste & Joyefull. . . . Bysechynge my sayd ladyes bounteou' grace to receyue this lityll boke in gree of me her humble seruaût/and to pardoune me of the rude and comyn englysshe. where as shall be found faulte For I confesse me not lerned ne knownynge the arte of rethoryk/ne of such gaye termes as now be sayd in these dayes and vsed : And that shall suffyse. Besechyng Allmyghty God to graunte to her mooste noble goode grace long lyffe/and thaccomplisshement of his noble and Joyes desires in thys present lyff : And after this short and transytorye lyff. euerlastynge lyff in heuen. Amen/[90]

Caxton's dedications, as those of England's first printer, are interesting in another connection—the dedication to a reading public. Collective dedicating was by no means a new thing. Both Bede[91] and Aelfric in the early time[92] had made use of the form and Robert of Brunne addressed his *Handlyng Synne:*

> To alle Crysten men vnder sunne,
> And to gode men of Brunne,
> And speciali, alle be name
> Þi felaushepe of Symprynghame
> Roberd of Brunne greteþ ʒow
> In al godenesse þat may to prow.[93]

Christine de Pisan, however, had an eye more closely to her readers when she directed *Le Dit de la Rose:*

> A tous le Princes amoureux
> Et aux nobles chevalereux,

[90] Blades, op. cit., I, 187.

[91] His *Life and Miracles of St. Cuthbert* is dedicated to "to the holy and most blessed Father Bishop Eadfrid, and to all the congregation of Brothers also, who serve Christ in the Island of Lindisfarne." (*Works,* ed. Giles, IV, 203.)

[92] His *Life of Aethelwold* was fitly directed to the "honorable Bishop Kenwulf and the brethren of Winchester," (Gem, op. cit., 166). Eddius also dedicated his *Vita Wilfridi Episcopi* to Bishop Acca, Abbot Tatbert, and others; (Raine, *Historians of the Church of York,* (R. S.), I, 1) and Reginald of Canterbury dedicated his *Life of St. Malchus* to Baldwin prior of St. Andrews, Rochester, and the brethren there. (*D. N. B.*)

[93] ll. 57 ff. ed. Furnivall, E. E. T. S., I, 2.

Que vaillantise fait armer,
Et a ceulz qui seulent amer
Tout bonté pour avoir pris,
Et a tous amans bien pris
De ce Royaume et autre part,
Partout ou vaillane s'espart:
A toutes dames renomées
Et aux damoiselles amées,
A toutes femmes honnorables,
Saiges, courtoises, agreables:
Humble recommendacion
De loyal vrage entencion.[94]

Hence, it is but a step that Caxton had to take when he made his reading public his dedicatee. The *Caton* is addressed:

"To the noble auncyent and renomed Cyte/the Cyte of London in Englond."[95]

and the *Kyng Arthur,* more directly

"vnto alle noble prynces/lordes and ladyes/gentylmen or gentylwymmen that desyre to rede or here redde of the noble and Joyous hystorye of the grete conquerour and excellent kyng."[96]

The dedication of books in the Middle Ages then is the continuance of the early tradition which sought to honor a friend or recognize and make some public return to a patron, and though the earlier ideal form of dedication was not unknown, but rather prevalent in the Middle Ages, the use of the dedication in commanding or soliciting patronage was also well known. Anyone in a position to become a patron was addressed: the opportunity for barter was recognized, and the advantages of multiple dedication at least essayed.

[94] *Oeuvres Poètiques,* ed. Roy, S. A. T. F., II, 29.
[95] Blades, op. cit., I, 169.
[96] Ibid., I, 180.

IX

PRESENTATION

When a medieval author did a work at request or spontaneously for a lord he wished to please and to whom he knew that literary works were acceptable, he took his production, upon which generally much care in writing and illuminating had been spent, and laid it at his feet. In fact, the presentation of a book is in actual deed, the dedication of it, and the custom rose naturally with those other spontaneus customs we have noted. In our view of dedications, the Roman idea of book dedications as gifts was noted, as well as the custom of presenting to the dedicatee the first copy of the work. Many references in medieval writings seem to indicate that a similar custom obtained, whether the work had a formal dedication or not. In old England Adamnan, Abbot of Iona, committed to writing all he had heard from the Frankish priest, Bishop Arculff, concerning what he had been on his travels to the Holy Land, the *De Situ Terrae Sanctae*. This book he took as a present (c. 701-3) to Aldfrith, King of Northhumbria, "and through his bounty it came to be read by lesser persons." We are told further that "the writer thereof was also well rewarded by him and sent back into this country."[1] Giraldus Cambrensis instead of gold and falcons that he might have brought from Ireland, sends, he tells us, a more worthy gift to a magnanimous prince, his *Topographia Hibernica*, which tells of all the glory of Henry and his progeny.[2] In four of the manuscripts of this book there is an epistle *Guillelmo Herefordensi episcopo*, which probably accompanied a presentation copy, explaining how to read the work profitably and pointing out the best chapters,[3] and in his *De Rebus a se*

[1] Bede, *Ecclesiastical History*, Ch. xv, (Bohn Lib.), 263.
[2] *Praefatio Secunda, Works*, ed. Dimock, (R. S.), V, 20-1.
[3] *Works*, ed. Brewer, (R. S.), V, 203. The Bishop is William de Vere, Bishop of Hereford, 1186-99.

Gestis, Gerald tells us that he presented some of his works to Pope Innocent III, whom he describes as a lover of letters and literary men.[4]

Layamon tells us that one of the works he used for the *Brut* was a work made by a French clerk named Wace:

> Þe wel couþe writen,
> & he hoe ȝef þare æðlen
> Aelienor þe wes Henries quene,
> Þes hiȝes kingis.[5]

and Roger Bacon, presenting his *Opus Magnum* to Pope Clement IV received only a rebuff for his pains. On the continent Petrarch alludes to the custom in commenting upon the request of his friend Philip for a copy of the treatise *On the Solitary Life* which was dedicated to him. "In truth" say Petrarch, "he asks what is only fair," and adds that delay has been due to bad copyists.[6] Eustache Deschamps, writing to his friend Guillaume de Machaut as to what disposition to make of his *Livre du Voir Dit* gives him good advice:

> Les grans seigneurs, Guillaume, vous ont chier,
> En vos choses prannent estabement.
> Bien y parut a Bruges devant hier
> A Monseigneur de Flandres proprement
> Qui par sa main reçut benignement
> Vostre Voir Dit selle dessur La range,
> Lire le fist; mais n'est nul vraiement
> Qui en die fors qu'a vostre louenge.[7]

Passing to England, some of Chaucer's works appear to have been meant for presentation. According to Shirley's rubric to the *Lak of Steadfastness:*

"this balade made Geffrey Chaunciers the Laureall Poete Of Albion and sent it to his souerain lorde kynge Richarde the secounde þane being in his Castell of Windesore,"[8]

---

[4] *Works,* ed. Brewer, I, 119.
[5] Ed. Madden, I, 3.
[6] Hollaway-Calthrop, *Petrarch,* 256.
[7] *Oeuvres Complètes de Eustache Deschamps,* ed. de St. Hilaire, S. A. T. F., I, 249.
[8] Spurgeon, *Five Hundred Years of Chaucer Criticism and Allusion,* Chaucer Society, Ser. II, xxviii, 148.

and of the *Legend of Good Women* it is said:

> And whan this book is maad, yive hit the quene
> On my behalfe, at Eltham, or at Shene.[9]

We should like to know of its dedication to Queen Anne, but it has not been given to us. It is not our purpose here to review the controversy as to the allegory of the *Legend,* other that to note this: that the choice of Alceste as Queen of the God of Love may be looked upon as evidence of Chaucer's adaptation of his material to the purpose of complimenting Queen Anne. If the poem, as we have seen, was to be presented to her, nothing could be more fitting than that the place of highest honor be given to a heroine who had distinguished herself for the particular kind of virtue exemplified by the queen, namely faithful and loving wifehood. If Alceste was selected by Chaucer as the Queen of the Court of Love because her virtues were those of Queen Anne, it is eminently fitting that she should bid Chaucer present his work with the compliments of the Queen of the Court of Love, to the Queen of England,[10] especially since Anne was a queen to whom it would be acceptable.

In the prologue to his *Chronicles* Froissart tells how he compiled a book of histories which he carried to England "and presented the volume thereof to my lady Phelyppe of Heynaulte, noble quene of Inglande, who right amyably receyved it to my great profite and avauncement."[11] In later years, wishing to revisit England, Froissart did much the same thing. He "engrosed a fayre boke, well enlumyned," he tells us, made up of his writings of the past twenty years, "whiche greatly quickened my desyre to go into England to se kyng Rycharde." The book, he adds, was bound with velvet and garnished with clasps of silver, and he "hadde suche a desyre to goo this voyage, that the payne and traueyle greved me nothyng." On arriving in England he

---

[9] Prologue B, 496-7. The passage is not in the A version.

[10] See Moore, "The Prologue to Chaucer's *Legend of Good Women* in relation to Queen Anne and Richard," *M. L. R.,* (1912), 490-1.

[11] *Berners' Froissart,* (Tudor Translations), I, 18.

bided his time for presenting his gift,[12] and when his time came, the king was much pleased.

"Whanne the kynge opened it, it pleased hym well, for it was fayre enlumyned and written, and covered with crymson velvet, with ten botons of sylver and gylte, and roses of golde in the myddes, with two great clapses gylte, rychely wrought. Than the kyng demaunded me whereof it treated, and I shewed hym howe it treated of maters of love; wherof the kynge was gladde and loked in it, and reed it in many places, for he could speke and rede Frenche very well; and he tooke it to a knyght of hys chambre, named syr Rycharde Creadon, to beare it into his secrete chambre."[13]

The famous fifteenth century feminist and the first woman of Western Europe to make her living by her pen, Christine de Pisan, tells us her story in her writings, how she was the subject of admiration of princes and nobles, who induced her to present copies of her works to the various members of the royal families and other distinguished folk. Among these works were *Le Livre du Chemin de Long Estude,* dedicated to Charles VI,[14] and the *Mutation de Fortune,* both of which, according to an inventory, were presented to the Duke of Berry.[15]

Both redactions of the *Confessio Amantis* of John Gower were meant for presentation, the first to King Richard and the second to Henry of Lancaster,[16] and the *Balades* were destined for the latter in later years when he became king. The one genuine poem of Henry Scogan, tutor to the sons of Henry IV was a presentation poem:

[12] On his first meeting he is careful to note that on this day he did not show his book because there was too much else to do. (*Berners' Froissart,* Tudor Translations, VI, 133.)

[13] Ibid., VI, 147.

[14] Ed. Püschel, 1.

[15] Concerning these the inventory reads:
"Le livre appelle de *Long Estude,* fait et compose par une femme appellee Christine, excript de lettres de court, le quel livre fu donne a monseigneur en son hostel de Nesle, a Paris, par la dessu dite Christine, le 20 mars 1402." . . . . .
"Un livre de la Mutacion de Fortune, excript en françois, ryme, de lettres de court, compile par une damoiselle apellee *Christine de Pizan,* historie en aucum lieux, lequel livre la dite damoiselle donna a monseigneur ou mois mars 1403 (1404)." (Thomassy, *Essai sur les Escrit Politiques de Christine de Pisan,* 115, and 123.)

[16] This povere bok I presente
Unto his hihe worthinesse.
    (Bk. VIII, ll. 3050* ff., ed. Macaulay, III, 474.)
This boke, upon amendment . . . .
I send unto myn oghne lord,
Which of Lancastre is Henri named. (ll. 83ff., ed. Macaulay, II, 6.)

> My noble sones, and eek my lordes dere,
> I, your father called, unworthily,
> sende un-to you this litle tretys here
> Writen with myn owne hand full rudely.[17]

Further, Lydgate's *Life of St. Edmund,* which we found him writing for his abbot for presentation to Henry, has, as one might expect, a presentation verse at the beginning:

> Souereyn lord, please to your goodly-heed
> And to your gracious Royal magnificence
> To take this tretys, which a-twen hope and dreed
> Presentyd ys to your hyh excellence!
> And for kyng Edmundis notable reuerence
> Beth to his chyrche dyffence and Champioun,
> Be-cause yt ys off your ffundacioun.[18]

Of the *Falls of Princes,* too, written for Humphrey of Gloucester, he tells us:

> I do present this boke with hand shakyng
> Of hole affection knelyng on my kne,
> Praying the lord one, two and thre,
> Whose magnificence no clerke may cōprēhede
> Sende you might grace and prosperite.[19]

Thomas of Walsingham presented his *Ypodigma Neustriae* to King Henry,[20] and Capgrave says significantly of his *Chronicle:*

"this werk send I to ȝow, where ȝe may turne and se schortly touchid the most famous thingis that have to do in the world. . . . O my benigne Lord, receyue this bok, thouȝ it be simpil: and lat that Gospel com in mynde, where the widow offered so litel, and had so mech thank."

Then he adds, "now wil I make ȝou pryvy what maner opinion I have of ȝoure persone in my pryvy meditaciones."[21]

Caxton again gives us much information. The *Recuyell of the Histories of Troy,* written at the urging of Margaret of Burgundy, he presented to her, and in the epilogue to the third book, he records:

"whiche book I haue presented to my sayd redoubtid lady as a fore is

[17] Ed. Skeat, *Chaucerian and Other Pieces,* 237.
[18] Horstmann, *Altenglische Legenden, Neue Folge,* 440.
[19] "The Wordes of the Translatour," end of Book IX.
[20] Ed. Riley, (R. S.), 3 ff.
[21] Ed. Hingeston, (R. S.), 1 ff.

sayd. And she hath well acceptid hit/and largely rewarded me/wherefore I beseche almyghty god to rewarde her euerlastyng blisse after this lyf."[22]

His *Life of Jason,* he says, was written under the shadow of the noble protection of his liege lord, but he does not presume to present his book unto his highness for he probably has the book in French already, but he does:

"entende by his licence & congye & by the supportacõn of our most redoubted liege lady/most excellent princesse the ,Quene to presente this sayde boke vnto the most fayr and my moost redoubted young lorde. My lord Prynce of Wales our tocomyng souayne lorde,"

that he may begin to learn English, who, he hopes, will accept it "in gree and thanke."[23] At the desire of Sire John Fastolf of Norfolk he translated into English the *Tully of Old Age* from a French translation made by Laurent de Premierfait at the command of Louis of Bourbon. This he has

"emprysed tenprynte vnder the vmbre and shadowe of the noble proteccion of our moost dradde/soueuerayn and naturel lyege lord/and moost Cristen Kyng Edward the fourth/to whom I most humbly byseche to receyue the said book of me William Caxton his moost humble subget and litil seruaunt/and not to desdeyne to take of me so poure ignoraunt & symple a persone."[24]

In 1481 he finished his *Godfroy of Boloyne,*

"whiche book J presente vnto the mooste Cristen kynge. kynge Eduard the fourth. humbly besechyng his hyenes to take no displesyr at me so presumyng,"[25]

and the *Order of Chivalry,* translated at the request "of a gentyl and noble esquyer," was duly presented:

"to my redoubted naturel and mast dradde souerayne lord kynge Rychard kyng of Englond and of Fraunce/to thende that he commaunde this book to be had and redde vnto other yong lordes kynghtes and gentylmen within this royame/that the noble ordre of chyualrye be hereafter better vsed & honoured than hit ben in late dayes passed."[26]

[22] Blades, op. cit., I, 134.
[23] Ibid., I, 139.
[24] Prologue, Epilogue, and Colophon, Ibid., I, 159-61.
[25] Epilogue, Ibid., I, 165.
[26] Ibid., I, 175-6.

Finally, to name no more examples in Caxton, the *Eneydos* was presented

"unto the hye born my tocomynge naturell & souerayn lord Arthur by the grace of god Prynce of Walys" etc.[27]

A little later, Stephan Hawes in his *Pastime of Pleasure* begs:

> Your noble grace and excellent highnes
> For to accepte I beseche right humbly
> Thys lytle boke, opprest wyth rudenes,
> Without rethorycke or coloure crafty;
> Nothing I am experte in poetry,
> As the monke of Bury, floure of eloquence,
> Whiche was in the time of great excellence
>
> Of your predecessour, the v. kyng Henry,
> Unto whose grace he did present
> Ryght famous bokes of parfit memory.[28]

The custom obtained everywhere; in Scotland, according to Sir David Lyndesay:

> . . . in the courte, bene present, in thir dayis,
> That ballatis, breuis, lustellie, and layis,
> Quhilks tyll our Prince daylie thay do present.[29]

Book presentation, however, had behind it a much more important purpose in the book world of the Middle Ages than merely pleasing the recipient; while, of course, in many cases the author was entirely satisfied with a gracious reception, he looked to is patron for another form of assistance. Drawing his evidence mainly from the correspondence of Petrarch and Boccaccio, Professor Root[30] has shown that the formal presentation of a book to a patron was virtually its 'release,' and that it constituted final and definite publication. The presentation copy after it had been approved by the prince was probably first shared among friends or the members of the court, and then sent forth to the public under the protection of the patron's

[27] Ibid., I, 191. This was Arthur, son of Henry VII.

[28] Percy Society, XXVIII, 2.

[29] *Testament of a Papyngo*, ll. 37 ff., *Monarche and Other Poems*, ed. Hall, E. E. T. S., 224.

[30] "Publication before Printing," *P. M. L. A.*, XXVIII, 417 ff.

name. The recipient of such a copy could, however, do with it what he pleased, lending it freely and permitting copies to be made; in fact, it seems that the patron was even under some obligation to further its circulation, and though his conclusions are drawn from fourteenth century Italy, Professor Root shows that in the more feudal north, where the author's dependence upon a patron was perhaps greater, the circumstances of publication were essentially similar. Nor is there anything to prevent such a system from operating in earlier times, and evidence is not lacking, for we have seen Adamnan in Saxon England as early as 701-3 presenting the book he had made to Aldfrith, through whose bounty it was copied and published abroad. Bede likewise sent his *Ecclesiastical History* to Ceolwulf to be copied and imparted to others more at large, and Aelfric sent his books of *Homilies* to Archbishop Sigeric to judge if they should be given to the faithful or cast aside.

In later times we hear less of the presentation of books from the authors themselves; at least they do not make a feature of their presentations, perhaps because book production by means of printing made a book a less notable gift, or more probably because the poet no longer looked to the patron as his publisher, but the custom persisted and remained as long as patronage was a fact.

From the instances cited above, especially in the case of Christine de Pisan, it is clear that a book need not be presented to a dedicatee exclusively, though by the nature of the case we may assume that he received a copy. Hoccleve we found writing a "Go, little book" balade to accompany a copy of the *Regiment of Princes* to the Duke of Bedford, in much the same manner as he did to his especial patron, Henry V,* and Christine, who made her living by writing at a time when all remuneration from authorship came by patronage, possibly did so largely by numerous presentation copies. When works were written for a lord at his command or desire, it is fairly evident that he received a copy of the work on its completion, for which,

---

* The *Regiment*, in fact, in one place is addressed: "O worthi princes two," (ll. 5363, ed. Furnivall, E. E. T. S., III, 193).

whether he received it or not, the author could expect something more than the traditional "well done, good and faithful servant." Froissart's presentation of his book of histories to Queen Philippa "to my great profit and advancement" has already been noted, and other instances of payment occur.[31]   That a reward for the presentation of books was customary practice is shown by this disappointed note of William Worcester's:

"1473, die 10 augusti presentavi W. episcopo Wyntoniensi apud Asher librum Tullii de Senectute per me translatum in anglicis, sed nullum regardum recepi de episcopo."[32]

On the other hand, we find in Erasmus' letter to Leo X concerning the dedication of his *Jerome:*

"I do not myself expect any other outcome of my exertions, but that Christian piety may obtain some aid from the memorials of Jerome. He for whose sake I undergo this labour will abundantly recompense me for it."[33]

But another letter disillusions us, for to Henry Bullock Erasmus writes:

"We sent last winter one volume to Leo, to whom it was dedicated, and if it has been delivered, I do not doubt that he will requite our vigils with the highest rewards."[34]

There is a phase of this matter of presentation of books which is so characteristic of the Middle Ages and its beautiful parchment, hand-made books, that it is not to be neglected: that is, the matter of manuscript illuminations.   Many of the gorgeous

---

[31] Jacques Raponde was given 300 francs by Philip le Hardi in 1403 "pour un livre francois de plusieurs histories des *Femines de bonne renommee* (Boccaccio's *De Claris et Nobilibus Mulieribus*) que ledit Raponde lui presenta en estrennes" (Doutrepont, *La Littérature Française à les Cours des Ducs de Bourgoigne,* 270).   Christine de Pisan is often the recipient of reward for her books.   On Nov. 17, 1407, she is given 50 francs of gold, "pour et en recompensacion de plusieurs livres en parchemin, contenans plusieurs notables et beaux ensengnemens, qu'elle a donnez at presentez pius peu en ca a ycelli sgr" (Ibid., 277.)   On June 17, 1408, 100 francs is paid her "en recompensacion de certains livres lesquelz all a faiz et donnez a ycelli sr, et pour certaines autres causes et consideracions a ce le mouvans" (Ibid., 277.)   Again Dec. 3, 1412, she received 50 francs "en recompensacion de pluseurs notables livrez qu'elle avoit presente et donne a mond sr."   (Ibid., 277.)

[32] *Itinraria Symonis Simeonis et Willielmi de Worcestre,* ed. J. Nasmith, (1778), 368.

[33] Epist. 323, Nichols, op. cit., II, 203.

[34] Epist. 441, Ibid., II, 331.

old books, made for presentation doubtless, have representations
of the author humbly offering his labor, often on bended knee,
to his lord, and in the better specimens at any rate, it may be
assumed that the pictures thus represented were intended for actual portraits. It is impossible to describe them: they must be
seen, and if possible, in their surroundings of crackling parchment and crabbed handwriting, or at least in a color reproduction,
in order to obtain their full meaning. Such illuminations usually
and appropriately accompany the dedication, if there is one; at
least they are among the first leaves of the manuscript, and from
the sumptuousness of the volumes among other things we may
assume that there were intended for presentation volumes. In
no case is the author presumptious enough, however, to present
himself or another receiving anything in return for his work.
Samples of this interesting device are very numerous, and to list
them would be impossible because of lack of space, and since they
are on the whole very similar when all is said, like everything
else in the Midde Ages, we shall be content with only a few which
are related to works of which mention has been made in connection with our study, of which mention will be made, or which
are of more than general interest to us.

Among the very earliest of these illuminations is one on the
dedication page of the treatise *De Virginitate,* a manuscript of
the eighth or ninth century, which pictures Aldhelm, the author,
presenting his work to the Abbess of Barking.[35] Another representing the old time, though itself of very late date, is the
representation of Hroswitha and Otto I, referred to earlier in
this study.[36] In Royal Ms. 16 G. v in the British Museum, a copy
of a French translation of Boccaccio's *De Claris Mulieribus,* is a
miniature representing Boccaccio presenting his book to Andrea,
Countess of Altavilla, beside the legend "Cy commence le liure
que fist Johan Bocace de Certalde des cleres et nobles femmes,
lequel il enuoya a Andree des Accioroles de Florence, contesse

---

[35] The manuscript is in the Lambeth Palace Library, but the illumination is reproduced in Trail and Mann, *Social England,* I, 307.

[36] Reproduced in Kemp-Welch, *Of Six Medieval Women,* and in Pollard, *Fine
Books,* 180.

de Hauteville."[37]   Another portrait of Boccaccio with Maghin-
ardho Cavalcanti is found in a fifteenth century manuscript of *De
Casibus Virorum.*[38]   A translator of Boccaccio, Laurient de
Premierfait, is represented as meeting his dedicatee in the street
in Ms. Cimel 38, Cod. Gall., 6 in the Münchener Kaiserliche
Hof-und-Staatsbibliothek.[39]   Deschamps is presented delivering
his book to Charles VI.[40]   Representations of Froissart are numerous, and the presentation of his book to Richard II we found
him so careful to tell of in his *Chronicle,* we find duly represented
in the manuscript.[41]   Harleian Ms. 6431 is a beautifully ex-
ecuted manuscript of many of the writings of Christine de Pisan,
and is doubtless the presentation copy which Christine is shown
offering to Isabelle of Bavaria.[42]   B. M. Arundell No. 38, undoubtedly a presentation volume, contains a portrait of Hoccleve
presenting a book to Henry V,[43] and another in Ms. Royal 17
D. vi shows him kneeling before Henry V as prince of Wales
with the *Regiment of Princes* which was written for the prince.[44]
Another Ms. of the *Regiment* which contains also a translation of
Vegetius *De Re Militari* made for "Sire Thomas of Berkeley"
shows the whole court assembled while Hoccleve presents his
work.[45]   Lydgate likewise is often so portrayed.   A manuscript
of his *Pilgrim* (Harl. 4826) contains a portrait of Lydgate and his
Pilgrim presenting the book to Thomas Montacute, earl of Salisbury,[46] another (Ms. Bodl. Digby, 232) represents Henry VI and

[37] *British Museum, Catalogue of Western MSS, in the Old Royal and King's Collections,* II.

[38] Reproduced in Hutton, *Boccaccio,* 34.

[39] Kobell, *Kunstvolle Miniaturen & Initialen . . . zu Munchen befindlichen Manu-
skripte,* (1890), 66.

[40] Frontispiece, Vol. II, *Oeuvres,* ed. St. Hilaire, S. A. T. F.

[41] Volume IV, pg. 174 of the Ms. Lindner, *Der Breslauer Froissart,* No. 45. Another miniature of Froissart presenting a work is reproduced in Humphrey, *Illuminated
Illustrations of Froissart selected from the MSS. in the B. M.,* I, Plate xvii, and still
another is mentioned as being in Royal Ms. 14 B, ii-vi in the British Museum *Catalogue*
referred to above, II.

[42] Roy, *Oeuvres Poètiques de Christine de Pisan,* S. A. T. F., II frontispiece, or
Shaw, *Dress and Decorations. . . . .* II, No. 43, where the illumination is reproduced in color.

[43] Shaw, *Dress and Decorations . . .* II, No. 41.

[44] Strutt, *Manners and Customs,* Plate xxx.

[45] Strutt, *Regal and Ecclesiastical Antiquities,* Plate xxxix.

[46] Ibid., Plate xlv, or Shaw, op. cit., II, No. 44. The legend in the Ms. reads:
"Lydgate presenting his booke called ye Pilgrime unto ye Earle of Salisbury."

Lydgate, while a manuscript containing the *Falls of Princes* (Ms. Harl. 1766.) is another variation on the theme.[47]   A manuscript of the *Life of St. Edmund* (Harl. 2278) which we found Lydgate writing for his abbot at St. Edmunds, contains a representation of Henry VI surrounded by his followers receiving the book from William Curteis, the abbot.   Beside it is Lydgate's prologue explaining the circumstances of writing.[48] Caxton is also portrayed in the act of presentation.   Once in a cut from an early copy for the *Recuyell of the Histories of Troye* we find him presenting a book to Margaret of Burgundy,* and again in a copy of the *Dictes and Sayings of the Philosophers* (Lambeth 265), a work which he printed for Anthony, earl of Rivers, we find him accompanying the earl when he presented the book to Edward IV and the court.[49]

Many others are interesting, but enough have been cited for our purpose.   There are a few curiosities, however, which are of especial interest.   Some of the early illuminations seem to regard the work of the monastery as a presentation to the patron saint of the monastery, and accordingly the saint is represented as receiving the book from the monk who presents it.   Such is the illumination in the St. Gallen Schriftsbibliothek Cod. 390/11 of the eleventh century which represents St. Gallus adorned by a halo receiving a book from a bowing monk,[50] and the one from a mid-twelfth manuscript of Bede's *Ecclesiastical History*, which formerly belonged to the Benedictine order of St. Martin of Köln, but now is Ms. CLXV of the Stadtsbibliothek in Liepzig, in which St. Martin, with a golden halo and a bishop's crosier, takes the book a kneeling monk offers, while St. Eliphius stands beside him and points to the volume.[51]   One of the most amusing of these illustrations is one which occurs in the pseudo-Aristotelian *Secreta Secretorum* mentioned in numerous connections above. Alexander, as will be noted, was the type of largess during much

---

[47] Trail and Mann, op. cit., II, 525.

[48] Strutt, *Regal and Ecclesiastical Antiquities*, Plate xli.

[49] Strutt, *Regal and Ecclesiastical Antiquities*, Plate xlvii; Besant, *Medieval London*, I, 262; or Traill and Mann, op. cit., II, 431.

* Ricci, *A Census of Caxtons*, frontispiece.

[50] Merton, *Die Buchmalerei in St. Gallen von neunten bis zum elften Jahrhundert*, Tafel LXVII, No. 1.

[51] Bruck, *Die Malereien in der Handschriften des Königreiche Sachsen*, 43.

of the Middle Ages, and we find Aristotle, dressed in proper medieval fashion, reminding one of the Squire in the Elsemere Chaucer, kneeling before his lord Alexander and presenting his book.[52] Concerning the "Anchiennes and Nouelles croniques dangleterre" there is an exceedingly interesting circumstance. The work was done at request of Edward IV, who is represented as receiving the book from the kneeling author. The Ms., however, is inscribed to Edward V. Edward IV probably died just before it was completed, and the ambitious author scratched out the original words and numeral and the line now reads: "Eduard de—Ve de ce nom."[53]

Nothing was more acceptable in the old time than a book, but not all persons who presented books were authors, and so not all who are so pictured are authors. Ms. B. M. Roy. 15 E. vi is a beautiful volume of romances in French, made to order for John Talbot, Earl of Shrewsbury, for presentation to Margaret of Anjou after her marriage to Henry VI of England. It is accompanied by a dedication, beside which is a beautiful miniature of Talbot, in the robes of the Garter, kneeling and presenting this huge clasped volume to his sovereign.[54]

The custom of representing the presentation of books in the work itself passed with the Middle Ages, though it is to be found even in the age of Elizabeth. Wood-cuts represent Alexander Barclay presenting his *Ship of Fools* and his version of Sallust's *Jugurtha* to his patrons,[55] and in a drawing from a manuscript translation of the tale of *Hemetes the Heremyte* into English, Italian, Latin, and French, "pronounced before Queen Elizabeth at Woodstock in 1575," (Ms. Roy. 18 A. xlviii) Gascoigne is shown presenting his works to the queen.[56] In later times at least, and with some princes, such presentation of manuscripts seems to have been expected from a man known as a wit or

[52] Rhodes, *Desc. Catal. of Fifty Mss. in Possession of H. Yates Thompson*, 257. (Ms. 47), and Lindner, *Der Breslauer Froissart*, 53.

[58] Ms. Roy. 15 E iv, Strutt, *Regal and Ecclesiastical Antiquities*, Plate xlvi.

[54] British Museum, *Reproduction from Illustrated Manuscripts*, Series II, Plate xxix; or Shaw, *Dress and Decorations*, II, No. 49.

[55] *Ship of Fools*, ed. Jameson, cxiv. and Pollard, *Fine Books*, 256.

[56] Traill and Mann, op. cit., III, 467.

litterateur, illustrated admirably by the familiar story of the introduction of Erasmus to the future Henry VIII. The trick was Thomas More's, who bringing Erasmus unawares upon the royal children, made his obeisance to the nine-year old Henry and presented him with a manuscript of his own. Erasmus had nothing to offer, but promised to compose something, and was especially chagrinned, when during luncheon, the prince sent him a note challenging something from his pen. "I went home," he writes, "and in the Muses spite, from whom I had been so long divorced, finished the poem within three days."[57] The poem, the *Prosopopoeia Brittanniae,* of course, said the proper thing, but was hardly worth three days labor.

[57] Nichols, *Epistles of Erasmus,* I, 201-2.

X

REWARDS

What Lodge expressed in his *Fig for Momus*, Ec. III, when
he said:

> The priest unpaide can neither sing nor say,
> Nor poets sweetlie write excepte they meete
> With sound rewarde, for sermoning so sweete,

was recognized in earlier days, and though in the Middle Ages
the profession of letters had not developed to the stage it reached
in the Elizabethan time, the problem of providing for literary
genius was no less a real one. Men, indeed, wrote often because they liked to or felt called to, but the man who looked for
compensation in an age when the cost of book production was
prohibitive to a living from book sales could not escape looking
to a patron. Fame, says Giraldus Cambrensis,[1] should be the
first great object of authors, and the *nobilium principum re-
muneratio* the second, and he quotes the classics to support his
view. Poor Gerald was forced by stress of circumstances to
find the first sufficient incentive, and though he denied that the
latter cause any longer had existence because there were no
learned princes and no honors to be won, his attitude, while
sometimes reiterated, is not the view of all medieval writers,
for they are by no means all so cynical. Generally the writer
realized the fact that has been to the advantage of writers since
the earliest times, that all princes are proud and hope for the immortality of their glory, and hence it often comes about that the
most glorious prince in deeds is also the most prized as a patron
of literature and the arts. And who is a better herald of fame
than the poet and the historian? Hence, among early writers the
conferring of immortality became a lucrative profession, and the

[1] *Topographia Hibernica, Works,* ed. Dimock, (R. S.), V, 3 ff.

idea that a good style and an aptness of phrasing in a dedication or in the body of a literary work conferred upon the lord so honored the admiration of future generations was preached, as we have seen, with naive openness and impressed upon princes. A firm consciousness of this power, however, did not manifest itself until the time of the Renaissance, but the fact was recognized even in the earliest times, and immortality was sold for the things of this world.

Our view of minstrel and troubadour patronage made evident the nature of rewards to these, and since remuneration for works of literature in goods rather than in money continued, further discussion of such manifestations of patronage may be deferred. Hélie de Borron boasts, as we have seen, that he got two castles from Henry II for his writings,[2] and it is interesting to note that Gower received in 1393 a comparatively cheap collar from Henry of Lancaster, though there apparently is no evidence of the gift's being due to an appreciation of Gower's poetry.[3] Even Poliziano, tutor and courtier at the Medici court, writes doubtfully serious verses beginning:

> Laurenti, vestes jam mihi mitte tuas.[4]

Caxton, we have seen, was promised a fee by the Earl of Arondel, of a buck in winter and a doe in summer,[5] and Dunbar, according to the accounts of the Lord High Treasurer, received a livery.[6]

This whole matter of rewards to poets is a subject upon which we are never on sure ground. Seldom are we sure that the

[2] Ms. Adds. 12,228, quoted by Ward, *Catalogue of Romances*, I, 365 ff.

[3] *Works*, ed. Macaulay, IV, xvi.

[4] Cotterill, *Italy from Dante to Tasso*, 387. There is an anecdote told of Dante by Michele Savonarola, the grandfather of the preacher, which is of interest here. "I will tell you the answer made by Dante to a buffoon at the court of the Lord della Scala of Verona, who, having received from his master a fine coat as reward for some piece of buffoonery, showed it to Dante, and said: 'You with all your letters, and sonnets, and books, have never received a present like this.' To which Dante answered: 'What you say is true; and this has fallen to you and not to me, because you have found your likes and I have not found mine. There, you understand that.' " (Quoted by Toynbee, *Dante Alighieri*, (1910), 145.)

[5] Preface to the *Golden Legend*.

[6] Small, ed. *Poems of William Dunbar*. (Introduction by J. G. Mackay), S. T. S., (1893), I, clvi, where the documents are quoted.

bounty is for literary work and not for other services rendered. When money is given there is difficulty in determining why, for if we judge from their context in the records, the entries might be for anything, and in only a few cases, where the records are explicit or there is direct mention in the author's works of a money gift can we be sure. Even when a payment is specifically made for books oftentimes we are not sure that the remuneration is not for copying or the mechanical labor of book production rather than for authorship. Hence, we will content ourselves with only a few instances. Suffice it to say, however, that money gifts were a frequent form of remuneration. Thus in a letter to Maghinardo Cavalcanti, September 13, 1373, Boccaccio, recovering from an illness, thanks him effusively for a vase of gold filled with gold pieces. Thanks to that, he says, he can buy a cloak for his poor feverish body.[7] Further, Amadis VI, Count of Savoy, is known to have given Guillaume de Machaut three hundred écus for an unidentified poem dedicated to him,[8] and in June, 1370 we find the Duchess of Brabant paying the sum of sixteen francs *uni Frissardo, do uno novo libro gallico*, probably a book of balades, romances, or love poems of which Wencelas and his good duchess were so fond.[9] Christine de Pisan likewise was the recipient of several money gifts. On February 20, 1406, John of Burgundy gave her a hundred écus, and in 1407, fifty francs, while on May 13, 1411, Charles VI gave her two hundred livres.[10] Jehan Waucquelin was given several sums in 1447 specifically "pour le fait de la translation de certaines livres et histoires que sondit seigneur lui avait fait faire" and two years later he receives thirty écus for "paines, travaulz, et services qu'il avoit fait et faisoit a sondit seigneur continuellement en descripture et translation de plusieurs cronicques."[11] In the time of the Renaissance spontaneous gifts of money were frequent. Guarino received a thousand florins from Nicholas V

[7] Hutton, *Boccaccio*, 201 n.

[8] Hoepffner, *Oeuvres de Guillaume de Machaut*, S. A. T. F., xxvii.

[9] Darmesteter, *Froissart*, (tr. Poynter, 1895), 34. Perhaps it was only for copying and not for composing; there is no evidence.

[10] Koch, *Leben und Werke der Christine de Pizan*, Anhang III.

[11] Doutrepont, *La Littérature Française à les Cours des Ducs de Bourgoigne*, 23, 24. Numerous payments are made to scribes. (Ibid., 23, 24, 472 ff.)

for a translation of Strabo and would have been paid five hundred more but for the death of the pope.[12] Perotti got five hundred ducats from the same prelate for Polybius,[13] and there is a well-known tale of how Filelfo got a purse of five hundred ducats (more than he deserved) for his outrageous satires. In vain Nicholas held out the offer of 10,000 gold pieces for a translation of Homer into verse. From Alfonso of Naples Poggio got six hundred gold pieces for Xenophon's *Cyropedia,* and Panorimita a thousand florins for instructing in Livy.[14] In short, whenever the popes or princes of the Renaissance could fasten scholars to them by money, they did so, and Vespasiano tells us Alphonso spent as much as twenty thousand ducats a year for such salaries.[15]

Turning to Scotland, there are several entries in the Treasurer's accounts which are doubtfully for literary service, but are of interest nevertheless, as they may deal with literary men. During the years 1489-91 a certain "blinde Hary" is mentioned as the recipient of sums ranging from five to eighteen shillings, though there is no indication of who he was or why he was paid, the only remark being that twice it is "at the King's command.[16] The author of the *Wallace* is recognized as Henry the Minstrel, who is reported to have been blind, but for all the records tell, this individual might have been a cobbler, gamer, usher, or trumpeter, but all that is to be assumed is that some person of the name was in the employ of the king during these years mentioned, and was paid for his services, the character of which we do not know. In the accounts also for the same period occur several entries to one Stobo, also sometimes "at the king's command." Perhaps *Stobo* was the *maker* to whom Dunbar alludes, but entries for particular services such as writing letters, indicate that he was a clerk as well, and a grant of a pension March 25, 1473 of £20 to "John Reide, *alias* Stobo" shows him

[12] Vespasiano, ed. Schubring, 290. Guarino, however, sought about for a dedicatee for his third book, and finally sent it to a Venetian nobleman, who, overjoyed, rewarded the scholar handsomely.

[13] Burckhardt, op. cit., I, 263.

[14] Ibid., I, 315.

[15] Ed. Schubring, 54.

[16] Schofield, *Mythical Bards,* 111.

to have been the well-known churchman and notary, Sir John Reide.[17] Further, a little later there are unspecified entries among others for fairly respectable sums to Maister William Dunbar, "be the Kingis command," in 1505-8, one of forty-two shillings, followed by three of £5 each, one for £3, 19s., and another for 42s.[18] Perhaps these are for no literary work at all.

In England under date of "Easter 19 Edward IV, 15th June" there is an entry in the Exchequer Roll:

"To William Caxton. In money paid to his own hands in discharge of 20£ for the Lord the King commanded to be paid to the same William for certain causes and matter performed by him for the said Lord the king."[19]

We should like to think the "certain causes and matters performed" were the printing of books, but there is no evidence. Most interesting, though late in the period with which this paper deals, are the Privy Purse expenses of Henry VII. There, among all sorts of entries is evident Henry's taste for books and painting, his love of plays and minstrelsy, together with bits of evidence of substantial patronage of letters. On December 27, 1491, there is a payment of £11. 13d. 4d. "to the scholars of Oxenford for their exebucion and for the making of two Baculers of Arte,"[20] an entry, among others, indicating that Henry was interested in the universities. Payments for general entertainment, often large, are frequent, but these concern us only in that sometimes bands of minstrels are designated by the name of a noble. There are also several entries to the printers at Westminster and others for book purchases. For our purposes the most interesting are the payments that are known to have been made to poets. On February 20, 1495, 10s. are paid "to a Walsheman for making a ryme"; on May 14 of the same year "to Master Peter for sertain bokes vpon a bille, £11. 3s. 5d."; no inconsiderable sum; on May 9, 1496, most munificently, £20 "to an Italian, a poete"; and on October 13, 1496, "to Master Peter the Poete for a currer of Florence in rewarde, 1£" where the

[17] Ibid., 112 ff.
[18] Small, op. cit., I, clv, where the records are printed.
[19] Blades, *Biography and Typography*, 160.
[20] Bentey, *Excerpta Historica*, 88.

entry is most specific. Bernard Andreas, tutor to Prince Arthur, of whom there is more to be said in another connection, is mentioned twice, once in September 20, 1496, as "the Blynde Poete," when he receives £3. 6s. 8d. and again as "Master Bernerd the blynde poet, £6. 13s. 4d." Perhaps Dunbar is the recipient of the two payments, both for £6. 13s. 4d. under date of December 31, 1501, and January 7, 1502, "to the Rymer of Scotland in rewarde." Some of these entries too indicate that poets were definitely attached to the royal family, one a payment, under date of December 3, 1497, of £3. 6s. 8d. "to my Lady the Kinges moder poete" and another February 4, 1498, of a similar sum, "to my Lorde Prince poete in rewarde." Thus enough has been said both here and in other places in this study to show that monetary gifts were not infrequent as rewards to poets in the Middle Ages, even though records are lacking or tantalizingly unspecific.

Another way of providing for the poet, a means not confined to medieval times either, was the pension. Again there is often no way of determining why the annuity was given, and as similar pensions were conferred upon political servants as upon literary ones, in the cases of men whose activity was both political and literary and both were worthy of reward, it is impossible to say why the pension was granted. In Renaissance Italy the custom prevailed, and Alfonso of Naples conferred upon Bartolomeo Fagi for his *Historia Alfonsi,* not only a present of 1,500 ducats, but a yearly income of five hundred, with the words, "it is not given to pay you, for your work would not be paid for if I gave you the fairest of my cities, but in time I hope to satisfy you."[21] In France in 1448 Jean Waucquelin was paid a hundred livres as a pension "pour consideration de la paine quil a souffert et soustenut et encorres soeffre et soustient à fair la translation de latin en franchois daucunes ystoires et croniques."[22] Putting aside the grants to minstrels which are numerous throughout the old time, grants to poets in England are unfortunately lacking. Henry III had among the retainers of his court a certain Henri

[21]Vespasiano, ed. Schubring, 54.
[22]Doutrepont, op. cit., 24.

d'Avranches, who is designated in the records as *versificator regis* and who was retained at a definite salary. On July 14, 35 Henry III (1251), there is an order to the treasurer for a payment to "nostro delecto nobis Magistro Henrico Versificatori centum solidos, qui ei lebentur de arreragijs stipendiorum suorum,"[23] even though the treasury is closed, and at another time another payment is made to him of £10.[24] Further, on May 20, 1257, there is a grant for life to Master Henry de Alvrincis, the king's poet *(versificator)*, of two tuns of the king's wines which are in the keeping of the chamberlains of London, to wit, a tun of vintage, and a tun of wine of rack.[25]

In Scotland, John Barbour, author of the *Bruce*, and arch-deacon of Aberdeen, received in 1388 from Robert II, an annual grant of £10, "pro suo fideli servicio nobis impenso," which is said to have been for the patriotic services of his pen.[26] Previously on March 14th 1377-8 he had a gift of £10, on August 29, 1378, a grant of a pension of 20s., as "dilecto clerico nostro," and in 1386 he received two more gifts from the king.[27] Clearly there is nothing to indicate what the grants were made for, and they are interesting only because they were made to a poet. Geoffrey Chaucer also had grants of money and pensions and official positions. There can be no virtue in giving a list of these in this place, since they are so well-known and especially since of none of them are we sure that the grant was made for anything but "la bone et agreable service." As far as evidence from the records goes, there is nothing to connect the official Chaucer and the author of the *Canterbury Tales*. Professor J. R. Hulbert has shown how erroneous are the statements usually made with regard to the connection between the grants and pensions made to Chaucer and the production of his literary work. Concerning the early grants his conclusions are that "so far as we know, Chaucer received no exceptional favors, and that his career was in practically every respect a typical esquire's career,"[28] and in

---

[23] Madox, *History and Antiquities of the Exchequer,* (2nd edn. 1769), I, 391.
[24] Ibid., I, 202.
[25] *Calendar of Patent Rolls, 1247-58,* 555.
[26] *Barbour's Bruce,* ed. Skeat, S. T. S., I, xxii, where the records are reprinted.
[27] Ibid., I, xvii ff.
[28] *Chaucer's Official Life,* 58.

regard to the later customs appointments his inferences are that he gave good service for all he received. In fact, in regard to the holdings of any of the medieval poets, the accounts in the records are so inadequate, and so little else has come down to us, that any opinions derived from them belong to the category of mere speculation. The medieval man of letters, as has been pointed out, was an author by avocation and not by profession, and though, as is possible in Chaucer's case notably, his poetic powers may have brought him to the attention of the great and thus contributed to his worldly advancement and prompted his superiors to assign him a position whereby he could support himself and perhaps have leisure for poetic composition, there is nothing to tell us one way or another.

Hoccleve, likewise had a pension, but whether it was for poetry or for his work in the office for the privy seal, is hardly doubtful: the latter reason seems most likely. On November 12, 1399, Henry IV granted him his patent *pro bono et laudabile seruicio quod dilectus seruiens noster* for £10 a year for life or until he should be promoted to an ecclesiastical benefice (without care of souls) worth £20 a year.[29] On May 17, 1409 there is a grant of £13. 6s. 8d. to Hoccleve instead of his former yearly £10,[30] where the grant again is clearly for his office work. When Henry V came to the throne he reneked his father's patent, provided that Hoccleve is not retained by anyone else,[31] and Henry VI did the same.[32] On July 4, 1424, the poet petitioned to the king that he supply "vostre treshumble clerc, Thomas Hoccleve," with the corrody that the late Nicholas Mokkyng had in the priory of Southwick, Hants, a petition that the king granted.[33] Such is the provision made for Hoccleve, all of the pensions being granted as the documents show, for good service in his office, and not for his literary works. The poetical means Hoccleve used to get his annuities paid is another matter and belongs to another part of this discussion, but the fact remains

[29] "Appendix of Hoccleve Documents," Furnivall, *Minor Poems of Hoccleve*, I, li.
[30] Ibid., lvi.
[31] Ibid., lix.
[32] Ibid., lxvi.
[33] Ibid., lxviii

that the original intention in them was to reward clerical labor. Of another clerk, William Dunbar, this time in the embassies of James IV, we cannot be quite so sure. On August 15, 1500, he obtained a pension of £10 for life or until he be promoted to a benefice of £40 or above, in 1507 this was increased to £20, and in 1510 to £80.[34] Speculation in Lydgate's case is more fruitful. The *Falls of Princes* was done by 1439 at the latest, and on April 22 of that year, there is a grant of•ten marks to be paid annually to the monk from the customs at Ipswich, which in the next year was increased to £7. 13s. 4d. from the proceeds of a farm of Waytefee.[35] Perhaps the pension came through Humphrey of Gloucester for whom the book was done. We do know, however, that Lydgate had money from Humphrey during the writing of the poem, for he sent a poetical petition to the Duke for it, and records his thanks in the work. In Lydgate's case, too, we know of one definite payment. Concerning the *Albon* and *Amphabel*, which we found him making for the abbot of St. Albans, we find among the *Expensae Abbatis Johannis Wethamstede Magis Notabiles*, the following entry:

> Item, cuidam monacho de Burgo Sancti Edmundi, propter translationem Vitae Sancti Albani in nostrum vulgare. . . . iii[li]. vi[s]. vii[d].[36]

Further, Capgrave, at the end of his prologue to the *Life of St. Katherine* says significantly:

> Ye that reed it, pray for hem alle
> That of this werk either travayled or payde,
> Þat from her synnes wyth grace thei may falle,
> To be redy to god whan Þat he wil calle.[37]

It has generally been supposed that Dunbar's poetic gifts were in large measure his main passports to the favor of the king,

---

[34] "Records Relating to Dunbar," Small, op. cit., I, cliv ff.

[35] "Documents relating to Lydgate" in Steele, ed. *Lydgate and Burgh's Secrees of Old Philosofrees*, E. E. T. S., xxiv. Lydgate's petition concerning this patent in which he calls himself "youre pouere and perpetuall oratour" is interesting in this connection, but tells us little.

[36] *Chronico Monasterii S. Albani : Annales Monasterii S. Albani a Johanni Amundesham, Monacho. . . . .* ed. Riley, (R. S.), 1871, II, 256.

[37] ll. 247 ff. ed. Horstmann, E. E. T. S., 17.

and the gifts we have seen Henry VII making to him about the same time of his first pension, if Dunbar is the "rymer of Scotland," lead us to suppose he was at least recognized as a poet in his own land. At the same time, however, Dunbar was not satisfied with his pension; he wanted his benefice and pleaded poetically and ardently for it, basing his claims, not on his poetic achievements, but upon his personal services to the king.[38] But in Scotland too, there were definite rewards for literary works, for when Bellendon and Stewart by royal command wrote a chronicle, though a little later than our period, there are entries in the accounts after this manner:

"Master John Ballentyne, be the kyngis precept, for his translating of the Cronykill,"

the sums varying from £6 to £30.[39]

But even if the grants themselves give us little information to our purpose, there can be little doubt of the possibility that literary work, while it may not be rewarded for itself, might lead indirectly to reward, by recommending the poet to the attention of the great and thus paving the way for his advancement. Such is most likely the case with Chaucer, if we are to assume patronage of him at all; perhaps it was so with Hoccleve, Dunbar, and others. Such a supposition is not unreasonable when we remember that medieval patronage was never so magnificent a thing as the policy of Maecenas, and when we note the number of works done at the bidding of the nobility by those attached to them. Often the poet is an ecclesiastic or becomes one. As in so many cases, the life of Giraldus Cambrensis is again of help. He tells of his doings in the *De Rebus a se Gestis* and how his fame spread because of his scholarship as much as anything else, and when Henry II went about pacifying Wales he summoned Gerald as counsellor, luring him with promises

[38] Most of the poems of Dunbar addressed to the king are poems of request. The best examples are "Schir, ȝit Remember as of Befoir"; "Of the Waldis Instabilitie"; "Dunbar's Remonstrance"; "To the King quhen mony Benefices Vakit"; and various poems "To the King." (*Poems of William Dunbar*, ed. Small, S. T. S., II, 104, 205, 208, 218, 220, 236.)

[39] *Buik of the Croniclis of Scotland by William Stewart*, ed. Turnbull, (R. S.), I, xiv.

and commands. Giraldus was reluctant about coming, "quia sicut scolarium vitam prae aliis appreciari sic curialium quoque detertari solet," but at last he came and became a clerk. But after many years of faithful service, with much profit for Henry's plans, there was little profit for Gerald, for he received nothing but empty promises while the king approved of his manner and fidelity and said again and again that if he were not a Welshman and so near kin to the kings of that country, he would reward him well with ecclesiastical dignities and rents and make a great man of him.[40] Too much is not to be made of this in regard to Gerald's literary powers, as the fact that he was a Welshman and knew Welsh had greatest bearing, as we may suppose, with Henry. Wace tells us that Henry II assisted him to compose his historical romance and gave him the prebend of Bayeux,[41] and he presented his translation of Geoffrey of Monmouth to Eleanor, the queen, according to Layamon, and perhaps the benefice was granted in anticipation, as recompense for this dedication. Geoffrey of Monmouth in the same group, was a domestic chaplain in the household of his patron, Robert of Gloucester.

The number of works written by private chaplains is enormous in the Middle Ages, and it is very likely when the lord shows some interest in letters that he selected his clerk with some eye to literature. To name only a few, Jean de Vignay calls himself "vostre petit religieux" in dedicating to Philip of France; Nicole Oresme, translating Aristotle's *Politics* at the request of Charles V of France, calls himself "doyen de vostre église de Rouen, vostre humble chapellain";[42] and in other works he calls himself 'chanoine,' 'trésorier,' or the two combined.[43] Whatever be the accuracy of these statements, he was made bishop of Lesieux by Charles in 1377;[44] whether his advancement was because of his literary work, again we do not know.

[40] *Works*, ed. (R. S.), I, 57.
[41] *Chron. Norm.* Bib. Reg. 4 C 11 quoted by Turner, *History of England During the Middle Ages*, I, 219.
[42] Meunier, *Essai sur la Vie et Les Ouvrages de Nicole Oresme*, 99.
[43] Ibid., 27.
[44] Ibid., 19.

In fact, in no case can we be sure which came first, the chaplaincy or the recognition of authorship. Further, Jehan Corbechon, dedicating his *Des Proprietez des Choses,* translated from Bartholomeus Anglicus, to the same prince, calls himself "son petit humble chapelain."[45] In England the translator of the *Orlogium Sapientiae* addressing his lady calls himself "ʒowre trewe chapeleyne."[46] John Trevisa, who translated much at the command of Thomas Barclay, was his "preest and bedeman,"[47] and according to the rubric to Lydgate's *Complaint for My Lady of Gloucester,* the poem is said to have been written by "a Chapellayne of my lordes of Gloucester humfrey."[48] The matter really all came about because in the Middle Ages there was little place for the learned or literary man outside of the church, and Petrarch, who is perhaps the first to determine upon letters as a career, was confronted by the problem that a man in his day could not live by his pen. At Florence and Bologna men of letters were largely lawyers; elsewhere they were nearly always churchmen, and Petrarch's course was obvious. He rejected the law and took minor orders which extended the hope of preferment in the church without hampering his liberty of action.[49] Even such a scholar as Erasmus in the later time was ready to do a like thing without much thought, and though at first blush this action of Renaissance scholars seems reproachful, it is clear that it was the custom of the age. But it is to be remembered that the church in the Middle Ages was the life of the community and took care of the intellects and the bodies of men as well as their souls. In her was all scholarship and all mental culture, and the place for the literary man and the scholar was within her ranks. The houses of the archbishops of Canterbury and other dignitaries in England, for example, were in the early time a substitute for the undeveloped universities. A notable example is the household of Archbishop Theobald in

---

[45] Ms. Roy. 15 E ii. British Museum, *Catalogue of Western Mss. in the Old Royal and King's Collections,* II.

[46] Ed. Horstmann, *Anglia,* X, (1888), 325.

[47] Epistle to the *Polychronicon,* ed. Babington, (R. S.), I, lxi.

[48] *Anglia,* XXVII, 398.

[49] Hollway-Calthrop, *Petrarch,* 27.

the reign of Stephan. About him were such figures as John of Salisbury, John of Poictiers, Thomas Becket, Roger de Pont Eveque, and Vacarius. Peter of Blois describes the group thus:

"Good master, you blame me for spending my days at court, when I might fructify in the scholastic camps. But this court in which I live is, I assure you a camp of God, none other than the house of God and the gate of heaven. In the house of the lord archbishop are most scholarly men, with whom is found all uprightness of justice, all the caution of providence, every form of learning."[50]

Thomas Becket's household as we hear of it through Herbert of Bosham, one of Becket's clerks, indicates that in his chaplains Thomas had a staff of professors on a small scale, and in the list of the *erudite Sancti Thomae,* Herbert puts such names as John of Salisbury, Robert Foliot, Ralph of Sarr, Lombardus of Piacenza, Reginald the Lombard, Gerard la Pucelle, Hugh of Monant, and Gilbert Glanville.[51]

The matter of caring for persons of literary genius outside the church became a very real problem during the Italian Renaissance, and in this period when medieval patronage was being put to the test and failing to provide, one may gather much information about what must have been general problems. The ideal of the Renaissance scholar was a single court, where there was only one lord to serve, to flatter, and to please, who richly rewarded for the privilege of retaining at his court a famous scholar who was an ornament to any court. At heart, then, the humanist was a monarchist, but in practice he generally served whatever party paid him best.[52] The relation between Petrarch and Robert of Naples was an ideal one; each knew why he honored the other, and the glory of Petrarch's laurel crown was not separable from the glory of the king. In the later practice the humanists were far from so ideal. At bottom the practice of retaining, and so enabling the scholar to do literary work, was not an unsound one, but it was open to abuses. With whom the fault lay that such a relationship became corrupt, cannot be determined. The

---

[50] Quoted by Stubbs, "Literature at the Court of Henry II," *Seventeen Lectures,* 143.
[51] Ibid., 143.
[52] Filelfo and Decembrio served the republic in 1447-50. (Ady, *History of Milan,* 292.)

author undoubtedly became grasping and inconsiderate, and the patron, not content with encouraging works of value, wanted works in his own praise. Whatever else the Renaissance scholar desired, freedom was foremost. Petrarch refused the office of Papal secretary because he was ashamed of it as a servitude,[53] and even the shameless Poggio appears to have hesitated in accepting it, though because he hoped for something better perhaps, for he wrote to Nicollo Niccoli:

"I have less esteem for the pontificate and its members than they imagine, for I wish to be a free man and not a public slave."

Erasmus, who perhaps had more "love letters" than any other humanist, likewise was shy of patronage, and his letters are full of similar statements. Writing to Battus in regard to the Lady de Vere, he says:

"I am as poor as a rat, but, as you know, I must and will be free."[54]

It is to be doubted if the average medieval writer felt the same way; more probably he was only too glad to accept patronage extended to him. From such statements, we see at least the evils to which medieval patronage of letters tended. In the Elizabethan Age these abuses were most apparent, for through printing, a literary profession had definitely grown up, and abject servility was the rule rather than the exception. Oftentimes, when the literary man's services might be of avail at court, he became an orator[55] or secretary. Thus Jehan d'Augin, dedicating his *Des Remedes de l'une et l'autre Fortune,* translated from Petrarch, to Charles, King of France, calls himself, "soñ très humble et très petit subject et orateur";[56] Gower, addressing Henry IV, calls himself "vostre orateur";[57] Lydgate, as we have seen, petitioned to the king for a grant as "your powere and perpetuall oratour," and Thomas Walsingham, dedicating to Henry V his *Ypodigma Neustriae,* is "suorum minimus oratorum."[58]

[53] Voigt, op. cit., II, 4, gives reference to his letters.
[54] Froude, *Life and Letters of Erasmus,* Ep. xxxvi, 56-7.
[55] Just what an 'orator's' duties were is not clear. Perhaps he was a spokesman, special envoy, or kind of professional advocate.
[56] Bruck, *Die Malereien in der Handschriften des Königreiches Sachsen,* 306.
[57] *Works,* ed. Macaulay, I, 335.
[58] Ed. Riley, (R. S.), 3.

During the Renaissance period there was much turmoil of
schisms and councils in the ecclesiastical world, and it was necessary to have the services of practical writers and orators, so that
just at the time when they could be of most help in furthering
knowledge, numerous secretaryships were created by the papacy.
These, of course, were filled with humanists from the times of
Martin V, and especially under Nicholas V was their number
exceedingly large. Petrarch no less than five times was offered
the secretaryship by different popes, and through Petrarch's influence it was offered to Boccaccio, who had strength enough to
refuse.[59] Filelfo continuously begged Nicholas for such an office,
and Poggio, appointed when he was twenty-three, served fifty
years,[60] holding his place under eight popes. He wrote a few
religious works, but on the whole he used his place as curiale as
a literary office. At Avignon, also, there were offices filled by
such humanists as Francesco Bruni and Salutatio. Of course,
there was trade in such positions,[61] and Pius II refilled the un-
necessary secretaryship and other offices with his friends, while
Paul III abolished them altogether, driving out even so famous
a man as Bartolomeo Sacchi da Piadena.[62] It is clear that secretaryships had developed into literary offices purely in the Renaissance period, and it is obvious that the duties would purposely
be slight when the office was conferred by a pope or prince interested in letters.

Private secretaryships held by men of letters also are numerous. In early England, Ingulph obtained favor with William the
Conqueror and became his scribe or secretary and tells us so
great was his authority that he ruled the whole of the duke's
court.[63] In later times Froissart, coming into England, entered
into the service of his countrywoman, Philippa, and became "once
of my said lady the quenes clerkes of her chambre,"[64] and the
same poet on his return to France became "chanon and treasourer

---

[59] Hutton, *Boccaccio*, 201.

[60] Voigt, op. cit., II, 7.

[61] Voigt, op. cit., II, 2 ff. gives prices for which they could be bought.

[62] Ibid., II, 236. Bartolomeo got even by writing a threatening work on the
reformer.

[63] *Ingulph's Chronicle*, tr. Riley, (Bohn Lib.), 14-8.

[64] *Berners' Froissart*, Tudor Translations, VI, 341.

of Chinay." [65]   When a noble was fond of books we find him retaining many secretaries for purposes of adding to his library. An excellent example is Philip le Bon of Burgundy, who retained Guy d'Augers, Daniel Aubert, de Hesdin, Droin Ducert, de Digon, and Jean Mielot for this purpose.[66] Laurent de Premierfait, dedicating his translation of Boccaccio's *De Casibus Virorum Illustrium* to Jehan, duc de Berry et d'Auvergne, calls himself, "clerc et vostre moins digne secretaire et serf de bonne foy," [67] and dedicating the *Decameron* to the same prince is "vostre humble clerc et subject voluntaire." [68]   The translator of Petrarch's *De Remediis utriusque Fortune,* dedicating to King Charles is "son très humble et très petit subject et oratour, Jehan Daudin, indigne chanoyne de la saincte Chapelle Royal a Paris."[69] The translator of *Les Chroniques de Brugues,* working at the commandment of Charles V, calls himself "son petit clerconnet frere Jehan Goulien," [70] and Alain Chartiers, famous for the kiss said to have been bestowed by Margaruite d'Escosse, saluting the lips from which came so many beautiful sentences, was secretary to two monarchs, Charles VI and VII, and in the dedication to his *Quadrilogue Invectif,* he calls himself "humble secretaire de Roy." [71]   The poet Jehan Lemaire de Belges was secretary to Louis de Luxemburg, clerk of finance to Pierre II of Bourbon, and historiographer to the "très noble et plus que très supperil-

---

[65] Ibid., VI, 398.

[66] David Aubert describes the duke and his following in an interesting manner: "Très renommé et très verteux prince Philippe duc de Bourgogne a dès long-temps accoutomé de journellement faire devant lui lirè les anciennes histoires et pour être garni d'une libraire non pareille à toutes autres il à des son jeune eaige en à ses geiges phisieurs translateurs, grands clercs, experts orateurs, historiens et escripvains, et en diverses contrées en gros nombre diligement laborans, tant que aujourd'hui c'est le prince de la chrestienneté, sans réservation aucune, qui est le mieus garni de autentique et riche libraire, come tout se pleinement apparoir: et combien que au regard de sa très excellente magnificence, ce soit petite chose, toutes fois en doit-il être perpetuelle à celle fin que se mirent vertus." (Barrois, *Bibliothèque Protographique, ou libraire des Fils de Roi Jean . . .* (1830), iv.)

[67] Hortis, *Studj sulle Opere Latine del Boccaccio,* 731.

[68] Ibid., 743.

[69] Meunier, *Essai sur le vie . . . . Nicole Oresme,* 133.   The work is usually attributed to Nicole Oresme, in spite of the pseudonym.

[70] Ms. Roy. 19 E vi. British Museum, *Catalogue of Western Mss. in the Old Royal and Kings' Collections,* II.

[71] Tourngeau, *Oeuvres de Alain Chartiers,* 40.

lustre princesse, Madame Marguerite," [72] and Jean Marot was secretary and poet of Anne of Brittany and afterward valet de chambre to Francis I, in which office he was succeeded by his son Clement.

Another convenient way of aiding the learned was to make them the tutors of the royal children, a custom which was followed extensively during the Renaissance when such figures even as Poliziano and Tommaso of Sarzana were intrusted with the care of the children of Lorenzo de' Medici and Rinaldo degli Albizzi respectively. In England the poet Scogan was the tutor of Henry IV's children, Bernard Andreas was tutor of Henry VII's son, Prince Arthur, while Skelton's scholarship caused him to be selected for the future Henry VIII.

The court of James IV in Scotland seems to have been thronged by all sorts of needy persons, and against these Dunbar wrote his bitter but humorous *Remonstrance*, beginning:

> Schir, ȝe haue mony servitouris,
> And officiaris of dyueris curis;

among whom he lists "rethoris and philosophouris," "artists and oratouris," "musicians and menstralis and mirrie singaris," "pryntouris, payntouris, and potingaris," all, he says:

> Quhilk pleisand ar and honorable;
> And to ȝour hienes profitable;
> And richt convenient for to be
> With ȝour high regale majestie;
> Deserving of ȝour grace most ding
> Bayth thank, rewarde and cherissing.

After this, remembering his own need, he launches forth in a diatribe most vitriolic against the rest:

> Fantastik fulis, bayth fals and gredy.[73]

One amusing phase of the custom develops in the Italian Renaissance when retainers at court were many and when places were not always easily found for them. The condottiere Sigismondi Malatesta had numerous scholars about him. For some

[72] Thibaut, *Marguérite d'Austriche et Jehan Lemaire de Belges*, 168.

[73] *Poems of William Dunbar*, ed. Small, S. T. S., II, 220 ff. His piece *Aganis the Solisitaris in Court* also describes those who flocked about James. (Ibid., II, 206.)

he provided liberally, while others were allowed to earn their livelihoods as officers in his army, and Bassinus of Parma, after the true Renaissance fashion, ridicules Porcellio and Tommaso Seneca as needy parasites who must play the soldier in their old age while he himself is enjoying his villa.[74]

It is clear, therefore, from the examples given above that the Middle Ages on the whole believed in allowing literature and scholarship to be a matter for leisure hours, while the practice of it was self-supporting by means of an office given the litterateur. This practice did not, however, exclude more gracious treatment of men of letters, and we find literati frequenting the society of the great much in the manner of courtiers and petty princes, less for honor perhaps, than for material profit which resulted. Genius was not unrecognized and its company was cultivated. Dante, discouraged in his hopes and with his friends, became a wanderer among the courts of northern Italy, where he found honor and protection, which he repaid by diplomatic service, more especially at the court of Can Grande della Scala of Verona and Guido Novello da Polenta at Ravenna. Petrarch was received with utmost cordiality by John of France, to whom he had been sent to congratulate on his release from his English prison, and he was invited to remain, but refused. The Emperor Charles IV, likewise, sent him a golden cup with the earnest invitation to settle at his court, and King Alfonso invited Lionardo d'Arezzo to his court with the stipulation, if it pleased him. Here definitely the literary man is no longer a suitor, but the sought, and when he did agree to settle, that he was cared for munificently goes as a matter of course. Filippo Maria Visconti had the poet Beccadelli at his court with a salary of eight hundred ducats. Machaut, Deschamps, and Froissart resigned themselves with a certain complaisance to the society of princes of the time, and Froissart is pleased to tell us of it, whenever he can, to let us know that he profited by his friendships. So complete are his descriptions and so interesting are the facts that it is well to insert them here as illustrating the medieval practice. He tells us how he went into Scotland in 1365:

[74] Burckhardt, op. cit., I, 320.

"car la bonne roine madame Philippe de Hainnau, roine d'Engleterre, m'escripsi deviers lettres le roi David d'Escoce, liquels fu fils au roi Robert de Brus, qui pour ce temps resgnoit, et au conte de Douglas et à messire Robert de Versi, signeur de Struvelin, et au conte de la Mare, liquel pour l'onnour et amour de la bonne roine desus ditte qui tesmongnoit par ses lettres séelees qu je estoie uns de ses clers et familyers, me requellièrent tout doucement et liement, et fuien la compagnie dou roi, un quartier d'un an."[75]

Contemplating a journey to visit the Earl of Foix, Froissart explains:

"I knewe well, that if I might have that grace to come into his house, and be there at leysar, I coude nat be so well enformed to my purpose in none other place of the worlde; for thyder resorted all maner of knightes and strange squyers, for the great noblenes of the sayd erle. And as I ymagined, so I dyd, and shewed to my redoubted lorde the erle of Bloyes myne entent; and he gave me letters of recommendacions to therle of Foiz."[76]

Such treatment is patronage of a high sort, and his reception by the Earl, and his occupation at his court, show that noblemen to have been a worthy medieval Maecenas:

"And the sayd erle, as soone as he sawe me, he made me good chere, and smylyng sayd howe he knew me, and yet he never sawe me before, but he had often herde spekyng of me; and so reteyned me in his house to my great ease, with the helpe of the letters of credence that I had brought unto hym, so that I might tarry there at my pleasure."

From him Froissart got much news, which the Duke graciously gave,

"seyenge to me howe thystorie that I had begon shulde hereafter be more praysed than any other, and the reason he sayd why, was this: howe that l. yere passed there had been done more marveylous dedes of armes in the worlde than in thre hundred yere before that."[77]

With him, Froissart tells us:

"I was more than xii. wekes, and my horse well entreated. The acquayntaunce of hym and of me was, bycause I had brought with me a boke, whiche I made at the contemplacion of Winslance of Boesme, duke of Luzenbourge and of Brabant, whiche boke was called the Melyader,

[75] *Chroniques de Jehan Froissart,* (Vatican MS.) ed. M. le Baron Kervyn de Lettenhove, *Académie Royale de Belgique,* Brussels, 1863, I, 84.
[76] *Berners' Froissart,* (Tudor Translations), IV, 86.
[77] Ibid., IV, 87.

conteyninge all the songes, baladdes, rundeaux and vyrelayes wiche the
gentyll duke had made in his tyme, whiche by ymagynacion I had gadered
toguyder, whiche boke the erle of Foiz was gladde to se. And every night
after supper I reed theron to hym, and while I reed there was none durst
speke any worde, bycause he wolde I shulde be well understande, wherin
he tooke great solace."[78]

Such is the picture of many a medieval court on long winter
evenings, and when Froissart says of Gaston that "he was large
and courteous of gyftes" we may assume that he spoke from
personal experience. Froissart tells us about all of his friends;
that "whan I came to Parys I founde there the gentyll lorde of
Coucy, a good lorde of mine . . . . whiche lorde made me good
chere,"[79] and he attributes the completeness and accuracy of his
Chronicle alone to his acquaintances:

"for God give me the grace to have the laysure to se in my dayes, and
to have the acquayntaunce of all the hyghe and myghty prynces and lordes
as well in Fraunce as in Englande. For in the yere of our Lorde God
a M. iii.C. iiii. score and x. I had laboured xxvii. yeres, a man beynge in
strength, and wel reteyned in every coost I was, for after my yonge dayes
I was in the kynge of Englandes courte v. yeres with the quene, and also
I was welcome to kynge John of Fraunce and to kynge Charles his sone,
myght well lerne many thinges; and surely it was always my chefe
ymagynacyon and pleasure to enquyre and to retayne it by writynge."[80]

Christine de Pisan likewise was in demand, and had tempting
offers to attach herself to various courts, among them that of
Henry IV of England, and Gian Galleazo Visconti of Milan, who
was most importunate, but she refused them all.[81] In later times,
Skelton wrote his *Garlande of Laurell* while living at the castle
of the Countess of Surrey.[82]

A promising youth often was fostered and trained by a nobleman of the neighborhood while young. Among those whose
names are familiar in the literary world are Henry of Huntingdon, who was trained in the household of Robert Bloet, Bishop
of Lincoln, and afterward became his Archdeacon. Richard

---

[78] Ibid., IV, 136.
[79] Ibid., V, 273.
[80] Ibid., IV, 478.
[81] Kemp-Welsh, *Of Six Medieval Women*, 123.
[82] *Cambridge History of English Literature*, III, 69.

Rolle of Hampole, the noted medieval mystic, was sent to Oxford by Thomas de Neville, afterward Archdeacon of Durham, and after he became a hermit he lived on the estate of Sir John Dalton, who supplied him with clothing and the necessaries of life. At the death of Dalton and his wife, however, Rolle wandered and became the advisor and instructor of the younger clergy, and at the same time began to write.[83]   Finally, George Ashby tells us in *A Prisoner's Reflections A. D. 1463:*

> I gan to remembre and revolue in mynde
> My bryngyng vp from chyldhod hedyrto,
> In the hyghest court that I coude fynd,
> With the king, quene, and theyr vncle also,
> The duk of Gloucestre, god hem rest do,
> With whome I haue be cherysshyd ryght well,
> In all that was to me nedefull euery dell.[84]

[83] Wells, *A Manual of the Writings in Middle English*, 444.
[84] ll. 57 ff. *George Ashby's Poems*, ed. Bateson, E. E. T. S., 3.

XI

HINTS FOR PATRONAGE AND THE EPISTLE MENDICANT

Just as the troubadour had the *sirvente* to bring his patron to terms, so the later medieval author wielded with no uncertain hand the weapon of satire and lampoon. Retention or reward of some kind was generally an expected thing in return for literary favors, and when it was not forth-coming the grumblings of the slighted author were not always slight. Even Dante heaves a sigh as he represents his ancestor Cacciaguida in Paradise telling him:

> Thou shalt make proof what salt and bitter fare
> Is bread of others, and what toils attend
> The going up and down another's stair,[1]

and in general, if the medieval author felt dissatisfaction he said so. If we bear in mind the abject humility and self-depreciation of the dedication and like forms as we view the complaint and the epistle mendicant, we feel that the author of the Middle Ages decidedly underestimated his "rude simplicity" and his power of using "eloquent terms subtle and couert." Boccaccio, visting Naples at the request of the wealthy Acciarolli, refused to compile his biography, and in consequence was treated shabbily, whereupon the indignant writer assailed him with all manner of satire and insult.[2] Tasso had a similar experience, and in more modern times, the incident is reminiscent of the more dignified coolness of Johnson to Chesterfield. Renaissance Italy, however, capable of anything, gives us a most notable example which is illustrative of what disappointed scholars were capable of. When the humanist Aeneas Silvius, became Pope Pius II there was

---

[1] *Paradiso*, XVII, tr. Anderson, (1921), 374.
[2] Cotterill, *Italy from Dante to Tasso*, 172.

much jubilation among scholars, to whom it seemed that a golden age had come again. Aeneas was himself a writer and perhaps more interested in own writings than in those of other humanists, but before he had the opportunity to manifest his patronage an unfortunate story got out on him, which made it impossible for Pius ever to be a patron. One day, as Ammanati tells the story, shortly after his election, Pius and two of his humanist friends, Ammanati and Campano, took boat and rowed to a monastery, and during the trip, Ammanati began reading a number of congratulatory, flattering verses that needy poets had sent to the new pope soliciting his favor. Stimulated by the verses the friends began improvising, and Campano reeled off a couplet to the effect that only those should be rewarded who had not asked; he had not asked, therefore he deserved a reward. Pius replied:

> If gifts, Campano, should not then be sought,
> You pray the deaf, *your* gain will be but nought.

Presently he added: "Here is something for your poets:"

> If poets wish but verse for verse to gain,
> Learn that we'll mend, but will not buy their strain.

Ammanati took the epigram up and altered it:

> Rhymsters who reel off their numbers for gold
> In dealing with Pius, will find themselves sold.

But Pius would not allow this to stand, and he at once varied the couplet so that it read:

> Learn rhymsters, who offer your verses for gold,
> From Pius great gifts you may hope to behold.

The least complimentary of these epigrams, "We'll mend, but will not buy your strain," unfortunately got abroad, and the clamor among scholars was great. Many uncomplimentary epigrammatic replies were circulated. The scholars at Rome became the pope's most bitter enemies. The worst of these was Filelfo; though Pius gave him a pension of two hundred ducats a year, he rewarded his benefactor with anonymous libels and attributed all the shameful vices of antiquity to him.[3] When Pius died,

---

[3] Boulting, *Aeneas Silvius*, 281 ff.

Filelfo composed a poem of jubilation: *Gratulatio de Morte Pii II Ecclessiae Romanae Pontificis*, which is a most outrageous piece of scandal.[4]

This kind of thing is not absent in England, and a notable example ocurs in a most interesting connection. Walter of Peterborough, a monk of Revesby Abbey in Lincolnshire, wrote an account of Edward's Spanish campaign of 1367, with a most fulsome panegyric on John of Gaunt. Knowing the Duke's treasurer, he hoped by his influence to be properly rewarded. But he was sadly disappointed and went empty away to regret having cast his pearls before swine, and to record his feelings at the end of his work.[5] It is of interest to us as the only connection of John of Gaunt with literature,[6] excluding the assumed relation with Chaucer, and to say the least, John did not acquit himself well.[7]

The examples just cited are of course extreme ones, for the medieval author generally contented himself with a mild com-

---

[4] Gaudeat orator, Musae, gaudete Latinae;
    Sustulit e medio quod ipse Pium
Ut bene consuluit doctis Deus omnibus aeque,
    Quos Pius in cunctos se tulit usque gravem.
Nunc sperare licet. Nobis deus optime Quintum
    Reddito Nicolem, Eugeniumve patrem.
    (Rosmini, *Vita de Francesco Filelfo*, (Milan, 1807), II, 320-1.)
[6] Wright, *Political Poems and Songs*, (R. S.), I, 97-122.
    Metra malas grates fero pro vobis ego vates,
    Inter primates sic modo, musa, scates.
Laudes sperabum, seu praemia danda putabam;
    Frustra sudabam, vos metra quando dabam.
Sed margarita nunquam fuit ulla cupita,
    Porco plus placita stercora dentur ita.
Ergo, libelle, vale; nomen cape non libro quale
    Munerat igne male te cocus absque sale.
[6] Nicholas of Lynne compiled a calendar "ad peticionem et complacenciam illustrissimi principes domini Johannis, regis Castelle et Legionibus, et ducis Lancastrie," (Moore, "Note of the Astrolabe," *M. P.*, X, 303 ff.) but this is hardly evidence of patronage of poetry; a calendar is hardly a literary work. Hoccleve eulogizes John in his *Regimen of Princes*, but for his prowess, and not for his connection with literature. Further evidence of John's connection with learning is the fact that the college of Corpus Christi and St. Mary, Cambridge, is described as "of the patronage of the king's uncle, John, Duke of Lancaster," May 1382. (*Calendar of Patent Rolls 1381-5*, 143.)

[7] Walter's verses are obviously pretty bad, but there is hardly warrant to assume with Armitage-Smith, (*John of Gaunt*, 413,) that Gaunt rejected them because Chaucer's were more to his taste.

plaint or was silent. Some of the more general of these poems of complaint have been dwelt upon as they have arisen; writers from Wace and Giraldus Cambrensis down have expressed their dissatisfaction with conditions. Most notable has been the commonplace expressed by Wace, Higdon, Jehan de Waurin, Gower, Lydgate, and others, of how much better times were formerly and how bad things have become at present. Hoccleve in later times says sadly:

> ffor if þat sothe schal confesse,
> The lak of olde mennes cherisshynge
> Is cause and ground eke of myn heuynesse,[8]

and Alexander Barclay devoting his fourth eclogue to a treatment "of the behauior of Riche men agaynst Poetes," has Minalcas, his needy shepherd poet, say:

> After inditing then gladly would I drinke,
> To reache me the cup no man doth care ne thinke:
> And ofte some fooles voyde of discretion
> Me and my matters have in derision,

adding also his word about courts and the numerous parasites there:

> To whom is vertue aduerce and odious.
> These be good Poetes forth of all courtes chase.[9]

On at least one occasion we know of an author's friend making his moan. John Shirley, famous for his manuscript collections, probably knew Lydgate, and of him he writes in a rhyming table of contents to Ms. Add. 16165:

> Lydgate þe munk cloþed in blacke—
> In his makyng. þe is no lacke—
> And thankeþe Daun Iohan for his peyne,
> Þat to plese gentyls is ryght feyne,
> Boþe with his laboure, and his goode:
> God wolde, of nobles he had ful his hoode.[10]

[8] *Regiment of Princes*, ll. 792 ff.

[9] *Certayne Eglogues*, ed. Spencer Society, XXXIX, 29 ff. Barclay's source, of course, in this eclogue is the fifth eclogue of Baptista Mantuanus, (ed. W. P. Mustard, (1911), 85.) where the theme is the same. A similar complaint is found in the October Eclogue of Spenser's *Shepheardes Calendar*.

[10] Quoted by Hammond, *Englische Studien*, XLIII, 12.

Again in a similar table of contents to Ms. Add. 29,729, Shirley semi-seriously mentions him:

> Yet for all his much konnynge
> Which were gret tresor to a kynge
> I mean this lidgate/munke dame John
> His nobles bene spent/I leve ychon
> And eke his shylinges nyghe by
> His thred bare coule/wolle not ly
> Ellas ye lordis/why nill ye se
> And reward his pouerte.[11]

It is clear that these complaints are in effect rather obvious hints for patronage, though often they are only broad, as many poems on princely liberality indicate, and Olivier Basselin assures his hearers:

> Si voulez que je cause et presche
> Et parle latin proprement,
> Tenez ma bouche tousjours fraische,
> De bon vin l'arrosant souvent;
> Car je vous dy certainment:
>   Quand j'ay seiche la bouche,
> Je n'ay pas plus d'entendement
>   Ni d'esprit, qu'une souche.[12]

In England there is an amusing early example in the *Owl and the Nightingale*. The debate is about over, and the two contestants have decided to take their troubles to "Maister Nichole þat is wis" through whose judgments "hit is þe betere in-to Scotlande." On one thing the owl and nightingale are agreed; he hasn't his desert:

> 'Certes' cwaþ þe hule, 'þat is soð:
> þeos riche men wel muche mis-doð,
> þat leteþ þane god man,
> þat of so feole þinge con,
> an ʒiueth rente wel misliche,
> an of him leteþ wel liht-liche,
> Wiðð heore cunne heo beoþ mildre.
> an ʒeueþ rente litle childre:
> swo heore wit thi demþ adwole.
> þat euer abid Maistre Nichole.[13]

[11] Ibid., 12.

[12] *Vaux-de-Vire d'Olivier Basselin et de Jean de Houx*, ed. "J. L. Jacob," (Paul Lacroix), 1858, 22.

[13] ll. 1769 ff. ed. Wells. (Belles Lettres Series.)

If Nicholas de Guildford is assumed to be the author, the passage
has amusing significance.

One of the cleverest and most interesting hints in all medieval
literature is to be found in Hoccleve's *Regement of Princes*.
In it the whole drama of literary mendicancy is laid before us.
More than a third of the poem, seventy-three pages out of a
hundred and ninety-seven, is taken up with Hoccleve's pre-
liminary talk about himself with the beggar he meets, and in it
the poet thinks aloud and develops his plan. For twenty-four
years he has been in the Privy Seal office, and Henry IV gave
him an annuity of twenty marks.

> But paiement is hard to gete adayes;
> And þat me put in many foule affrayes. (ll. 825 ff.)

Matters will get worse as time goes on; when he's old he won't
get it at all, and when he can't work, he'll lose all his friends and
suffer. Writing is such hard work, scribes can't sing or talk as
other workmen do, but must keep to the sheepskin and get pains
all over and spoil their eyes. He never was clever, he says, but
his wits were good so long as he had cash, but with a steadily
decreasing income, his wits grow dull. But, asks the beggar,
have he and his fellows no one to look to:

> ȝis, fadir, ȝis! þer is on clept 'nemo';
> He helpeþ hem; by hym ben þei chericëd:
> Nere he, þey weren porely cheuyced;
> He hem auanceth; he ful hir frende is;
> Sauf only hym, þey han but fewe frendes. (ll. 1487 ff.)

Can't some lord help him, asks the beggar:

> What, fadir? what? lordës han for to done
> So mych for hem-self, þat my mateere
> Oute of hir mynde slippith away soone.
> The world is naght swich now, my fadir deere,
> As ye han seene; farwel, frendely maneere! (ll. 1793 ff.)

In short, there's nothing for poor Hoccleve to do, "or begge, or
stele, or sterue." He's ashamed to beg, and though the beggar
advises:

> Compleyne vnto his excellent noblesse,
> As I haue herd þe vn-to me compleyne: (ll. 1849 ff.)

he doesn't like to be so undignified, even though the prince is his "good gracious lord." Besides, a complaint will help little; he'll get nothing this year, but he'll follow advice and write a book worthy of any prince:

> Writtë to hym a goodly tale or two,
>> On which he may desporten hym by nyghte,
>> And his fre gracë schal vp-on þe lighte.
>
> Sharpë thi penne, and write on lustily;
>> Lat se, my sonë, make it fresh and gay. . . .
>
> But of a thyng be wel waar in al wise,
>> On flaterië þat þou þe nat founde. (ll. 1902 ff.)
>
> Looke if þou fyndë canst any tretice
>> Groundid in his estates holsumnesse;
>> Swych thing translate, and vnto his hynesse,
>>> As humbly as þat þou canst, present;
>>> Do thus my sone", "fadir, I assent." (ll. 1949 ff.)

And though Hoccleve speaks and writes poorly, he means well, and so begins his *Regement:*

> Hyë and noblë princë excellent,
>> My lord the prince, o my lord gracious,
>> I, humble seruaunt and obedient
> Vnto your éstate hye & glorious,
> Of whiche I am full tender & full ielous,
>> Me recommaunde vnto your worthynesse,
>> With hert entier, and spirite of mekenesse. (ll. 2017 ff.)

When he talks of princely liberality, however, Hoccleve can't restrain himself; not content with his shameless prologue, he begins again. He can't get on unless Henry helps him:

> My yearly guerdoun, myn annuite,
> That was me graunted for my long labóur,
> Is al behynde, I may naght payëd be,
> Whiche causeth me to lyuen in languor.
> O liberal prince! ensample of honour!
> Vnto your gracë lyke it to promoote
> Mi poore estat, and to my woo beth boote! (ll. 4383 ff.)

"I love you," says Hoccleve, "look"!:

> In al my book ye schul naght see ne fynde,
> That I youre dedës lakke, or hem despreise;

> But for I wolde þat ye hadde in mynde
> Swich thing as your renoun myghte vp areyse,
> I write as my symple conceyt may peyse;
> And trustith wel, al þat my penne seith,
> Proceedeth of good herte and trewe, in feith.   (ll. 4397 ff.)

And Prince Henry, if you give a man a pension, don't stop payment! (ll. 4789 ff.)

Getting that annuity paid seems to have been a very real problem to our poet for he complains again and again about it in his verse. *La Male Regle de T. Hoccleue* is just another complaint.

> My body and purse been at oones seeke,

he says, addressing this time the Lord Fourneval, the treasurer.[14] So also is the *Balade to My Lord the Chancellor, the Balade & Chanseon . . . a mon Meistre H. Somer, quant il estoit Souztrèsorer,* and the *Item au Roy,* written for himself and two companions of his office. He begs Henry not to stop his bounty, for:

> gold hath us in swich hate,
> þat of his loue and cheerte the scantnesse
> Wole arte vs three to trotte vn-to Newgate.[15]

Hoccleve's *Complaint* has already been noted. This piece was prefixed to several tales, written as he says, to please Duke Humphrey, but really addressed to Lady Westmorland. In this collection is a treatise, *How to Learn to Die,* which has a further history. Another manuscript of the work exists, in which the piece is prefixed by three amusing roundels:

> "Cy ensuent trois chauncheons/lune compleynante a la Dame monoie/& lautre la response dele a cellui qui se compleynt & la tierce/la commendacion de ma dame."

In the first Hoccleve develops the theme:

> Well may I pleyne on yow, Lady moneye,
> þat in the prison of your sharp scantnesse
> Souffren me bathe in wo and heuynesse,
> And deynen nat of socour me purueye.

When he had the key to her prison, did he keep her straight?

---

[14] *Hoccleve's Minor Poems,* ed. Furnivall, E. E. T. S., I, 25 ff.
[15] Ibid., I, 62. The *Balade to my Maister Carpenter,* mentioned in another connection, is likewise a plea for aid to keep him out of jail.

No! God witness; he let her escape and she now lets him die!
Come back, and bring comfort on this Christmas-tide. But Lady
Money is a bit perverse:

> Hoccleue/I wole/it to thee knowen be,
> I, lady moneie/of the world goddesse,
> Þat haue al thyng vndir my buxumnesse,
> Nat sette by thy pleynte risshes three.

When she was in Hoccleve's slippery grasp he showed her no
kindness; she grew emaciated and worn out by his largess.
Since great lords obey her:

> Sholde I me dreede/of thy poore symplesse?
> My golden heed akith for thy lewdnesse.
> Go, poore wrecche/who settith aght by thee?

But though he is treated scornfully, Hoccleve cannot help praising her. Her golden forehead is full narrow and small, her
brows are like to "dym reed coral," her eyes are jet,

> Hir bowgy cheekes been as softe as clay,
> with large Jowes and substancial.

She has a pentice nose, her mouth is nothing scant, her lips are
grey, and her chin may not be seen at all. Finally, her comely
body is shaped like a foot-ball:

> And she syngith/ful lyk a papeJay.

Then, adds the poet:

> After our song/our mirthe & our gladnesse
> Heer folwith a lessoun of heuynesse:

and he begins the tract *How to Learn to Die*.[16] Doubtless this
version with its prologue was sent to one or more moneyful lords
who Hoccleve hoped might restore to him the capricious Lady
Money.

Alexander Barclay in the *Egloge* quoted above follows another
ingenious device. His theme is the ill-treatment of needy poets
by those who are rich and powerful, and he introduces into this
context a lament, the *Towre of Vertue and Honour*, for Sir
Edward Howard, son of Thomas, Duke of Norfolk, who met

---

[16] For these poems from the Ashburnham Ms. of Hoccleve's work I am indebted to
Sir I. Gollancz, who is editing them for the Early English Text Society.

his death off Brest in April 1513 as Lord High Admiral in the war with France. Minalcas, the poor shepherd, sings this poem, and after it is finished, Codrus, the wealthy one, properly touched, exclaims:

> Minalcas, I sweare by holy Peters cope
> If all thing fortune as I haue trust and hope,
> If happy winde blowe I shall or it be longe
> Comfort thy sorowe and well rewarde thy songe.[17]

That this matter of literary mendicancy is an old device goes without question. Seldom was the medieval poet ashamed to beg, even if he was ashamed to starve, and though there is little that is poetic in the word 'money,' upon it the Muses seemed very easily inspired. In fact, verse based on the principle "ask and it shall be given to you" has been a recognized form in all ages. We have had occasion to note it among the ancients and among the Arabs and Persians; it served the purpose of the troubadour, trouvère, and minnesinger, and of the minstrel, and it had a definite place in Byzantine literature.[18] It was quite natural then for other medieval poets to take up this form. Among the songs of the goliardi of the twelfth century are numerous examples of its use by needy students, some of which are most amusing. In one, the first three or four strophes are of a religious character on the general theme of doomsday, good works, and the prettiest of virtues—generosity. Then: all this, says the poet, his audience knows already. He is satisfied of that; but as to his desires, he's poor, but not bad, and his single fault is that he gladly receives a present and doesn't deny himself more. The beautiful cloak he wears he can't sell—it's the present of the most generous of bishops; he'd rather go hungry. Therefore, won't his audience please make him a gift; he takes anything:

> aurum, vestes, et his similia,

let each one bestow as he sees fit.[19] Another poem, directed to

---

[17] Op. cit., 38.

[18] *Dietrich*, K, *Geschichte der Byzantinischen und Neugriechischen Litteratur*, (1902), 53, gives examples.

[19] I. "Lingua balbus, hebes ingenio," Grimm, *Geschichte des Mittelalters*, 49. ff., and Spiegel, *Vaganten*, 14.

Reinold of Cologne, complains of being crowded in the performance of literary work undertaken for the chancellor. The writer
says that anything his patron wants he will compose, only he
must have time. What Homer and Virgil couldn't do fully in
five years, he's expected to turn out in a short week. One must
await the right inspiration to write poetry—true, sometimes the
verses flow easily from his pen, but such inspiration doesn't last
long and he can't work because he comes from a knightly class.
He's ashamed to beg or steal; he can only lament. Luckily
German lords have a feeling for poetry, but even these protect
uncultured jugglers instead of bestowing their gifts upon poets
such as himself. May they stick to their knights! The bishops
belong to poets. Cursed be the avarice of Italian prelates, but
praised be the generosity of the German, and especially of the
archbishop-elect of Cologne! He is our poet's only hope; his last
gift was well used, won't he continue his patronage? Heaven
send him a long row of issue, and our poet a well-advised mouth
to sing of them![20] Another of the most shameless sort is the
one beginning:

> Dum redeo didica populi tocius ab ore,
> quod tua sistribuas solo pietatio amore;
> per mundum redoles tanto bonitatis odore,
> *cesaris* adjutor, speciali dignus honore.[21]

Of greatest interest, however, is the begging petition from the
Carmina Burana, translated by Symonds in *Wine, Women, and
Song.* It seems to have been a kind of circular letter, for the
suppliant, after complaining not for himself, but for learning:

> Literature and knowledge, I
> Fain would still be earning,
> Were it not that want of pelf
> Makes me cease from learning,

addresses his plea to:

> Oh, thou pride of N—
> By thy worth I pray thee
> Give the suppliant help in need,
> Heaven will sure repay thee.

[20] IV. "Archicancellarie, vir discrete mentis," Grimm, op. cit., 54; Spiegel, op.
cit., 18.
[21] IV, (b). Grimm, 62, Spiegel, 21.

The N—— of the piece may possibly signify 'nomen,' where the name of any town or castle may be inserted for the afflicted one's need.[22] There are others in this same delightful shameless vein,[23] but enough has been said of them for our purpose.

Turning to the use of such verse in a literary connection, we find a pleasing example in Rutebeuf's *Lay of Poverty:*

> Je ne sai par où je coumance
> Tant ai de matyère abondance
> Por parlier de ma povertei.
> Por Dieu vos pris, frans Rois de France, (Louis IX.)
> Que me doneiz queilque cheevance.

He suffers greatly; he lacks food, he has no bed, he has a cold, and he is maltreated; in short:

> N'a si povre jusqu' a Senliz.[24]

More violent is the complaint of Colin Muset to his patron, beginning:

> Sir Cuens, j'ai viele
> Devant vos en vostre ostel;
> Si me m'aves riens done
> Ne mes judges aquites.
>   C'est vilanie,
> Foi que doi sainte Marie!
> Ensi ne vos sieve je mie:
>   M'aumoniere est mal garnie,
> Et ma borse mal fussie. . . .[25]

Walter von der Vogelweide begs Frederick most delightfully for a fief, and poetically thanks him for it.[26] In a similar vein Neidart von Reuenthal begs his lord Frederick for a tiny house.[27]

---

[22] *Carmina Burana,* xci. Bibliothek des Litt. Vereins. in Stuttgart, XVI, 50 ff. Symonds, *Wine, Women, and Song,* (King's Classics), 59 ff.

[23] The Digby Ms. version of a poem printed by Wright, *Latin Poems attributed to Walter Mapes,* Camden Society, 152, has an appeal to a patron, Fulmarus. It is printed by Wright, *Anecdota Literaria,* 39. Another is Carmina cxciv, op. cit., 74.

[24] 'C'est de la Povertei Rutebeuf,' *Oeuvres Complètes de Rutebeuf,* ed. Jubinal, (1874), I, 1 ff.

[25] Tarbé, *Chansonniers de Champagne aux XIIe et XIIIe Siècles,* 78 ff. One should not miss Synge's delightful translation of this poem which ends: "It's a full purse, I tell you, makes a man lord in his own house." *Works,* II, 248.

[26] Lachmann, *Gedichte Walther von der Vogelweide,* 28, and 31. Other mendicant complaints of Walther's are to be found on pp. 19, 20, 26, 27, 28, and 84, and in Schroeter, *Gedichte Walther's von der Vogelweide,* 144-5 and 148.

[27] Nicholson, *Old German Love Songs,* 107.

In almost all of the poems of this nature, the writer makes clear
how humiliated he is, but necessity forces him; and sometimes,
presenting himself at the court of a king, the poet comes not to
beg—oh, dear me, no; that is unthinkable—but to borrow. Thus
François Villon presented himself to Jean II, Duke of Bourbon,
who kept his court at Moulins. On one occasion he had been
given six écus, but this was soon spent, so he applies again:

> Le mein seigneur & prince redoubté
> Fleuron de Lys, royalle geniture,
> Françoys villon, que trauail a dompté
> A coups orbes, par force de bature,
> Vous suppliè par ceste humble escripture,
> Cui lui faciez quelque gracieux prest.
> De s'obliger en toutes cours est prest:
> Si ne doubtez que bien ne vous contente
> Sans y auoir dommaige n'interest,
> Vous n'y perdrez seulement que l'attente.

He swears that he has had a fee from no one else and that the
six écus were all spent on food and not on frivolity. All—everything—will be repaid:

> Car, si du glan recontre en la forest
> D'entour Patay, & chastaignes ont vente,
> Paié serez sans delay ny arrest:
> Vous n'y perdrez seulement que l'attente.

Such is the tenor of his plaint, and his balade is sent off with:

> Allez, lettres, faictes vng sault,
> Combien que n'ayez pié ne langue;
> Remonstrez en vostre harangue
> Que faulte d'argent si m'assault.[28]

Before this both Eustache Deschamps[29] and Guillaume de
Machaut[30] had availed themselves of this means of getting funds,

---

[28] *Oeuvres Complètes de François Villon,* ed. Longuon, 129. The poem is well
translated by Stacpole, *François Villon: His Life and Times,* 89.

[29] *Requête aux dux d'Anjou et de Bourgoigne, 1380; Oeuvres inedites d'Eustache
Deschamps,* ed. Tarbé, (1849), 42, and *Plainte d'Eustache Deschamps 1381;* Ibid., I, 55.

[30] '*Complainte, Guillaume de Machaut': Poesies Lyriques,* ed. Chicmaref, I, 262.

> Et aussi qui vous me deistes,
> Quant secretaire me feistes,
> Com nobles princes et entiers
> Que vous m'aideriés voluntiers,
> Se j'avoie nécessité.

and in England Geoffrey Chaucer, whether pleading for patronage or only his wages as an official, represented himself :

shave as nye as any frere,

in his *Complaint to his Empty Purse.*[31]   Both Hoccleve and
Lydgate beg consistently, and in the case of Lydgate, there is
an example definitely connected with literature, the result of which
we are able to follow.   As has been noted, Lydgate translated
his *Falls of Princes* for Humphrey of Gloucester, and among his
poems is preserved a "litera Dompni Johannis Lydgate Monachi
monasteriis Sancti Edmundi de Bury, missa ad ducem Gloucestrie
in tempore translaciones libri Bochasii Pro oportunitate Pecunie."
It is an elaborately metaphorical sportive little poem beginning :

Riht myghty prynce | and it be your wille
Condescende | leiser for to take
To seen the content | of this litil bille
Whiche whan I wrot | myn hand I felte quake
Tokne of mornyng | weryd clothis blake
Cause my purs | was falle in gret rerage
Lynyng outward | his guttys | were out shake
Oonly for lak | of plate | and of coignage.

I souhte leechys | for a restoratiff
To whom I found | no consolacioun
Appotecaryes | for a confortatif
Dragge nor *dya* | was tournyd vp so doun
A *laxitif* | did hym so gret outrage
Made him slendre | by a consumpcion
Oonly for lak | of plate | and of coignage.

"Ship" was there none, he says; there was no token sent down
from the tower; Sol and Luna were both in eclipse; and no
cross was evident,

But ye my *lord* | moy al our soor recure
With a receyt | of plate and of coignage,

[31] Skeat (I. 562) suggests that Chaucer in his *Compleint* may have had in mind
those of Deschamps and Machaut, but the influence, if any, may be looked upon as
unimportant.   A convention, such as the complaint device, was well known to all ages
where literature flourished under patronage and these conventions were common alike
to the work of Chaucer and that of his French contemporaries.   In fact, Chaucer's
poem is more dignified than those of the Frenchmen.

for

> Gold is a cordial | gladdest confecciou*n*
> Ageyn Etiques | of oold co*n*sumpciou*n*.

Then Lydgate catches himself and unbraids his poem:

> O seely bille | why are thu nat ashamyd
> So malapertly | to shewe out thy constreynt.[32]

How could anyone, especially the liberal Duke Humphrey, refuse a plea like that? Humphrey we know was liberal on this occasion, and in the prologue to Book III of the *Falls of Princes* the refreshed Lydgate sings a song of joy and thanksgiving in praise of the duke. Ignorance and indisposition assailed him, and coupled with this was his light purse,

> fful pale of chere astonid in my looke
> My hand gan tremble my pen I felt quake
> That disespeirid I had almost forsake
> So grete a labour dreedfull & importable,
> It to parfourme I fond mi silff so on able.
>
> Twene the residewe of this grete iornee
> And litil part ther of that was begun*n*e
> I stood checkmaate for feere whan I gan see
> In mi weie how litil I had run*n*e.

But when he was about to abandon the task, he says, Hope and Trust returned to him and bade him rely on his "lordis freedom and bounteous largesse":

> And thus releuid bi the goodlihede
> And throuh the noblesse of this moost knihtli man
> Al mistis clerid of dispeir and dreede
> Trust hope and feith in to my hert ran
> And on my labour anon forth I gan.[33]

Without doubt the *Falls of Princes* cost Humphrey a pretty penny before it was finished, and Lydgate added an envoy to his work dealing with the ideal conditions for composing literary

---

[32] This version of Ms. Harley 2255 is reprinted by Hammond, *Anglia*, XXXVIII, 125. A variant version, containing the latin rubric quoted above, is to be found in Halliwell, *A Selection from the Minor Poems of Lydgate*, Percy Society, II, 49.

[33] Ms. Roy. 18 D. v., quoted by Hammond, *Anglia*, XXXVIII, 129.

work in a "Chapitle of þe Gouernance of Poetis," ending with another plaint:

To descryue | the dispocioun
Of al Poetis | be old ordynaunce
Thei shold be quiett fro worldli mocioun
And it sequestre | out of ther remembraunce
ffare compotent | vnto ther sustenaunce
Drynk wyn [among] | to quile ther diligence
Support of princes to fynde hem her dispence.

Courage dulleth, thinks Lydgate, when there is want of the necessities of life and of cash in coffers:

What mihte beste | ther sorwes recompense
Support of princes | to fynde hem her dispence.

The lords of the earth have dominion, churchmen have gold in abundance, knights have renown, merchants their gain:

But poetis | god sheeld hem fro myschaunce
May now adaies | for ther Jmpotence
ffor lakke of support | go begge ther dispence.

Dante, Virgil, Petrarch, and even Chaucer "fond vertuous suffisance" through support of princes. But note, Humphrey:

O well of fredom | enclyne thyn eris down
And of thi bounte | yiue sum attendaunce
To heere of merci | my supplicacioun
In releuyng | of myn hertis greuaunce
Oppressid with pourert | & han no purueiaunce
Sauff to resorte | to this magnificence
Onli be support | to fynde me my dispence.[84]

In the Renaissance such complaints became common things and such humanists as Poggio, Filelfo, and even Erasmus did not hesitate to state their needs frankly. Of these Filelfo is the most shameless. Great genius, which Filelfo undoubtedly had, he felt should make great claims upon life, and he lived in luxury while he begged consistently. At one time when he was especially clamorous in his mendicancy and his complaints against poverty, he had six horses, lived brilliantly, and dressed in costly garments. He complains that poverty oppresses him, his posses-

[84] Ms. Bodley, 263, Ibid., 133 ff.

sions are pawned, his daughter has no dowery, and he threatens to leave Milan and to go where he will be appreciated, even to the Turks, because in Italy virtue and worth are not honored.[35] Whenever he needed money to outfit a daughter, wished to take a journey, or had to expend a sum of money, he begged, or rather tried to borrow, promising to repay in verses, thus exchanging immortality for paltry gold. His letters abound in impudent demands, lamentable outcries against poverty, and violent threats if his salary remained in arrears. In short, so bad was he that even a contemporary, in Rennaissance Italy, be it remembered, said:

> "He is calumnious, envious, vain, and so greedy of gold that he metes out praise or blame according to the gifts he gets."

Coming to England at the invitation of Henry Beaufort, Bishop of Winchester, Poggio was sadly disappointed in his reception. The country and the people displeased him; there were no classical manuscripts to be found and a search of the principal libraries yielded only one book that was worth saving. And Beaufort gave him nothing, while Poggio began earnest importunity. "At length," says he, "the mountain labored and produced a mouse," for Beaufort gave him a benefice, the nominal value of which was only 120 florins, and Poggio, disgusted, returned to Italy.[36]

But the humanists were not all so bad as Filelfo and Poggio, Even Petrarch was not above subterfuge to gain his laurel crown,[37] but though a shameless beggar at times, Erasmus perhaps represents the most ideal of the Renaissance scholars. In his letters to his "dear Battus" he is the flatterer, thoroughly conscious of himself and willing to go pretty far in his beslavering to get what he wants, if he can get it as he wants it. Dignity

---

[35] Voigt, op. cit., I, 527.

[36] Shepherd, *Life of Poggio Bracciolini*, 123.

[37] In a letter to Dionesio, Jan. 4, 1339, he writes: "I have resolved, all things being considered, to be indebted for it (the laurel) to no one else than the king of whom we have just been speaking (Robert of Naples). If I shall seem sufficiently worthy in his eyes for him to invite me, all will be well. Otherwise, I may pretend to have heard something which will explain my coming, or I will, as if in doubt, so interpret the letter which he sent me containing such friendly and flattering recognition to an unknown man, that I shall appear to have been summoned." (Robinson-Rolfe, *Petrarch*, 102.)

has been thrown to the winds, learning is in danger, and as a
desperate suitor, while careful to select the psychological moment
for his plea, he states his demands deliberately and with assurance.   He is even willing to play upon the sympathies of his
patrons: "Point out" he writes to Battus,

> "that I make complaint in my letters of suffering from a like affliction
> as that which troubled Jerome, *viz.* loss of eyesight, and that the prospect
> before me is of being compelled to study, as Jerome used to do, with ears
> and tongue alone.   Coax her with the neatest words you can command
> into sending me a sapphire or some other gem that is good for weak eyes."[38]

A letter to Colet shows us clearly that he carried on equally high
in England, being so importunate that even he himself felt he
could take no more from Warham, while his friend Linacre
besought him to spare Mountjoy.[39]   Erasmus recognized that
all this was not congenial to his character,[40] but when he reflected
upon how much more his patrons would receive from him in
fame and immortality, he could lift his head.   "I am busy" he
writes, "with a book that will live forever, . . . the books I
am writing will be read in every land." [41]

It is entirely unfair to the humanist to hold him blameworthy in
these matters, for if there was anything he realized fully it was
that through him the cause of learning was advancing, and none
of these men can be accused of being lazy or unproductive.   That
he was sincere in his belief in the permanent value of his work
there can be no doubt, and the relation of these men to their
patrons was an ideal one, not reducable to commercial terms at
all.   To contribute to the support of learning was a privilege,
and to beg for it no undignified or dishonorable thing.

But such proceedings were not confined alone to the humanists.   In Scotland, Dunbar was most anxious about his benefice,
as we have seen, and it was not for want of pressing his claims
upon the king and queen that he was baulked of his reward.
About his complaints and his begging poems, there is a tone of

---

[38] Capey, *Erasmus*, 38.
[39] Nichols, *Epistles of Erasmus*, II, 36.
[40] Letter to Battus, Ibid., I, 255.
[41] Capey, op. cit., 37.   Another example of his style of begging and flattery is a
letter addressed to the Princess of Vere.   (Froude, op. cit., 78 ff.)

anxious sincerity, which, in spite of the semi-humorous manner of all such pieces, arouses one's sympathy. He welcomes the Lord Treasurer, and with him his benefice and his rents; he explains his poverty *To the Lordis of the Kingis Chaker;* and *To the King* he complains:

> Sanct Saluatour! send siluer sorrow;
> It grevis me both evin and morrow;
> Chasing fra me all cheritee;
> It makis me all blytheness to borrow;
> My panefull purss so pricliss me.[42]

He wishes he were Johne Thomsounis man, and *Quhen mony Benefices Vakit* he pleads:

> Schir, quhidder is it mereit mair
> To gif him drink thot thristis sair,
>   Or fyll ane fow quhyll he brist,
>   And lat his fallow de for thrist,
> Quhylk wyne to drynk als worthie war?[43]

and in another address points out:

> Sum swelleis swan, sum swelleis duke,
> And I stand fastand in a nwke,
>   Qwhill the effect of all thay fang thame:
> Bot, Lord! how petewuslie I luke,
> Quhen all the pelfe thay pairt amang thame.[44]

His indignation is righteous, "gud consciens cryis reward thairfoir," but what can he do:

> In sum parte on my self I plenȝe,
> Quhen vdir folkis dois flattir and fenȝe;
> Allace! I can bot ballatis breif,
> Sic bairneheid biddis my brigdill renȝe:
> Excess of thocht dois me mischeif. . . .
> May nane remeid my melady
> Sa weill as ȝe, schir, veraly;
> Ffor with a benifice ȝe may preif,
> And gif I mend nocht hestely:
> Excess of thocht dois me mischeif.[45]

[42] *Poems of William Dunbar,* ed. Small, S. T. S. II, 129.
[43] Ibid., II, 205.
[44] Ibid., II, 208.
[45] Ibid., II, 104 ff.

But though the majority of his pieces are in dead earnest and righteously indignant, Dunbar was not without a saving sense of humor. In his plaint *Of the Waldis Instabilitie,* he complains of vain service and general bad conditions and then recurs to his old theme:

> I knaw nocht how the kirk is gydit,
> Bot beneficis ar nocht leill devydit;
> Sum men hes sewin, and I nocht ane;
> Quhilk to considder is ane pane.

He fears it has gone astray, it is so long in coming, or maybe it has turned back! Quhilk to considder is an pane, but:

> The formest hoip ȝit that I haue
> In all this warld, so God me saue,
> Is in ȝour Grace, bayth crop and grayne,
> Quhilk is ane lessing of my pane.[46]

Most delightful, however, is the *Petition of the Gray Horse, auld Dunbar,* which is a plea of an old horse who has become gray in service, quite in the strain of the other complaints of the poet. To this, however, he amusingly affixes a "Responsio Regis":

> Eftir our wrettingis, thesaurer,
> Tak in this gray horss, Auld Dunbar,
> Quhilk in my aucht with schervice trew
> In lyart changeit is in hew.
> Gar howss him now aganis his ȝuill,
> And busk him lyk an beschopis muill,
> For with my hand I have endost
> To pay quhat euir his trappouris cost.[47]

At the same court, Sir David Lyndesay, acting on the recognized principle that:

> Ane dum man ȝit wan neuer land,
> And in the court, men gettis na thyng
> Withoute inopportune askyng,

made his complaint to the king for recognition of past services.[48]

This matter of poetical petitions did not, however, pass with the Middle Ages, though as a rule, it seems safe to assume that

---

[46] Ibid., II, 226 ff.
[47] Ibid., II, 215 ff.
[48] *Monarche and other Poems,* ed. Hall, E. E. T. S., 303 ff.

it fell so into disuse until it became an extinct species of verse,
not perhaps because patronage became so lavish that such verses
were a superfluity, for such was far from the case, but because
men found a more delicate manner of letting their wishes be
known. We find it fairly late, however, and in no less a poet
than Ben Jonson in

> The Humble Petition of Poor Ben;
> To the Best of Monarchs, Masters, Men,
> King Charles.
> —Doth most humbly show it,
> To you majesty, your poet:
> That whereas your royal father,
> James the blessed, pleas'd the rather,
> Of his special grace to letters,
> To make all the Muses debtors
> To his bounty; by extension
> Of a free poetic pension,
> A large hundred marks annuity,
> To be given me in gratuity
> For done service and to come: . . . .
> Please your majesty to make
> Of your grace for goodness sake,
> Those your father's marks, your pounds:

and let those who are envious and spiteful do their worst, who
cares! [49]

[49] *Underwoods,* xciv, *Works,* ed. Gifford-Cunningham, IX, 30. There are numerous
other examples in Jonson's work. In France, too, the custom persisted. There are
some delightful verses which Margaret of Navarre sent to Clement Marot instead of
gold, when he complained to her of persecution of his creditors. He showed them to
the vultures and wrote an epigram in answer, describing the effect to Margaret.
(Costello, *Specimans* . . . 201 ff.)   Marot, likewise has a few Epigrams addressed
"au roy" which beg for cash. (*Oeuvres de Clement Marot,* ed. D'Hericault, (1857), 225.)

XII

PATRONS OF LETTERS IN ENGLAND

To list all the patrons of letters in the Middle Ages, besides being a tedious and unprofitable task, would also be an impossible one, if one went about it with the intention of doing justice to each name. Suffice it to say that patrons were numerous, and that whenever we hear of a glorious and brilliant court, it is almost safe to put it down as one at which arts and letters flourished, for patronage was a thing of fashion.

> At a court one should not live,
> Save to get or else to give;
> And niggard hearts if courtly fashions cloak,
> 'Tis not a court, but crowds of worthless folk,[1]

sang Sordello, and it would be rare indeed if one were praised and not beneficent to letters. Hence, since our study has dealt primarily with England and the conditions of the literary man there, it is not amiss to confine ourselves to listing the most important medieval English patrons and reinforcing what has been said about each in the various connections in which they have been mentioned as our study proceeded. It will be, however, a sad business. Many of the men with whom one must deal no longer loom large on the horizon, and in spite of the promises of immortality for which they may have sold their patronage, their names now may not even be distant memories. On the other hand, figures which are great as patrons of letters sometimes are not great as the world counts greatness, and some princes now looked upon as infamous stand out because of their connection with literature. This, however, is not the rule; ordinarily the prince hailed now as immortally great has a good record as art patron. In short, in spite of all this, our final

[1] Smith, *Troubadours at Home*, I, 264.

chapter on medieval patronage must be largely a chapter of exploded reputations.

Because much of the early literature had its birthplace in the church, and because the clergy in the Middle Ages comprised the cultured class in whose keeping the preservation of literature and education, as well as the care of the soul, was intrusted, it is well at the beginning to view in a small way the record of the princes of the English church as art patrons. Northumberland first attracts our attention. Under King Ecgfrid, in the seventh century, monasteries had been founded, and when the Venerable Bede was only a child, such churchmen as Benedict Biscop and Wilfrid had already kindled learning on the banks of the Wear and Tyne, and fame of knowledge of architecture, music, and illumination, recently brought from Italy, spread. In Whitby Abbey, the English poet Caedmon found a patroness in the abbess Hilda, who, we are told,

"embracing the grace of God in the man, instructed him to quit the secular habit, and take upon him the monastic life, which being accordingly done, she associated him to the rest of the brethern in her monastery, and ordered that he should be taught the whole series of sacred history."[2]

Wilfrid, the archbishop of York about the same time, besides being a zealous builder, was also a patron of learning, and to him perhaps is due the flourishing of those schools which produced Bede and Alcuin. In the next generation Bishop Acca of Hexham is known as the man to whom Bede addressed much of his work, and to him also among others, Eddius Stephanus addressed his *Vita Wilfridi Episcopi*.[3] Bede likewise dedicated to others, among them John and Eadfrid. Not long after, Folcardus wrote his *Vita Sancti Johannis Episcopi Ebrocensis* at the request of Archbishop Aldred.[4] In the south about the middle of the tenth century, Odo of Canterbury demands attention, both as a man of learning and as a patron. For him Fridegode wrote his metrical *Life of Wilfrid* when Odo conveyed the relics of that saint to Canterbury.[5] About the same time Dunstan, hav-

---

[2] Bede, *Ecclesiastical History*, tr. Giles, 218.
[3] *Historians of the Church of York*, ed. Raine, (R. S.), I, 1.
[4] Ibid., I, 239.
[5] *D. N. B.*

ing been a patronized youth in the household of Edmund, Edred and Edgar, was coming to the fore. When he came to the see of Canterbury, the many monasteries he founded became so many schools of learning. He is the dedicatee of literary works repeatedly, and from Abbo of Fleury's *Passion of St. Eadmund,* we learn something of his method of patronage. Abbo tells Dunstan he writes at the urging of his brethern, who argue that the life of Edmund, besides being edifying to future generations and a serviceable momento to Abbo, would be acceptable to the archbishop. They urge this, he adds, because they had heard the story of this passion, which is known to most people and written by no one, related by Dunstan, in Abbo's presence, to the Bishop of Rochester and the Abbot of Malmesbury, "and to other brethern there assembled in accordance with your practice, whom you cease not to nourish with the food of God's word, alike in Latin and in the mother tongue."[6] Lanfranc, who became archbishop of Canterbury after the Conquest when William deposed the Saxon clergy in favor of his own followers, has a good record. Monkish writers extol him for his liberality and affability, and William of Malmesbury records of him:

"nec pudebat archiepiscopum, alte succinctum, pauperibus cibos opponere, et tenuioris fortunae scholares ad disputationum pugnam committere. Post verba utrique laeti abibant, dum et victor scientiae praemium et victus acciperet verecundiae solutium."[7]

To him Goscelin of St. Bertin dedicated his *Life of St. Edith,* and recognizing likewise other great figures of his age, the same writer dedicated his *Historia Translationis S. Augustini* to Anselm, and his *Life of St. Ives* to Herbert de Lozenga, afterwards Bishop of Norwich, at whose desire he had written it.[8]

In later times the archbishops of Canterbury carried on the tradition. We have seen Giraldus Cambrensis carefully aware of the power of these prelates and dedicating hopefully to several, and Joseph of Exeter addressed his *De Bello Trojana* to Baldwin of Canterbury.[9] In fact, in later years, in the courts of

---

[6] Ed. Hervey, *Corolla Sancti Eadmundi,* 7.
[7] *De Gestis Pontificum Anglorum,* ed. Hamilton, (R. S.), 69.
[8] *D. N. B.*
[9] *D. N. B.*

these prelates were to be found the promising youth of the land, and about them as secretaries and chaplains was much of the literary talent. Nor were the lesser churchmen idle. The Bishops of Lincoln and of Winchester, especially, appear to have had good records. Geoffrey of Monmouth we have seen dedicating his *Prophecies of Merlin* to Alexander of Lincoln; a later anonymous *Vita Merlini* is addressed to his successor, Robert de Chesney.[10] Henry of Huntingdon first lived under the patronage of Robert Bloet, Bishop of Lincoln, and afterwards his successor Alexander, for whom he wrote his *History*. The great Robert Grosseteste was also of the see of Lincoln and attestations to his fostering of literature are numerous. Robert Mannyng assures us of his fondness for the harp and for music, for he had his harper's chamber next his·study,[11] and Matthew Paris in his praise of him calls him "scolarium sustentator."[12] Nigel Wireker we find addressing the notorious William Longchamp, afterwards both bishop of Ely and chancellor of England in Richard's absence; William of Ramsey addressed his *Life of Guthlac* to Henry de Longchamp, abbot of Croyland, and his *Life of St. Birin* to Peter de Rupibus, Bishop of Winchester. Further, Osmund, bishop of Sherbon, besides collecting a large library, received with great liberality every clerk that was distinguished for learning and persuaded him to reside with him.[13] Abbots of monasteries are often mentioned as patrons of letters, but enough has been said perhaps to indicate that in the church the author could find sufficient encouragement in the early time for his literary work. Later, of course, court patronage far eclipsed the patronage of the ecclesiastical princes, but it by no means died out, and even Gower recognized an archbishop of Canterbury as patron in his *Vox Clamantis*.[14]

At the same time that the various churches in Northumbria were becoming famous as centres of learning and as fosterers of literature, the Northumbrian kings of the seventh century

[10] Ward, *Catalogue of Romances*, I, 285.
[11] *Handlyng Sinne*, ll. c. 400 ff.
[12] *Chronica Majora*, ed. Luard, (R. S.), V, 407.
[13] William of Malmesbury, *De Gestis Pontificum Anglorum*, 184.
[14] *Works*, ed. Macaulay, VI, 1.

were likewise coming to the fore as patrons of letters. In fact, in early Saxon times Northumbria was the literary centre of Europe. Under King Aldfrith, peace and order were brought about, and being a man of learning himself, this king fostered and encouraged such enterprises in his subjects. To him Aldhelm addressed his treatise on versemaking, *Liber de Septenario et de Metris,* which is really a long letter, and the very fact that he should have done so goes to prove that Aldfrith was interested in matters literary. His old teacher Adamnan, as we have seen, presented to him his version of Bishop Arculf's account of the holy places, which the king caused to be copied, while he handsomely rewarded Adamnan. In fact, so ideal are the qualifications of Aldfrith as a great patron of letters that Professor Cook[15] looks to him as a possible begetter of the *Beowulf* and *Widsith.* The date of *Beowulf* is usually conceded to be c. 700, and hence it was written within the reign of Aldfrith, and possibly at his court. It is recognized of the poet of *Beowulf* that he was a man connected in some way with an Anglian court, who possessed an actual knowledge of court life and addressed himself to an aristocratic or loyal audience.[16] He further points out that there are traits in Aldfrith's character that might have been converted by the poet to his uses, and that perhaps it was this king who prompted and encouraged the poet in his undertaking after the manner described in the *Widsith.* The use of the same names in the *Widsith* and the *Beowulf* argues similar date and provenance, if not common authorship. Be that as it may, there can be no doubt of the literary activity in Northumbria both at this time and later. Bede at the conclusion of his *Ecclesiastical History,* which is dedicated to a Northumbrian king, gives us a picture of the peace and tranquility of Northumbria:

"Such being the peaceable and calm disposition of the times, many of the Northumbrians, as well of the nobility as private persons, laying aside their weapons, rather incline to dedicate themselves and their children to

---

[15] "The Possible Begetter of Old English *Beowulf* and *Widsith*," *Trans. of the Conn. Acad.,* XXV, (1922), 281 ff.

[16] Klaeber, *Beowulf,* cxxii.

the tonsure and monastic vows, than to study of martial discipline. What will be the end hereof, the next age will show."[17]

His own age, however, showed, for in it flourished the poet Cynewulf, and under the great archbishops of York, Egbert and Aethelbert, the scholar Alcuin, who at the call of Charlemagne went to the continent to be with the emperor. The next century in England did produce a great patron, the greatest of the Anglo-Saxons, Alfred, of whom something has been said before concerning the great work of keeping alive learning during the Dark Ages. The early years of Alfred's reign were occupied by the wars with the Danes, but the moment he was free to do other things he set to work to collect the few scholars, all Mercians, yet to be found in England, and to invite others from outside his own territory. One has but to read Asser's *Life* to feel to the full exertions of a patron of letters such as Alfred was. He gave England an educated governing class, and the impulse which began with him lasted for at least three generations.

Concerning the Conqueror William, opinons differ. According to Warton, "the conqueror himself patronized and loved letters. He filled the bishoprics and abbacies of England with the most learned of his countrymen, who had been educated at the University of Paris."[18] Mary Bateson, on the other hand, says that the "indifference of William I to the poets is recorded by one who wrote under the patronage of his daughter Adela. William was concerned rather to choose active men of affairs for the public offices of his new kingdom than to extend his patronage to learning."[19] She points out that the men of affairs attached to Norman churches and in offices of all kings were without exception men of learning and were all of William's own choosing. Further than this it is hardly safe to make any statement. Ingulph, as we have seen, tells us in his chronicle that he was scribe and secretary to William and in favor with him, even to the extent of having the whole court at his will,

[17] *Ecclesiastical History*, tr. Giles, 293.
[18] Warton, op. cit., I, 209.
[19] *Medieval England*, 21.

much to the envy of other courtiers, but there is nothing to show that Ingulph held his position of scribe or secretary because he had literary talent. Nor does the fact that William's minstrel Berdic received three parishes in Gloucestershire as his fruit of the victory[20] argue any deep seated attachment to learning. Perhaps to a practical man such as William, literature and learning was something to be used, rather than petted and pampered. His daughter Adela, however, was the friend both of historians and of poets. She urged Hugues de Sainte Marie, monk of Fleury, to write his *Chronicle*, in which he attests her love of literature :

> Una tamen restat quâ praesit filia patri,
> Versibus applaudit, scitque vacare libris.
> Haec etiam novit sua merceo esse Poëtis.
> A probitate sua nemo redit vacuus.
> Rursus inest illi dictandi copia torrens,
> Et praeferre sapit carmina carminibus.[21]

Her brother Rufus, however, did not have her tastes. His education was military, and his reign too troublous for one to expect much in the way of patronage.

It is in the court of his brother, Henry I, that we find a patronizing court for the first time in England. Alfred's patronage before him had been the patronage of one man rather than of an entire court, but about Henry and his queen grew up a coterie which in its entirety was interested in letters. To describe their activities, William of Malmesbury says:

> "scarcely Cicero himself, whose eloquence is venerated by all the Western world, would attempt it in prose; and in verse, not even a rival of the Mantuan Bard."[22]

Indeed, "the good peace" that Henry "made in the land," as the *Peterborough Chronicle* speaks of it, brought forth good fruit in the way of literary patronage. Literature and culture, as has been indicated, found a welcome around Henry, but not the king, rather his queens, were the greatest encouragers of it. Under

---

[20] *Domesday Book, Gloucestershire*, referred to by the Abbe de la Rue, *Archaelogia*, XII, 300.
[21] *Histoire Litt. de la France*, VII, 153.
[22] *Chronicle of the Kings of England*, tr. Giles, 424.

the patronage of the Anglo-Norman ladies at Henry I's and Henry II's court, the first poetry distinct from minstrel recitation arose. Matilda, Henry's first queen, was fond of the poems, not of minstrels, but of scholars, and we have noted her extreme prodigality to clerks of melodious voice. Crowds of scholars came to her court, and "happy did he account himself who could soothe the ears of the queen by the novelty of his song."[23] Though William complains just a bit that her patronage was extended mostly to foreigners who might make her famous, even her devout piety did not prevent her from gouging her tenants to pay her poets. Adelaide of Louvain, the princess Henry married after the death of Matilda, was no less interested in letters, though her patronage appears to have been extended more directly to romantic compositions. For her, according to Gaimar, one David composed in the vernacular a rimed history of Henry's achievements, which he set to music, and though Gaimar boasts that he knew more tales than David ever knew or than Adelaide had in books, the loss of the work is to be regretted. To her also, Philippe de Thaun addressed his *Bestiaire*. For another lady of the court, one "Custance li Gentil," Gaimar wrote his *Estoire des Engles*, in which he tells us that she had paid a mark of silver for a copy of David's work which she kept in her chamber. About the same time Sanson de Nanteuil translated the *Proverbs of Solomon* into French for another court lady, Adelaide de Condé, nor were the men of the age entirely unsympathetic. It is Henry's natural son, Robert of Gloucester, who must stand out as the greatest individual of the time. To him has accrued lasting fame through William of Malmesbury's dedications, in which he is described in terms of unbounded praise for his devotion to literature. Concerning Henry I himself, his surname "Beauclerc" and William of Malmesbury's unlimited praise of his learning indicate that he carefully lived up to his proverb that "an illiterate king is a crowned ass." His connection with literature itself is not so well attested as that of his wives; we know that he put out the eyes of Chevalier Luc de la Barre because he wrote a satire against him which indicates that

[23] William of Malmesbury, *Chronicle of the Kings of England*, 453.

he was at least mindful of his fame and perhaps would have rewarded a panegyric. In all likelihood his learning was that of the administrative man, and while he was not at all unfriendly to literature, his reign gave him little time to be actively a patron.

Stephan, of whom we are told that he was a "mild man, soft and good, and did no justice," was fitted neither by inclination nor circumstance to carry on any patronage of learning his predecessors had begun, in spite of the fact that his mother, Adela, was a famous patroness. The second Henry, however, was a shining light, and the new poetry of the age found ample patronage. It has been estimated that nearly two-thirds of the French writers of the period were connected with the English court and that the whole romantic movement which characterizes medieval literature had its nucleus in England in the latter half of the twelfth century.[24] Both Wace and Beneoit we have found declaring that poetry was essential to the formation of respectable reputations, and it is clear that Henry's palace was the centre of learned talk and writing, even if Henry himself was home for only two or three days at a time. It is possible also that his sojourns at Oxford were an influential cause of fixing the university there. His household, we are told, was a byword for confusion and discomfort, to which Henry was utterly indifferent, if he could have about him literary associates, of whose discussions he was very fond. Hence, he had the reputation of being the most highly educated man in Europe. His taste was catholic, and not only did historians such as Roger de Hovedon, Giraldus Cambrensis, Peter of Blois, and John of Salisbury, gain his ear, but also such minglers of truth and legend as Wace, Beneoit de Sainte-Maure, Robert de Borron, and wits like Walter Mapes and Nigel Wireker. As a further attestation to his patronage we find Osbert de Clare in a *Poema ad Regem Henricum Secundum,* hailing him as "Maecenas" after the manner of the classic poets. In Eleanor of Acquitaine, famous as a munificent patroness of troubadours, Henry had a wife well fitted to him in taste. We have found her frequently the subject of troubadour songs, and it is not difficult to imagine that Provencal poets visited a queen who had always been favorable to them, in her new home. Unquestionably, throughout Henry's reign there was close connection between England and France. The court language was French, as were the tastes, and perhaps it was this intercourse which gave the English people and English literature (by reflection from the French) the breadth and polish that developed in the next century. However widespread that influence may or may not have been, the children of Henry and Eleanor were all well-educated, and in most cases appear to have had a sympathy for letters. Of the daughters little is known save that they all married princes who were themselves cultured and who were patrons of culture. Matilda, the eldest, became the wife of Henry of Saxony, Eleanor married Alfonso of Castile, and Johanna, William of Sicily. Of the sons, Henry, while he was devoted to arms, was also devoted to letters, and one book we know was written for his amusement, the *Liber Facetiarum* of Gervase of Tilbury, which is lost. In Richard, the second son, the cultured tastes of his parents bore most fruit, and we find him both a troubadour and a generous patron of troubadours. His brother, Geoffrey of Brittany, appears to have been in close connection with Giraut de Clanson and Bertran de Born, and the "comte Geoffroi" to whom Gace Brulé addressed some of his chansons seems to have been this prince. Finally, as to John's scholarship and interest in literary matters, apparently all we have to base his reputation upon is his indifferent reception of Giraldus Cambrensis' address to him of the *Conquest of Ireland* and the fact that he once borrowed a book from the Abbot of St. Albans.

Henry III's court was likewise one at which literature flourished. According to the account of Denis Pyramus,[25] who seems to have lived at Henry's court, French court poetry, and especially wild romantic tales, were much in request. He tells us how in his youth he had dedicated his talents to pleasing the knights and ladies, but has now repented and will write serious

---

[25] *La Vie de Seint Edmund, Memorials of St. Edmund's Abbey,* ed. Arnold, (R. S.), II, 137, ll. 1 ff.

works. The author of *Parthenope of Blois,* he says, wrote much wild fiction, as did Marie de France, but their verses were well-liked by the king, barons, counts, and courtiers. Henry's interests were largely artistic; there are numerous records of paintings that he ordered made in his palace and elsewhere, and he is especially interesting as the first king who had a "versificator regis," to whom he granted a stipend. His wife, Eleanor of Provence, doubtless brought with her the Provençal love of poets and poetry.

Edward I also seems to have shown some interest in letters. Pierre Dubois dedicated to him his *De Recuperatione* . . ., a work on the recovery of the Holy Land, and Guido della Collonna is said by Borton of Bury to have written his *De Bello Trojana* at Edward's command, though the work is dedicated to another. Girard of Amiens tells us that his subject was given him by a Spanish princess, queen of England, who is undoubtedly Eleanor of Castile, Edward's wife. His son Edward II was hardly fitted by temperament to have any serious interest in anything, though he seems to have cared a great deal for minstrels, and we find him beseeching the abbot of Shrewsbury to send him a good fiddler to teach his rhymer to crowd. He was likewise devoted to the stage, and Reynolds first won his favor by his skill "in ludus theatralibus."[26]

In the court of Edward III we find a number of poets. The good Queen Philippa, as we have seen, had Froissart in her service, and the various manifestations of her patronage of her countryman, both in aiding him materially, and in aiding him to get the information he required for his book, have been discussed. So great was her help to him and his appreciation of it, that Froissart says of her:

> Elle me fit et crea.

At the same time there was the Duchess Blanche of Lancaster, whose connection with Froissart and Chaucer has been mentioned, but concerning Edward himself there is no evidence which indicates a taste for literature.[27] He did, however, patronize

---

[26] *D. N. B.*

[27] Moore, "Chaucer and Edward III," *P. M. L. A.,* XXVI, xxvi.

William of Wykeham, whose genius for architecture was attractive, making him his chaplain,[28] though in this case, too, Philippa perhaps was as much his friend as Edward. But even if Edward was not a munificent patron, his old tutor, Richard de Bury, who occupied a high position in the kingdom, and who corresponded with Petrarch, amply attoned for his deficiency. In his *Philobiblon*, Richard tells how after his duties as chancellor and treasurer were discharged, he searched out the hiding places of old books. His fame spread, he tells us, and "it was reported, not only that we had a longing desire for books and especially for old ones, but that anybody could more easily obtain our favor by quartos than by money."[29] About him as chaplains grew up many learned men, and throughout his book, it is evident that his sympathies were with those who were impeded by poverty. Of most interest, however, is his plan of a Hall at Oxford, given as a perpetual almsdeed for his own soul and the souls of Edward III and Philippa, which is in substance the plan of a circulating library.[30]

Concerning Richard II, the evidence is far more conclusive and interesting, for he is apparently the first English sovereign to encourage the writing of poetry in English. We know that he encouraged Gower to write, that he was pleased when Froissart presented him with a beautiful book, and perhaps Chaucer enjoyed his patronage. Two of his poems are said to have been addressed directly to Richard, while the *Legend of Good Women* apparently was written for his queen, Anne. Henry IV, though his reign was a troublous one, was nevertheless a friend of poets. The poet Scogan was tutor to his children, Gower addresses him several times and dedicates one redaction of the *Confessio* to him, but most to Henry's credit is his invitation to Christine de Pisan to come to his court. Finally, among other things, a book on hunting, called *Mayster of the Game*, by Edward, Duke of York, is addressed to him.

Henry V's connection with literature was likewise brilliant, and for him the most celebrated of the Chaucerians undertook

---

[28] Hardy, *Philippa of Hainault*, 238.
[29] Tr. Morley, Chapter VIII.
[30] Ibid., Chapter XIX.

comparatively ambitious works. Lydgate wrote for him the *Troy Book,* Hoccleve his *Regiment of Princes,* and Jean de Gallopes dedicated to him a French prose translation of Bonaventura's *Pilgrimage of the Soul.* About him, too, was a court of folk interested in giving commissions to the famous court poet, Lydgate. Perhaps in a more settled reign, Henry VI might have been notable, but his connection with letters seems slight. Edward IV is notable for his connection with Caxton, and though Caxton dedicated his *Order of Chivalry* to Richard III, Richard on the whole seems not to have been at all connected with letters.

It is in Henry VII that we again have a brilliant patron. The extracts from his privy purse expenses show him to have been liberal; he was a reader of romances, an admirer of French players, but he is of interest most for his recognition of Bernard Andreas, called Poet Laureate and Royal Historiographer. Henry's mother, the "venerable Margaret" as Gray called her, Countess of Richmond and Derby, was likewise a munificent patroness, as her relations with Caxton and others has shown, and John Fisher's funeral sermon attests the fact that

"All Englonde for her dethe had cause of wepynge. The poore creatures þat were wonte to receyue her almes, to whome she was alwaye pyteous and mercyful. The studyentes of bothe the vnyversyties to whome she was a moder. all the lerned men of Englonde to whome she was a veray patronesse."[31]

So good and noble was she that it has been said of her that the worst thing she ever did was to try to draw Erasmus from his Greek studies to train her untoward stepson, James Stanley, to be Bishop of Ely.

One coterie of patrons must be mentioned. Professor Samuel Moore[32] has pointed out the existence of a group of persons connected by ties of acquaintance and interest in East Anglia, who were causing works to be written, and rewarding authors who wrote them. Among these were the Paston Family, Sir John Fastolf, Sir Miles Stapelton and his lady, the Duke and

[31] *The English Words of John Fisher,* ed. Mayor, E. E. T. S., I, 301.
[32] "Patrons of Arts and Letters in Norfolk and Sufolk c. 1450." *P. M. L. A.,* XXVII, 188 ff. and XXVIII, 79 ff.

Duchess of Suffolk, the Countess of Hugh, and other ladies and gentlemen, for whom such poets as Lydgate, Metham, Bokenham, and others were writing. Professor Moore's opinion, however, is that besides being a notable stimulus to literature, this patronage amounted to very little in the end.

What may be said of the early Renaissance in England and its fostering by English patrons? The record is not commendable. We have noticed how Poggio came to England at the invitation of Cardinal Beaufort, and how he quitted it again in disgust. Whatever moved Poggio in the first place to come to a land looked upon by Italians as a remote corner of ignorance and barbarity is not clear. Perhaps England, in comparison with Italy, was a kind of unenlightened island, and it is evident that the various stimulants to intellectual reawakening which operated in Italy were not present in England, but it is not necessary to accept Poggio's diatribe upon the country as unexaggerated when he complains that the Englishmen thought of nothing but eating and drinking. But one fact that he states is interesting in our connection. "The nobles of England," he writes, "deem it disgraceful to reside in cities, and prefer living in retirement in the country. They estimate the degree of a man's nobility by the extent of his estates."[33] Perhaps this arrangement prevented anything larger than a coterie interest in literature from developing, but at any rate there is only one patron in England who can be looked upon as even an approximation to the great Italian patrons, Humphrey, Duke of Gloucester, but Humphrey's interest in the new learning was not shared by his countrymen. Perhaps, as Vickers points out,[34] while he himself was ready for the Renaissance, Humphrey did not grasp its true significance in England, because he was cast in the Italian, rather than in the English mould, and hence had no sympathy with the popular movement. Not until after Humphrey's death were the Renaissance ideas fully understood, so that Humphrey stands as a inaugurater of a new system. Henry V, with all his interest in literature, was interested in such men as Hoccleve and Lydgate

[33] Shepherd, *Life of Poggio Bracciolini*, 127.
[34] *Humphrey of Gloucester*, (1907), 341.

and theological writers and not in works of classical origin, while Humphrey found his inspiration in Greece and Rome and his model in Italy. His importance lies in that he was a son of the Renaissance before ever that movement had penetrated England; there was no one to teach him, and "what Petrarch did for the world, Humphrey did for England."[35]   About him he had numerous secretaries and orators who wrote and translated diligently, and he imported scholars from Italy. Antonio de Beccaria, a Veronese, translated into Latin from Greek Dionysius' *De Situ Orbis* as well as six tracts of Athenasius, a copy of which has the inscription in Humphrey's hand: "Cest livre est a moi Homfrey Duc de Gloucestre: le quel je fis translater de Grec en Latin par un de mes secretaires Antoyne de Beccara nè de Verone,"[36] and Tito Livio da Forli is described as the poet and orator of the Duke of Gloucester. Lydgate in his *Falls of Princes* praises his communion with learned clerks, and compares him to Julius Caesar, who in spite of the cares of state, was not ashamed to enter the rhetorical school of Cicero at Rome.[37]   Aeneas Silvius, writing to Adam Moleyns, complimented him on his style, and marvelled how the reformed Latin style had thus early reached England:

"For this progress thanks are due to the illustrious Duke of Gloucester, who zealously received polite learning into your country. I hear that he cultivates poets and venerates orators, and thereby many Englishmen have become really eloquent. For as are princes so are servants, who improve by imitating their masters."[38]

John Wethamstede, Abbot of St. Albans, was employed by Humphrey to collect books for him, while his monks accused him of neglecting their affairs by his intellectual pursuits, and Candido Decembrio was his commissioner on the continent. Humphrey's name was also familiar in Italy, due perhaps to his friendship with Zano Castiglione, Bishop of Bayeaux, whom he

---

    [35] Ibid., 348.
    [36] MS. Roy. 5 F. quoted by Warton, op. cit., III, 51. A copy of Capgrave's *Commentary on Genesis* bears the inscription: "Cest livre est a moy Humfrey duc de Gloucestre du don de frere Jehan Capgrave, quy le me fist presenter a mon manoyr de Pensherst le jour . . . de l'an. MCCCXXXVIII." (Ibid., III, 49.)
    [37] Warton, op cit., III, 50.
    [38] Epist. lxiv., quoted by Vickers, op. cit., 349.

commissioned to buy books, and who seems to have praised him highly to the humanists. From his correspondence [39] and the numerous dedications to him,[40] we may judge that Humphrey had a large number of protégés, among whom were Leonardo Bruni of Arrezzo, Peter de Monte, Piero Candido Decembrio, Antonius Pacinus, and Lapo da Castiglionchia, and with Decembrio especially, he carried on an animated correspondence about his immortality, and from all received the most flattering dedications. Hence, his reputation with Italian humanists was widespread, and though he himself was probably not wholly conscious of the results of his interest in scholarship, yet he occupies a significant place as the originator of the Renaissance in England.

But Humphrey was more than a patron of foreign scholars, as we have seen; he was an acknowledged leader in the literary world of fifteenth century England, encouraging all who were interested in writing. Hence, he became the medium of introducing these new Italian ideas to English writers, though on the whole it must be admitted he met with little response. Commending his activity, the university authorities at Oxford, writing in 1441, speak of his fame both in England and abroad as a patron and the flood of literature translated from the Greek and Latin and dedicated to that prince, as well as the production of works in the vernacular, and they add that under his patronage, Greek has revived, and that they now can study in the original the works of Plato, Aristotle, and other great philosophers:

"patrocinio vestro Grece, que multis jam seculis littere sepulte fuerant, revixere. Nunc Grecos philosophos, bene vivendi magistros, Platonem, Aristotelem, ceteros quoque non superficie tenus, et intute uti per priores translaciones, sed intus et in profundo [Latinis] cernendi copia datur."[41]

Surely if many virtues can confer immortal fame, it will be Humphrey's.

[39] Borsa, "Correspondence of Humphrey Duke of Gloucester and Piero Candido Decembrio," *English Historical Review,* XIX, 509 ff.; Creighton, "Some Literary Correspondence of Humphrey, Duke of Gloucester," Ibid., X, 99 ff., and Newman, "Correspondence of Humphrey, Duke of Gloucester," Ibid., XXI, 484 ff.

[40] Macray, "Early Dedications to Englishmen by Foreign Authors and Editors" *Bibliographica* I, 324 ff.

[41] *Epistolate Academicae Oxon.*, ed Anstey, I, 203.

Though Humphrey was the most important of the supporters of the Renaissance he was not altogther alone. The "fierce executioner and beheader of men," John Tiptoft, Earl of Worcester, by his combination of cruelty and scholarship, may be looked upon as an early specimen of the Italianate Englishman being a devil incarnate. Vespasiano leads us to believe that he was looked upon as a kind of Maecenas during his stay in Italy, where he gathered books and generally favored the new learning. He was a friend of Guarino and Lodovico Carbo, and attended lectures during his stay in Italy, and Francesco of Arrezzo dedicated a translation of a work of Lucian to him, while the Earl, according to Caxton, himself translated Cicero into the vernacular.[42] But his interest seems to have terminated when he left Italy, and beside the eulogy of Caxton, we hear nothing of any literary activity. Henry VII likewise seems to have been known abroad, for we find him eulogized by Gulielmus Parronus of Piacenza in the dedication of a curious little astrological treatise as a king possessing all six of the regal virtues: wisdom, prudence, justice, fortitude, temperance, and clemency, and Cardinal Hadrian a Castello, the papal ambassador in England and Scotland, who later became bishop of Herford, Bath, and Wells, dedicated to Henry his *De Vera Philosophia ex quatuor Doctoribus Ecclesiae,* shortly after his coming to England. Later, of course, patrons of the new learning increased in numbers, and such names as Archbishop Warham, Henry VIII, John Clymond, and others, are known as the dedicatees of no less a person than Erasmus, while both students and interested persons were found throughout England.

As might be expected, an interest in things intellectual on the part of the nobles manifested itself in patronage of the universities, as well as in patronage of literature. On the continent, the pope or emperor in many cases granted their charters, though lesser, but still powerful princes also acted as patrons, and throughout the Middle Ages we find the various colleges dependent upon royal or papal bounty.[43] In England a similar state of affairs

---

[42] Prologue to *Tully of Friendship*, Blades, op. cit., I, 162.

[43] See Rashdall, *The Universities of Europe in the Middle Ages*, 2 vols. in 3, Oxford, 1895.

existed. In 1229 when, because of difficulties between students and citizens of Paris, scholars and masters were removing to other places, Henry III, apparently aware of the benefits to accrue from an influx of scholars, on July 16, 1229 issued an invitation in the form of a patent for masters and students to reside in England,[44] and seeing that Oxford would be preferred, had conveniences provided for them there. William of Durham who came on this occasion from Paris, founded University College in 1249, by a bequest of 310 marks,[45] and Balliol College grew out of certain payments made about 1260 by John Balliol for the support of poor students at Oxford, as well as the activity of his wife.[46] Similarly in 1264 Walter de Merton maintained twenty students at Malten in Surrey, from which foundation in 1274 the "House of the Scholars of Merton" grew.[47] In 1314 Stapledon Hall was founded by Walter de Stapledon, Bishop of Exeter, for poor students, and from this grew up Exeter College.[48] Interesting indeed is the founding of Queen's College. The founder of the "Hall of the Scholars of the Queen" was Robert of Eglesfield, chaplain and confessor to Queen Philippa, who had forethought enough to vest the "avowdson" of his new hall in his royal mistress, and thus to place it under the perpetual patronage of the Queens consort.[49] Philippa procured for it from her husband various revenues, and donations credited to "domina Regina" are recorded.[50]

Part of the students invited to England by Henry III settled in Cambridge, and there formed a community of teachers and pupils. Peterhouse was founded through the benefactions of Hugh de Balsham, Bishop of Ely, (1257-1286), who basing his plan upon that of Merton at Oxford, introduced a group of secular scholars under his patronage into the Hospital of St. John, but differences arose, and in 1284 he separated his scholars from the hospital, assigning them the church of St. Peter and

[44] *Calendar of Patent Rolls*, 1225-1232, 257.
[45] Clark, *Oxford*, 3.
[46] Ibid., 25.
[47] Ibid., 59.
[48] Ibid., 76.
[49] Rashdall, op. cit., II, (2), 495.
[50] Clark, op. cit., 127.

certain revenues,[51] the foundation being known as "the Scholars of the Bishops of Ely." Edward II maintained thirty-two boys under their master at Cambridge, and his successor erected for his pensioners a special hall of residence, called King's Hall.[52] In 1388 Elizabeth de Burgh, countess of Clare, and grand-daughter of Edward I, came forward as a benefactress of the university and especially of the foundation known as University Hall, which because of her endowments, became known as Clare Hall, the present Clare College.[53] Pembroke College is likewise due to the benefaction of a woman, Marie de Saint Paul, wife of Audomare de Valentin, Earl of Pembroke, who among other works of piety, founded the college in June 1384.[54] To Henry VI are due both Eton and King's College at Cambridge,[55] and to his wife, Margaret of Anjou, is due the foundation of Queen's, which its real founder, Andrew Dokett, placed under her patronage much as Queen's College, Oxford, had been placed under the patronage of Philippa,[56] Margaret's work being completed by Elizabeth Woodville in 1465. Finally, to name no others, the great foundations of Christ's College and St. John's are lasting monuments to the munificent Lady Margaret of Richmond and Derby,[57] who also founded the Lady Margaret professorships in Divinity at both Oxford and Cambridge, one of which was held by Erasmus during his early stay in England. Other grants and foundations are too numerous to mention, and from the correspondence of the officers of the University of Oxford with various lords of the time,[58] it is clear that such aid was ardently solicited, return to be made by prayers for the benefactors' souls or in the immortality he would attain by his munificence. In the early fifteenth century, the Duke of Bedford, the Bishop of Winchester, the Archbishop of Canterbury, and in later times Prince Edward and the Bishops of Exeter, Norwich, and Wor-

---

[51] Stubbs, *Cambridge and Its Story*, 76-7.
[52] Ibid., 97.
[53] Ibid., 99-100.
[54] Ibid., 107.
[55] Ibid., 141 ff.
[56] Ibid., 158 ff.
[57] Ibid., 210 ff.
[58] Anstey, *Epistolae Academicae Oxon.*, 2 vols., passim.

cester are all addressed, generally as possible patrons who will supply the university's needs, or as patrons to whom the foundation is eternally thankful. To Humphrey, Duke of Gloucester, more letters are addressed than to anyone else. Most often they are solicitations for funds, with promises of eternal glory and everlasting memory of future generations, promises that undoubtedly appealed to the good duke's temperament, and we find an equally large number of letters of thanks for gifts of books and money. To him also matters of discipline were referred, and repeatedly we hear of him—"you are our harbor of refuge in every trouble"—the letter inclosing a statement of the circumstances which disturb the peace. Further, in 1436, Humphrey founded lectureships in the seven arts and the three philosophies, for which the authorities beg him to provide the continual maintenance. Most interesting are the gifts of books which Humphrey made, some of which are still in existence, and for which Humphrey is repeatedly thanked, for they have given "light of life, warmth, and nourishment to our studies." Occasionally, too, there are appeals for funds for students and rewards for their labors, lest the pursuit of literature be at an end.

Throughout the Middle Ages wealthy religious houses defrayed the charges of selected students of their orders, and William de Kilkenny, Bishop of Ely (d. 1356-7), bequeathed two hundred marks to the priory of Barnwell in trust for the payment of ten marks annually to two priests studying divinity at Cambridge, and William of Durham, archbishop-elect of Rouen about 1250 bequeathed three hundred and ten marks to Oxford for the maintenance of ten or more masters studying theology.[59] To found a chantry for the maintenance of a priest to say mass for the founder's soul was also a common practice. Before 1243 Alan Basset deposited eight marks a year with the prior and convent of Bicester for the maintenance of two chaplains to say mass for his and his wife's souls, and at the same time study at Oxford or elsewhere.[60] To maintain or 'exhibit' a scholar at

[59] *Cambridge History of English Literature*, II, 352, and Rashdall, op. cit., II, (2), 558.

[60] Rashdall, II, (2), 469.

the university was also a recognized "good work" in medieval times, as we have seen; so was the foundation of a 'chest' from which needy masters and scholars could borrow by giving books or plate in security.[61]   In short, it is clear that the universities as well as individual writers and scholars were largely dependent upon the bounty of the wealthy throughout the Middle Ages, and it is of interest to note that those figures we have seen to be patrons of literature in the old time are likewise the patrons of the universities and of needy scholars studying there.

At least one remnant of the patronized poet that has come down to us in modern times deserves treatment here.   The office of poet-laureate, though it did not have actual existence until after the Middle Ages in the time of James I of England, when it became definitely an office of patronage, (a significance which has long since passed), at least had its beginnings in the retained poet of which we have spoken.   He was a regular officer of the household, and Professor Broadus, the recent historian of the office, shows that "it is no straining of terms to say that the Anglo-Saxon *scop* is the first poet-laureate."[62]   As our discussion has shown, the patronized poet from even the earliest times was careful to cater to the tastes and wishes of his lord, and hence sang of

> old unhappy far-off things,
> And battles long ago.

The line of the laureate is doubtless through the retained minstrel and the *citharista regis,* the *ioculator regis,* and the *mimus regis,* or more correctly, derived from the *versificator regis,* Henri d'Avranches, to whom we have seen Henry III giving a stipend and a grant of wine.   But being an office of court minstrelsy, the office of *versificator regis* did not become permanent, and it is nearly two centuries before there is again such an official in the records.   The tradition, however, was only deflected to the universities, where from the thirteenth century on an office of poet-laureate had been in existence.

[61] "The Ordinance of the Exeter Chest" founded by John, Duke of Exeter, in 1441 is printed in Anstey, op. cit., I, 205.

[62] *The Laureateship.* (1921), 1.

But in spite of the fact that the laureateship is a late office, there exists a tradition that several medieval poets held it. Robert Baston, said to have been poet laureate of Oxford, has been described as "poet-laureate to Edward II," due to the legend that he accompanied Edward on his Scotch campaign, was captured, and made to make a song for ransom.[63] Chaucer, too, is traditionally a laureate, partly because of the application of the title to him shortly after his death by his fellow poets.[64] It is clear, of course, that the references are to the custom of crowning poets of great fame, like Petrarch, and as applied to Chaucer mean no more than what Lydgate expressed when he spoke of his master:

> That worthy was the laurer to haue
> Of peetrie and the palm attaine.[65]

or as Walton hopes:

> Þat þe laurer of oure englishe tonge
> Be to hym ȝoue for his excellence.[66]

Be that as it may, when in 1688 the laureateship was officially established in England, Chaucer is named in the document as one of Dryden's predecessors in office, and Dryden himself called Chaucer "laureate to three kings."[67] Gower also, upon no basis, is included in the tradition, as is "Lydgate Laureat," who, as we have seen, was much of a court poet. Further, one Johan

---

[63] Ibid., 15.

[64] Shirley calls him "the Laureall Poete of Albion" in the headline to the *Lak of Steadfastness*. James I in the *Kingis Quair* speaks of Gower and Chaucer "superlative as poetis laureate." (Spurgeon, op. cit., 34.)

[65] Spurgeon, op. cit., 19.

[66] Spurgeon, 20. One might be led to suppose, remembering that French was current in Chaucer's time, that the term *laureate poet* signifies no more than *l'aureate poet*, by the simple loss of an apostrophe. Chaucer's followers are extravagant in their praise of his rhetoric and the "golde dewe droppis of speche and eloquence," or as Dunbar calls it, his "sugurit lippis and tongis aureate." In fact the headline to the *Complainte to Pite* calls Chaucer "the Aureat Poete," and the *Book of Curteyse* speaks of his "laureate seyence." Caxton, too, seems to have had this quality in mind when he wrote in the Prohemye to the second edition of the *Canterbury Tales:* "the whiche for his ornate wrytyng in our tongue maye wel haue the name of a laureate poete / For to fore that he by his labour enbelysshyd / ornated and made faire our englisshe." (Blades, op. cit., I, 172 ff.) But unfortunately, a search fails to reveal that the word *l'aureate* in the proper sense existed in Old French.

[67] Broadus, op. cit., 17-8.

Kaye, dedicating a translation of a Latin history, *The Dylect-able Newesse and Tythynges of the Gloryous Victory of the Rhodjans agaynst the Turkes,* to Edward IV, calls himself "hys humble poete lawreate, and most lowly seruant."[68] He was probably only poet laureate of Oxford, adopting the same title in addressing the king. Skelton, of course, was also laureate of Oxford, as was Bernard Andreas, but in the case of the latter in 1486, the king, granting a patent of ten marks annually, styles him *poet laureate,* and according to Bale, Andreas was officially appointed court poet. A few years after, he received the additional office of historiographer royal.[69]

Hence, while the office of poet-laureate cannot be said to have actual existence until the time of Ben Jonson, though Spenser, Drayton, and Daniel were traditional laureates, it will be seen that the tradition was firmly established by the end of the Middle Ages, and that it grew out of the medieval patronage system of retaining a bard for the amusement of the king.

[68] *Cat. Lib. Mss. Bib. Harl.,* II, 252.
[69] Broadus, op. cit., 25.

CONCLUSION

After our discussion of the various aspects of medieval patronage and the social conditions in which it flourished, it is only
natural to ask: what was the effect of this patronage on the
general literary history of England? This is a question which
is not easily answered, for it is impossible to isolate the influences
upon England from the more general and universal effects upon
all Europe. Patronage, as we have seen, knew no national
bounds, and the uniformity of all things medieval makes it more
evident that England shared in the general effects. The plan
adopted for presenting the mass of evidence concerning literary
patronage in the Middle Ages has laid special emphasis upon
the various phases of the custom, and has called attention to certain general results and functions of the system. To summarize
for a moment: it as been seen that literary patronage arises
from individual appreciation of art side by side with the more
impersonal public appreciation of it, and that patronage itself is
due to an aristocratic fostering spirit which arises from such
appreciation. If literary patronage in classcal times be compared with medieval patronage, a continuous tradition is revealed
which is modified only slightly by a difference in social and
economic conditions. The same marks of patronage exist,
similar conditions are similarly met with, and like results are
due to like causes. A view of the patronage accorded to the
scop, the scald, and the bard, their privileges and general high
esteem, has confirmed the fact which was noted of early patronage, that it is a universal custom. Minstrel patronage has
testified to a love for amusement and a hope for widespread
glory, which the minstrel could fulfill through his songs. Though
no fast distinction between the itinerant and the retained minstrel
can be said to have existed in the Middle Ages, there were some
who were domesticated and became *ministri* in the true sense. As

235

there was no place in the social status of the Middle Ages for a man of intellect or genius outside the church, such men had to depend upon court patronage, and often became retained entertainers. From these hall minstrels, perhaps developed the later men of letters. Further, a view of the patronage of the troubadours, trouvères and minnesingers as the producers of literature definitely connected with the courts, has shown the custom in an ideal form and has made clear that the singers of love were amply remunerated for their activity—in fact, were dependent upon princely largess for their maintainence.

Passing now to the man of letters in the Middle Ages more specifically, as distinguished from the more general entertainer, a survey of the economic conditions has shown that aside from uncertain and capricious patronage, nothing material could come to the author for his work. The Middle Ages were content to allow literature to be the occupation of an idle hour rather than a profession to which a man might devote all his talents and his life. To practice letters as a profession, therefore, was highly impractical unless the author had other means of support, and many of the medieval poets had remunerative positions which supplied their needs and yet gave them leisure in which to write. The impracticality, so often characteristic of poets and scholars, however, led many under the impulse to write to devote themselves to literature anyway. A good many writers are without other visible means of support than patronage. Hence, there is complaint upon complaint over neglect, and innumerable instances of shameless importunity and open begging of authors. To be sure, there was a reading public in the Middle Ages, but not a well-developed book-buying public, and until the invention of printing the author expected not only remuneration from his patron, but a hearing and an introduction to a public. Not all books in the Middle Ages, of course, were patronized works; authors in all ages have written because of an urge within or for self-satisfaction, but if the author sought remuneration, patronage was his only hope. Hence, it is perhaps the result of these conditions that so many books in the Middle Ages are the works of practical men who wrote only one book, and that with the painful care of the amateur rather than the skill of a trained writer.[1]

As the evidence produced shows, medieval writers, like authors in all ages, prefixed to their books dedicatory epistles, extolling the virtues of the prince or noble who is the patron, and expecting the only reward that could come to a medieval author, the largess of the great. Fame abroad and the immortality hopefully promised by needy authors to princes through their connection with literary enterprises, has been seen as the great cause of patronage. Doubtless, a sincere love of letters on the part of many princes did exist, but in the case of as many more it was the intense craving for renown and remembrance that made the lord willing to pay. The naive concern of both author and patron in the old time about immortality and eternal fame to arise as reward for the fostering of literature, and the simple frankness with which such doctrines were preached, brings a smile to us of the twentieth century. But it should be remembered that in the Middle Ages good repute meant everything, and what the author promised, if he could pay it, was worthy of the remuneration he received.

Very often, as we have seen, in a prosperous and unified district, the patron was expected to act as publisher and to show the author's work to his friends, who might be interested and either desire copies or suggest new subjects, and such a condition was obviously favorable to literary production. The presentation of the volume, so often pictured in the old illuminations, therefore, constituted its 'release,' and though essentially different from the modern method of advertisements, advance notices, and book reviews, it was a no less momentous occasion. An influential patron lent not only currency to a work, but authority as well, and the selection of the proper dedicatee was of as much importance as the selection of the proper publisher is now.

The first general effect, then, of patronage in the Middle Ages is upon production. The very fact that the man of letters was encouraged to write at all is itself a fact of momentous effect, especially since through patronage alone could he expect

[1] Cf. Moore, *P. M. L. A.*, XXVIII.

profit from his pen. To imply, however, that had there been no
patrons there would have been no books, is, of course, to go
too far, for there are other compensations for writing besides
material ones, but much of the literature preserved to us would
not have come into existence without encouragement.

Further, it is evident that the dependence of medieval writers
upon the generosity of the wealthy was an important factor in
their choice of subject, their style, and sometimes even in their
choice of words. Hence, it comes about that such effects of
patronage are usually the result of the wish of a coterie or of a
single patron at least in the beginning, however widespread they
may afterward have become. The influence of the coterie of
patrons about the court of the early Norman kings and the consequent development of romantic literature has been commented
upon. There can be little doubt that such courtly subjects were
chosen because of the hope of pleasing a high lord or winning
his favor, and in many of the *romans courtois* we have a mention of the nobleman who protected the poet. Li Rois Adenez,
Geoffrey Gaimar, Chréstien de Troyes, Marie de France, Girard
de Cambrai, and Gautier d'Arras, to mention only a few, all
mention with great praise the lord for whom they undertook
their works, or to whom they expect to present them. But by
no means all the *chansons* have such mention, and the reason is
not far to seek. According to M. Bedier, many of these tales
grew up, not from the folk or through the interest of individual
patrons, but through a kind of hand and glove arrangement
between the jongleurs and the various monasteries along the
principle pilgrim routes, and this theory explains beautifully the
problems of the existence of such works:

"les chansons de geste va-t-on-répétent, ont été composées principalement pour la "classe guerriere", s'addressent principalement au mond
seigneurial: s'il en fut ainsi, pourquoi ne trouvet-on jamais, dans une
chanson de geste de la bonne époque, comme on en trouve dans le romans
courteois, chez Chrétien de Troyes, par example, la mention d'un haut
seigneur qui aurait protégé le poète, ensouragé son entreprise? Pourquoi
les jongleurs de geste, soils s'addressant de préférenne à un public
aristocratique, n'one-ils jamais employé ce genre de flatterie, connu depuis
le temps de Pindare, qui aurait consisté a rattacher à la lignee de Renaut

de Montauban, ou de Girard de Roussillon, ou d'Ogier telle ou telle des familes illustres du XIIe et du XIIIe siècle? Mais l'auter de la *Chevalrie Ogier* semble avoir eu un Mécène, et ce fut un abbe l'ordre de Saint-Benoit."[2]

Hence, because of the influence of the patron upon subject matter, schools of authors fostered by groups of patrons may be conceived of as growing up. The courts of the Norman kings, for example, fostered romances for amusement, and chronicles for political purposes primarily. The idea of entertainment was by no means absent in compositions such as these, for the trouvère David wrote his history and set it to music. Other coteries of patrons doubtless existed, though traces of them are lacking or not clearly marked. In the fifteenth century one is recognized in East Anglia, which undoubtedly stimulated the local production of literature, but beyond this its influence is negligible. It fostered no special type of writing of its own, nor was it instrumental in originating anything, but it is obvious that the conditions were ripe for something worthwhile to be produced. Intensely interesting also is the suggestion of the connection of patronage with the sudden revival of alliterative poetry about 1350.[3] As this revival seems to have taken place in western and northern England, it seems possible that there should have been a group of patrons of letters in that district. Evidence, unfortunately, is only fragmentary. There is one school of poets, however, whose existence can be traced definitely to patronage, the school of Scottish Chaucerians. James I of Scotland, himself a poet, was during the early years of the fifteenth century a prisoner in England, just at the time when Chaucer's works and the works of his imitators were in vogue, and when he returned to his native land the influence of these writers showed itself in his *Kingis Quair*. But the influence of James and his fostering of Chaucerian verse did not bear immediate fruit. Before James there was almost a dearth of Scottish literature, but about the middle of the century, there is a brilliant period, and then the influence of Chaucer is definitely

[2] *Les Legendes Epiques*, (1908), II, 302.
[3] Moore, *P. M. L. A.*, XXVIII, 103.

established. This came about under the patronage particularly
of James IV, a prince interested in everything, but not particularly or vitally in anything, so that the impulse given by
James I's solitary effort was followed.

Coming more directly to the influence of individual patrons,
the field is so large that it might well be made the subject of
another study. It is clear that many of the lives of saints in
England at least, were composed for devout patrons or patronesses. During the Middle Ages it can hardly be said that a
national literature had been developed; certainly there was not
yet a unified reading publc. Little groups of literary con-
noisseurs, however, were in existence, each satisfying its own
particular taste by an intelligent patronage, and it is to the
credit of the medieval patrons that such a love of letters was
kept alive. As soon as printing was introduced and the number
of books multiplied, these groups were merged, and a development of national taste became a possibility. Individual authors,
however, still looked to the patron to supply their needs, but a
more powerful patron was merely waiting to be courted, the
public.

The development of the lyric, likewise, was influenced by patronage, though in a very indirect fashion. It is generally conceded that the lyric of the Middle Ages had its origin ultimately
in Provence, and developing in the eleventh century in the
hands of the troubadours, it became something definitely aristocratic. It has been seen that the troubadour was in most cases
a patronized poet, who took up his residence wherever he could
find sustenance, and though this courteois poetry spread over all
Europe rapidly, it is to be recognized that its spread was due in
large measure to the existence of munificent princes, who not
only enjoyed the *gai saber,* but were willing to encourage it
materially. In regard to the influence upon England, there can
be no doubt that the double marriage of Eleanor of Acquitaine was
an important means of diffusing this poetry northward, first to
the court of France, where she presided as queen for fifteen
years, and then to the court of Henry II of England. Strangely
enough, while lyrics continued to be written in French as the court

language, it is not until the late thirteenth and early fourteenth centuries that the lyric may be said to develop in English, in the poems such as are preserved in Harleian Ms. 2253, and here definitely there is troubadour influence. Also the earlier Hymns to the Virgin exhibit French influence unquestionably.

Besides influencing the author's choice of subject the patron doubtless influenced the author's style and diction. From the very earliest times book dedications are accompanied by references to style, as will be recalled, and the dedications themselves are marked efforts to be elaborate, dignified, and proper, the style generally rising in proportion to the dignity of the person addressed. Professor J. C. Mendenhall[4] has shown that the poet's choice of language was influenced by his dedicatee, and that it is in works dedicated to a nobleman or known to have been written on commission, that one finds embellishment of style. His conclusions are well borne out by our notice of the excusatory epilogue appended to many works, in which the author very abjectly and modestly apologizes for his "rude and simpil endyting" and bids his little book be not overbold, but quake in dread before so noble and erudite a personage as the one to whom it is being sent. Caxton's prologues also, it will be recalled, carry on this tradition. But the evidence produced tells us more. It will be noted that there are many prose reductions of works originally in verse which are done on commission, a fact which leads to speculation as to how far the transition from verse to prose, effected in the Middle Ages, is due to patronage and the desires of persons to whom verse romances were tiresome and prose a fresher medium. Patronage undoubtedly had its effect. The matter of style and form is in any case merely a desire to present a subject worthily, and that patronage should have been an influence in forming it is not strange. In addressing a noble the author naturally dipped his pen in "aureat lycour" and heightened his style, and the patron probably gave his orders and knew what he liked or wanted without any great amount of critical judgment or knowledge of why he liked it.

In another respect patronage had a very wide-spread effect,

---

[4] *Aureate Terms: A Study in the Literary Diction of the Fifteenth Century.* (1919), 61 ff.

that of the fostering of the new art of printing. At no time was there so considerable a number of works to be saved from destruction, and at no time could the invention of printing have been rewarded more munificently and hence more rapidly extended. Evidence shows that in no case did the early printers enter upon their new adventure without good and able patronage. Gutenberg, as far as one can get beneath the myth which surrounds him, seems to have been able to interest moneyful folk in his enterprise, and when the art spread it seems to have been fostered in all places. Colard Mansion was munificently patronized early in his career, though apparently deserted when he fell on bad days. Evidence shows that Piero de' Medici wrote to a local goldsmith, Bernardina Cenini, and to John of Maintz, inviting them to Florence and promising them protection and provision,[5] and though they were not able to accept until after 1471, after the death of Piero, Lorenzo, his son, extended his patronage to printing, financing Cenini's scheme of casting type in metal. Lodovico Sforza encouraged the new art in Milan, Lodovico Gonzago patronized a press in Mantua, Aldus Manutius in Venice received patronage from many hands, and Borsa, first Duke of Ferrara, increased the fame of his town by introducing a press. In England, Caxton likewise was patronized amply, as we have seen, and of him we have a complete list of patrons, for he appears to have recorded in prologue or epilogue the names of the persons by whom he was employed, mentioning likewise any special favors accorded to him. That he found the occupation remunerative is not to be doubted. It is hardly possible to overestimate the importance of the printing press in its influence upon literature and literary taste, to say nothing of its influence upon civilization in general, and it is of great interest to see that such an enterprise in its beginnings, was cradled by the same fostering spirit that has kept alive literature from the earliest times.

Hence, if account be taken of the record of medieval fosterers of art and learning in a time when patronage meant everything, it is evident that the age which produced such patrons can hardly with justice be passed with the designation "dark."

[5] Smeaton, *The Medici and the Italian Renaissance*, 130.

INDEX